EATCS
Monographs on Theoretical Computer Science
Volume 17

Jan Paredaens Paul De Bra
Marc Gyssens Dirk Van Gucht

The Structure of the Relational Database Model

With 53 Figures

Springer-Verlag
Berlin Heidelberg New York
London Paris Tokyo

Authors

Jan Paredaens
Paul De Bra
Marc Gyssens
Department of Mathematics and Computer Science
Universiteit Antwerpen, Universiteitsplein 1
B-2610 Antwerpen, Belgium

Dirk Van Gucht
Computer Science Department, Indiana University
Bloomington, Indiana 47405-4101, USA

Editors

Wilfried Brauer
Institut für Informatik, Technische Universität München
Arcisstrasse 21, D-8000 München 2, FRG

Grzegorz Rozenberg
Institute of Applied Mathematics and Computer Science
University of Leiden, Niels-Bohr-Weg 1, P.O. Box 9512
NL-2300 RA Leiden, The Netherlands

Arto Salomaa
Department of Mathematics, University of Turku
SF-20500 Turku 50, Finland

ISBN 3-540-13714-9 Springer-Verlag Berlin Heidelberg New York
ISBN 0-387-13714-9 Springer-Verlag New York Berlin Heidelberg

Library of Congress Cataloging-in-Publication Data
The Structure of the relational database model / Jan Paredaens ... [et al.]. p. cm. –
(EATCS monographs on theoretical computer science ; v. 17)
Bibliography: p. Includes index.
ISBN 0-387-13714-9 (U.S. : alk. paper) 1. Data base management. 2. Relational data bases. I. Paredaens, Jan, 1947- . II. Series. QA76.9.D3S758 1989 005.75'6–dc 19 89-5967 CIP

Printing: Beltz, Hemsbach/Bergstr.; binding: J. Schäffer, Grünstadt
2145/3140-543210 – Printed on acid-free paper

Preface

This book presents an overview of the most fundamental aspects of the theory that underlies the Relational Database Model. As such it is self-contained though experience with formal models and abstract data manipulating on the one hand and with the practical use of a relational system on the other hand can help the reader. Such experience will offer the reader a better understanding of and a motivation for the different concepts, theories and results mentioned in the book. We have focussed on the most basic concepts and aspects of the relational model, without trying to give a complete overview of the state of the art of database theory.

Recently a lot of books on databases in general and on the relational model in particular have been published. Most of them describe the use of database systems. Some clarify how information has to be structured and organized before it can be used to build applications. Others help the user in writing down his applications or in finding tricky ways to optimize the running time or the necessary space. Another category of books treat more fundamental and more general aspects such as the description of the relational model, independent of any implementation, the decomposition in normal forms or the global design of distributed databases. Few, however, are the books that describe in a formal way some of the subjects mentioned above. Nevertheless, such a formal approach is required for the following reasons:

- a formal framework in which the concepts can be described unambiguously;
- a language or an environment for formally-oriented people to discuss database problems;
- a textbook on databases for mathematically-oriented disciplines;
- a clarification for database designers that are looking for exact definitions of widely accepted concepts.

The authors hope that this book fulfills these needs.

For a long period, ad-hoc database software has been developed. Until 1971 databases were part of computer science, without being supported by a general and formal framework. In that year E. F. Codd published two small papers in which he introduced the relational model. This model was a real breakthrough for the fundamental understanding of databases. It offered a tool to express different properties, characteristics, theorems and results. It was the hard core of the basic research on databases until the mid 80ies, and it still influences the market of database packages nowadays. Even for those who are interested in more recent trends in database theory, such as functional, rule-based and object-oriented databases or knowledge bases, a knowledge of the basic concepts of the relational model is indispensable.

The book can be divided in two parts.

The basic material is contained in Chapters 1 to 4. Chapter 1 gives a general description of the relational model. In particular, the dynamic evolution of a database is considered. Chapter 2 is devoted to relational query languages. Three of them, algebra, calculus and a subset of SQL are discussed and shown to be equivalent with respect to their expressive power. In Chapter 3 we elaborate the constraints. While the emphasis is on functional, multivalued and join dependencies, some other types that are studied in the literature are briefly discussed to provide for a broader context to handle issues such as the implication problem and the existence of an axiomatization. Finally in Chapter 4, it is shown how constraints can give rise to the vertical decomposition of a database. The various normal forms are discussed, as well as the trade-offs that have to be made between maximal decomposition information preservation and constraint preservation.

Chapters 5 to 8 deal with some assorted research topics. They discuss various issues of database design in the context of the relational model. Even if the reader would consider working with non-relational systems, insight into the problems that are discussed here remains essential. We hope that these chapters can provide this insight. In Chapter 5 another method of optimizing the structure of a relational database is discussed: horizontal decomposition. Instead of replacing relations by some of their projections, relations are replaced by some of their subrelations. The study of horizontal decompositions gives rise to some new types of constraints which are discussed in detail. The problem of representing incomplete information is subject of Chapter 6. Various categories of null values are distinguished, depending on their semantics. In Chapter 7, an extension of the relational model is introduced. A disadvantage of the relational model is its inability to represent hierarchical information. In order to remedy this situation, the relational model was extended to the nested relational model. An overview of various aspects of this model is given. Finally in Chapter 8, we deal with updating a relational database, which, in our opinion, has been an area too much neglected in database theory.

In order to facilitate reading this book, many examples are inserted, illustrating the various concepts and techniques we introduce. At the end of each chapter, a list of exercises may help the reader to test to which degree he has familiarized himself with the contents of the chapter.

We thank all those who helped us in writing this book. Our clarifying discussions were a necessary and continuous stimulation.

Antwerp, Belgium
Bloomington, Indiana, USA
November 1988

Jan Paredaens
Paul De Bra
Marc Gyssens
Dirk Van Gucht

Contents

Chapter 1

Relational Database Model

A database system is a collection of programs that run on a computer and that help the user to get information, to update information, to protect information, in general to manage information.

The first fundamental aspect of a database system is the way data or information is represented. For instance, it would be very nice for English speaking human beings if all the information would be represented in English sentences like *John is the father of Tim. He lives in Brussels and he is married to Nicole.* However such sentences can be ambiguous. (As a matter of fact the sentences we mentioned are ambiguous.) Furthermore, it does not seem very interesting to represent information by English sentences, since at the actual state of the art we cannot use a human language as an interface with the computer.

During the last three decades different approaches were made and three famous models were proposed: the *network model*, the *hierarchical model* and the *relational model*. In the network model the structure of the information is represented by a directed graph, whereas in the hierarchical model a set of trees is used.

In this book we will study the relational model, in which the information is stored in a very natural way in tables, called relations.

The relational model was introduced by E. F. Codd in 1970. [29] It has since been used as a theoretical and practical basis for many investigations and studies. The advantages and disadvantages have been discussed on many occasions. Many fundamental problems have been treated as to the structure, the characteristics and the userfriendliness of the representation of the information in the relational database model.

In this first chapter we will describe formally what we mean by a relation, by its scheme and its instances. We define a relational database. Finally we express a not-so-small example of a database that will be used throughout the book.

1.1 Relation Schemes

Suppose we are interested in the following: we want to handle some information about some friends. We are interested in their first and their last name, the town they are living in, the country they are living in and their international phone number. Say we have a friend called *Tom Tillery* living in *Paris*, *France*, whose phone number is 33-1-876-55-89. Another friend is *Jeff Johannes* living in *Amsterdam*, *Holland*, whose phone number is 31-20-822-56-78. Finally, there is also *Pietro Picavillo* who lives in *Torino*, *Italy*. His phone number is 39-11-678-41-72.

We could represent this information in the table called *FRIENDS* in Figure 1.1.

LAST-NAME	*FIRST-NAME*	*TOWN-WHERE-LIVING*	*COUNTRY-WHERE-LIVING*	*PHONE-NUMBER*
Tillery	*Tom*	*Paris*	*France*	33-1-876-55-89
Johannes	*Jeff*	*Amsterdam*	*Holland*	31-20-822-56-78
Picavillo	*Pietro*	*Torino*	*Italy*	39-11-678-41-72

Figure 1.1: *A table of FRIENDS*

Since we get new friends very often, our table becomes bigger and bigger nearly every week. This implies that we add new rows to *friends*. Notice that the width of our table is not changing, nor the headings of the columns.

The contents of a table such as the one in Figure 1.1 is called an instance of a relation. Note that this notion of relation is different from the mathematical relation. We will give the formal definition of an instance of a relation later on in this chapter. You see however that at each moment there is a relation instance. This instance is unique at each moment but it can change from moment to moment. All the possible instances of a given relation have some common properties. All these properties together form, at least intuitively, the type or the scheme of the relation.

We shall formalize this notion in two steps. First of all, we shall incorporate the "basic facts" about the table format of our relation in a primitive relation scheme.

In the example of Figure 1.1 the following basic facts should be subsumed by the primitive scheme corresponding to the relation *FRIENDS*:

- every instance contains five columns respectively headed by: *LAST-NAME*, *FIRST-NAME*, *TOWN-WHERE-LIVING*, *COUNTRY-WHERE-LIVING*, *PHONE-NUMBER*;
- the column headed by *LAST-NAME* only contains last names;
- the column headed by *FIRST-NAME* only contains first names;

- the column headed by *TOWN-WHERE-LIVING* only contains names of towns;
- the column headed by *COUNTRY-WHERE-LIVING* only contains country names;
- the column headed by *PHONE-NUMBER* only contains legal phone numbers.

Formally, we define:

Definition 1.1 A *primitive relation scheme* is a three-tuple

$$PRS = (\Omega, \Delta, dom)$$

where

- Ω is a finite set of *attributes*; the attributes are the headings of the columns;
- Δ is a finite set of *domains*; each domain is a set of values which may be infinite;
- $dom: \Omega \rightarrow \Delta$ is a function that associates with each attribute a domain. For each attribute, only the values of the corresponding domain may appear in the column that is headed by that attribute.

□

There are however other common properties of all possible instances of a relation than those described above. E.g. in the case of *FRIENDS* we have the following properties:

- the meaning of the rows of the table: every row represents a friend and for each friend we know his (or her) last name, first name, the town and the country he (or she) lives in, and his (or her) phone number. But we do not know the street he (or she) is living in for instance;
- the town in which a friend is living must be in the country he (or she) is living in;
- the prefix of the phone number must agree with the corresponding town and country.

We are now ready to give the formal definition of a relation scheme.

Definition 1.2 A *relation scheme* (or briefly a relation) is a three-tuple

$$RS = (PRS, M, SC)$$

where

- *PRS* is a primitive relation scheme;
- *M* is the *meaning* of the relation. This is an informal component of the definition, since it refers to the real world and since we will mostly describe the meaning in a human, natural language. In nearly all theoretical studies the *M* component of a relation scheme has little importance. However, we include it in the definition of a relation scheme since it is a fundamental time independent property of the relation;
- *SC* is a set of *relation constraints* or conditions. The significance of these conditions will be explained later on when we introduce the relation instances over a relation scheme in Definition 1.4.

□

So, a relation scheme is a three-tuple the first component of which is a three-tuple in turn. However, whenever the intermediate step of a primitive relation scheme is not relevant in our discussions, we shall denote a relation conveniently as a five-tuple $RS = (\Omega, \Delta, dom, M, SC)$.

Example 1.1 Recall the example of Figure 1.1. The relation scheme which is associated with the relation of that example is $FRIENDS = (\Omega, \Delta, dom, M, SC)$ with

- Ω = {*LAST-NAME*, *FIRST-NAME*, *TOWN-WHERE-LIVING*, *COUNTRY-WHERE-LIVING*, *PHONE-NUMBER*};
- Δ = {set of last names, set of first names, set of names of towns, set of names of countries, set of legal phone numbers}. All these sets have to be defined properly. They can be defined by enumeration or by giving their syntactical structure;
- the function *dom* associates the set of last names with *LAST-NAME*, the set of first names with *FIRST-NAME*, the set of names of towns with *TOWN-WHERE-LIVING*, the set of names of countries with *COUNTRY-WHERE-LIVING* and the set of legal phone numbers with *PHONE-NUMBER*;
- M is the meaning of the relation. This meaning has to be as exact and as unambiguous as possible. Here the actual friends of the first author of the book are included. For each friend the last name, the first name, the town, the country and the phone number are given;
- the set SC includes at least the condition that the town in which a friend lives is in the country he lives in. The condition that verifies the prefix of the phone numbers is also included in SC.

□

Example 1.2 Consider a hotel that wants to store information about its rooms. For each actual room the hotel management is interested in the room number, the number of beds in the room, whether or not there is a bath in the room, on which floor the room is and last but not least its rate.

A relation scheme that can be used for this purpose is

$$ROOMS = (\Omega, \Delta, dom, M, SC)$$

with

- Ω = {*ROOM-NUMBER*, *NUMBER-OF-BEDS*, *BATH?*, *FLOOR*, *RATE*};
- Δ = {set of room numbers, set of positive integers, {*true*, *false*}, set of floor numbers};
- *dom* is straightforward. Note that the set of positive integers is associated with both *NUMBER-OF-BEDS* and *RATE*;
- The meaning M of this relation scheme describes some information about the rooms of the hotel. For each room its room number is given, the number of beds, whether or not there is a bath, on which floor the room is located and its rate per night;

- SC can include different conditions such as:
  - every room has a different room number,
  - there are only 8 floors and the first digit of the room number indicates the floor,
  - every room on floor 2 has a bath,
  - a room with a bath has a rate of over 150,
  - no floor has more than 20 rooms,
  - the average number of beds per room is at least 1.60.

□

1.2 Relation Instances

In Section 1.1 we introduced the relation scheme in order to specify the structure of the relation. The actual information which is stored in the relation is described by relation instances. A relation instance can be viewed as a table like the one in Figure 1.1. As such it is a set of rows the order of which is not important. Each row has several entries, one for each attribute in the scheme. Furthermore each entry must belong to the appropriate domain. Consider the first row in Figure 1.1. Its *LAST-NAME*-entry is *Tillery* and it belongs to the set of last names. Its *COUNTRY-WHERE-LIVING*-entry is *France* and this belongs to the set of country names.

A row of a table is called a tuple. It is actually a function that associates with each attribute its corresponding value. The first tuple of the relation instance of Figure 1.1 is a function that associates *Tillery* with *LAST-NAME*, *Tom* with *FIRST-NAME*, *Paris* with *TOWN-WHERE-LIVING*, *France* with *COUNTRY-WHERE-LIVING* and 33-1-876-55-89 with *PHONE-NUMBER*.

In analogy with the previous section, we shall distinguish between sets of tuples satisfying only the requirements encoded in some primitive relation scheme and sets of tuples satisfying also the additional constraints in a relation scheme containing that primitive scheme. The latter sets of tuples are relation instances of the scheme under consideration.

Definition 1.3 Let $PRS = (\Omega, \Delta, dom)$ be a primitive relation scheme.

- A *tuple* over the primitive relation scheme PRS is a function t, $t : \Omega \rightarrow \bigcup_{\delta \in \Delta} \delta$ such that for every attribute A of Ω, $t(A) \in dom(A)$.
- A *possible relation instance* of the primitive relation scheme PRS is a set of tuples over PRS.

□

Definition 1.4 Let $RS = (PRS, M, SC)$ be a relation scheme.

- A *relation constraint* of the relation scheme RS is represented by a boolean function that associates with every possible relation instance of PRS the value *true* or *false*. If that function associates the value *true* with a possible relation instance of *PRS*, then we say that the possible relation instance satisfies the relation constraint. As we indicated in Definition 1.2, the set *SC* contains the relation constraints of a relation scheme.

- A *relation instance* of the relation scheme *RS* is a possible relation instance of *PRS*, that satisfies all the relation constraints of *SC*.

□

In the sequel, we denote primitive relation schemes and relation schemes with capitals; possible relation instances and relation instances are denoted with small letters.

We represent a (possible) relation instance by a table with one column for each attribute, and one row for each tuple. It follows from Definition 1.3 and Definition 1.4 that the order of the rows in the table is irrelevant and that all the rows of the table are different. Also the order of the columns (together with their heading attribute) does not influence the relation instance that is represented.

Example 1.3 The table in Figure 1.1 represents a relation instance of the relation scheme of Example 1.1. It contains three tuples.

Recall the relation scheme of Example 1.2. Suppose that *prs* is a possible relation instance over the relation scheme *ROOMS*. The six relation constraints together with the boolean functions that represent them are:

- every room has a different room number:
  $f_1(prs) = true$
  iff
  $\forall t_1, t_2 \in prs$ holds that
  if $t_1(ROOM\text{-}NUMBER) = t_2(ROOM\text{-}NUMBER)$
  then $t_1 = t_2$;

  (Such a constraint is called a *key dependency*; keys are discussed in Chapter 4.)

- there are only 8 floors and the first digit of the room number indicates the floor:
  $f_2(prs) = true$
  iff
  $\forall t \in prs$ holds that
  $1 \leq t(FLOOR) \leq 8$ and
  for every positive integer n holds that
  if $t(ROOM\text{-}NUMBER)$ div $10^n = 0$
  then $t(ROOM\text{-}NUMBER)$ div $10^{n-1} \in \{0, t(FLOOR)\}$;

- every room on floor 2 has a bath:
  $f_3(prs) = true$
  iff
  $\forall t \in prs$ holds that
  if $t(FLOOR) = 2$
  then $t(BATH?) = true$;
- a room with a bath costs over 150:
  $f_4(prs) = true$
  iff
  $\forall t \in prs$ holds that
  if $t(BATH?) = true$
  then $t(RATE) > 150$;
- no floor has more than 20 rooms:
  $f_5(prs) = true$
  iff
  for all $fl, 1 \leq fl \leq 8$ holds that
  the number of elements of $\{t \in prs \mid t(FLOOR) = fl\}$ is at most 20;
- the average number of beds per room is at least 1.60:
  $f_6(prs) = true$
  iff
  the sum of all $t(NUMBER\text{-}OF\text{-}BEDS)$ with t in prs, divided by the number of elements of prs is at least 1.60.

□

Example 1.4 Recall again the relation scheme of Example 1.2, and suppose that *SC* only contains the six given relation constraints. The table in Figure 1.2 gives a representation of a relation instance of the relation scheme *ROOMS*. Although it is a possible relation instance of the primitive relation scheme *ROOMS*, the table in Figure 1.3 however does not represent a relation instance of *ROOMS*, for three reasons:

- the first row says that there is a room with number 505 on floor 3. This violates the second relation constraint;
- the second row says that there is a room on floor 2 without a bath. This violates the third relation constraint;
- the third row says that there is a room with a bath for only 100. This violates the fourth relation constraint.

The table in Figure 1.4. does not represent a relation instance of *ROOMS* either since the average number of beds is only 1.33.

□

ROOM-NUMBER	*NUMBER-OF-BEDS*	*BATH?*	*FLOOR*	*RATE*
101	2	*true*	1	200
201	3	*true*	2	155
202	2	*true*	2	190
303	1	*false*	3	100
203	2	*true*	2	170

Figure 1.2: An instance of *ROOMS*

ROOM-NUMBER	*NUMBER-OF-BEDS*	*BATH?*	*FLOOR*	*RATE*
505	2	*true*	3	160
202	1	*false*	2	200
301	2	*true*	3	100

Figure 1.3: Not an instance of *ROOMS*

ROOM-NUMBER	*NUMBER-OF-BEDS*	*BATH?*	*FLOOR*	*RATE*
101	1	*true*	1	200
102	2	*false*	1	100
103	1	*true*	1	200

Figure 1.4: Not an instance of *ROOMS* either

Example 1.5 Time now for an example that is a little more abstract. Let

$$ABSTRACT = (\Omega, \Delta, dom, M, SC)$$

with

- $\Omega = \{A, B, C\}$;
- $\Delta = \{\text{set of integers, set of prime numbers, set of minuscules}\}$;
- $dom(A)$ is the set of minuscules, $dom(B)$ is the set of integers, $dom(C)$ is the set of primes;
- SC contains the following relation constraints:
  - for every tuple its B-value is smaller than its C-value,
  - for every tuple its A-value is either the first letter of the English word for its B-value or the first letter of the English word for its C-value,
  - there are no two different tuples with the same B-value,
  - the sum of the B-values of all those tuples that have the same C-value is greater than that C-value.
- M is not considered here.

Figure 1.5 shows an example of an instance of *ABSTRACT* and Figure 1.6 shows a set of tuples that is not a relation instance of *ABSTRACT*.

□

A	B	C
s	6	7
s	3	7
t	20	43
s	11	17
t	2	43
s	7	17
f	22	43

Figure 1.5: Instance of *ABSTRACT*

A	B	C
f	14	17
t	2	19
t	21	19

Figure 1.6: No instance of *ABSTRACT*

ROOMMAID-NUMBER	*ROOM-NUMBER*
$M05$	101
$M05$	201
$M05$	202
$M05$	203

Figure 1.7: An instance of *ROOMMAIDS*

1.3 Database Schemes and Database Instances

When we want to represent the information structure of a situation by the relational database model, we will mostly use several relations that contain independent information. Suppose for instance that in Example 1.2 we want to include the names of the roommaids, together with the rooms they are responsible for. Therefore we consider a second relation, with two attributes. In Figure 1.7 an instance for such a relation is shown. Hence in general a database instance consists of several relation instances. In the same way the database scheme is composed of several relation schemes. Furthermore we suppose that if the same attribute is used in two different relation schemes of the same database scheme, then these two attributes really have the same intuitive meaning and hence must have the same associated domain. We define:

Definition 1.5 A *primitive database scheme* PDS is a finite set of relation schemes $\{RS_i = (\Omega_i, \Delta_i, dom_i, M_i, SC_i) \mid i \in I\}$ such that for all $i, j \in I$ and $A \in \Omega$, $A \in \Omega_i \cap \Omega_j$ implies $dom_i(A) = dom_j(A)$. Hence all the functions dom_i can be extended to one function $dom: \bigcup \Omega_i \mapsto \bigcup \Delta_i$.

□

Note at this point that the meaning of a database is not entirely covered by the meanings of all the relations it contains; something has to be said about what these relations have in common. Similarly, there sometimes are constraints that deal with several relations at a time. These constraints cannot be described within the various relation schemes. Therefore a database scheme must also include a set of database constraints. Hence we define a database scheme as follows:

Definition 1.6 A *database scheme* (or briefly a database) is a three-tuple

$$DS = (PDS, DM, SDC)$$

where

- PDS is a primitive database scheme;
- DM is the *meaning* of the database;
- SDC is a set of database constraints of DS, which are defined in Definition 1.8.

□

As to the actual contents of a database, we define:

Definition 1.7 Consider a primitive database scheme PDS. A *possible database instance* of PDS is a set *pds* of relation instances, such that there is exactly one relation instance in *pds* for each relation scheme in PDS.

□

Finally, we have:

Definition 1.8 Consider a database scheme $DS = (PDS, DM, SDC)$.

- A *database constraint* is represented by a boolean function that associates *true* or *false* to each possible database instance of DS. If this function associates *true* to a possible database instance, we say that the possible database instance satisfies this database constraint.
- A *database instance* of DS is a possible database instance of PDS that satisfies all the database constraints in SDC.

□

Example 1.6 Recall Example 1.4, and consider another relation scheme $ROOMMAIDS = (\Omega', \Delta', dom', M', SC')$ with

- $\Omega' = \{ROOMMAID\text{-}NUMBER, ROOM\text{-}NUMBER\}$;
- $\Delta' = \{\text{set of employee numbers, set of room numbers}\}$;
- dom' is obvious;
- M' indicates that every tuple denotes the employee number of a roommaid together with a room she is responsible for;
- the only two relation constraints in SC' are that every roommaid is responsible for four rooms and that no two different roommaids can be responsible for the same room.

$ROOMSDB = (PDS, DM, SDC)$ is a database scheme where

- $PDS = \{ROOMS, ROOMMAIDS\}$;
- DM says that an instance of $ROOMSDB$ indicates the assignment of roommaids to rooms in a hotel;
- SDC consists of only one database constraint which says that roommaids can only be responsible for rooms that appear in the instance of $ROOMS$.

Figures 1.2 and 1.7 together show an instance of the database scheme *ROOMSDB*. Figures 1.2 and 1.8 are instances of the schemes *ROOMS* and *ROOMMAIDS* respectively. Hence together they are primitive database instance of the primitive database scheme contained in the database scheme *ROOMSDB*. However they do *not* represent a database instance of *ROOMSDB* since the database constraint of *SDC* is violated.

□

ROOMMAID-NUMBER	*ROOM-NUMBER*
$M05$	201
$M05$	202
$M05$	203
$M05$	204

Figure 1.8: An instance of *ROOMMAIDS*

1.4 Dynamic Schemes and Evolutions

As we have seen in the preceding section, a relation scheme has at each moment a unique relation instance. This instance is changing regularly. If we want to keep track of this evolution, we have to consider the sequence of consecutive instances which are associated with the relation scheme in the course of time. It could be that this sequence has to fulfill some additional conditions, namely conditions on the updates of each instance. In Example 1.2 for instance we might claim that a bath in a room must never be removed. Hence in no consecutive instances there is a room with a bath in the first instance and without a bath in the second one. Such conditions on updates of relations are called dynamic relation constraints. Formally they are boolean functions on the set of sequences of instances of the relation scheme.

Definition 1.9

- A *dynamic relation scheme* is an ordered pair $DYDS = (RS, SDYC)$, where RS is a relation scheme and $SDYC$ is a set of *dynamic relation constraints*. Each of these constraints is represented by a function that associates *true* or *false* with each sequence of relation instances of RS. We say that a sequence of relation instances satisfies a dynamic relation constraint if the representing function returns *true* for that sequence.
- A *relation evolution* of the dynamic relation scheme DRS is a sequence $rs_0, rs_1, rs_2, \ldots$ of instances of RS for which every dynamic relation constraint in $SDYC$ is satisfied.

□

Definition 1.10

- A *dynamic database scheme* is an ordered pair $DYDS = (DS, SDYDC)$ where DS is a database scheme and $SDYDC$ is a set of *dynamic database constraints.* Each of these constraints is represented by a function that associates *true* or *false* with each sequence of database instances of DS. We say that a sequence of relation instances satisfies a dynamic database constraint if the representing function returns *true* for that sequence.
- A *database evolution* of the dynamic database scheme $DYDS$ is a sequence $ds_0, ds_1, ds_2, \ldots$ of instances of DS for which every dynamic database constraint in $SDYDC$ is satisfied.

□

Example 1.7 Recall Example 1.2 and suppose that we claim that a bath must not be removed from a room. However rooms may be annulled. The dynamic relation scheme is $DYROOMS = (DYDS, SDYC)$ with $DYDS = ROOMS$ and $SDYC$ only consisting of the dynamic relation constraint that says that no bath may be removed from a room. This constraint is represented by a boolean function *noremove*. The reader is invited to give a formal definition of *noremove*. Verify that *noremove* returns *true* for the instance of Figure 1.2 and the empty instance, and returns *false* for the instances of Figures 1.2 and 1.9 in that order. □

ROOM-NUMBER	*NUMBER-OF-BEDS*	*BATH?*	*FLOOR*	*RATE*
101	2	*false*	1	250
201	3	*true*	2	160
202	2	*true*	2	200
303	1	*true*	3	171
203	2	*true*	2	170

Figure 1.9: Part of an illegal evolution of *rooms*

Example 1.8 Recall the database scheme $ROOMSDB = (PDS, DM, SDC)$ of Example 1.6. Let $DYROOMSDB = (DS, SDYDC)$ with $DS = ROOMSDB$ and $SDYDC$ consisting of the dynamic database constraints saying that

- if some roommaid is responsible for a room of more than 180, then there is always some maid responsible for that room in the future;
- a bath may not be removed from a room.

Note that it is possible that only one relation is involved in a dynamic database constraint.

$(\{\text{Figure 1.2}, \text{Figure 1.7}\}, \{\text{Figure 1.2}, \text{Figure 1.10}\})$ represents a database evolution but $(\{\text{Figure 1.2}, \text{Figure 1.7}\}, \{\text{Figure 1.2}, \text{Figure 1.11}\})$ does not.

□

ROOMMAID-NUMBER	*ROOM-NUMBER*
$M06$	101
$M06$	202
$M06$	203
$M06$	303

Figure 1.10: Part of a legal evolution of *roommaids*

ROOMMAID-NUMBER	*ROOM-NUMBER*
$M06$	101
$M06$	201
$M06$	203
$M06$	303

Figure 1.11: Part of an illegal evolution of *roommaids*

1.5 Classification of Constraints

It results from the preceding sections that there are different types of constraints. We already distinguished relation constraints, database constraints, dynamic relation constraints and dynamic database constraints.

Let us first discuss relation constraints. A relation constraint determines which sets of tuples are relation instances. In order to verify whether a given constraint is satisfied for a set of tuples, sometimes we have to look at the whole relation at once, sometimes we can verify the constraint tuple by tuple. In the latter case we call the constraint a *tuple constraint.*

Example 1.9 Recall Example 1.2. The relation constraints "there are only 8 floors and the first digit of the roomnumber indicates the floor", "every room on floor 2 has a bath" and "a room with a bath costs over 150" are tuple constraints. The other three relation constraints of the example are not tuple constraints. □

Obviously every tuple constraint is a relation constraint. But furthermore every relation constraint in a relation scheme of a database scheme is equivalent to a database constraint of that database scheme. The former only specifies the relation instances of the given relation and does not say anything about the relation instances of the other relations of the database.

In almost the same way every relation constraint is equivalent to a dynamic relation constraint and every database constraint is equivalent to a dynamic database constraint.

Figure 1.12 summarizes the foregoing. The arrows have the meaning "are equivalent to a subset of".

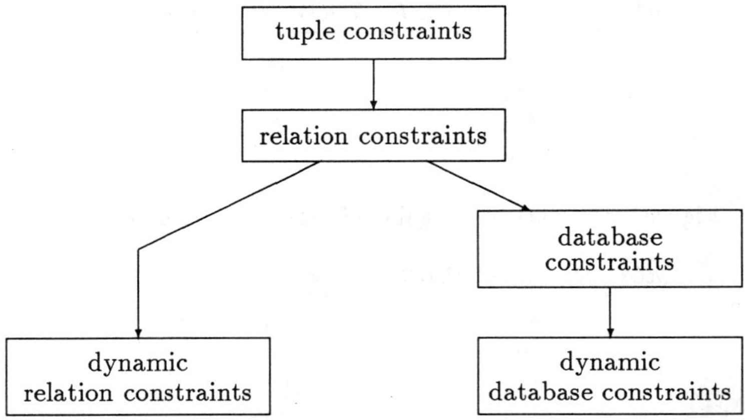

Figure 1.12: Classification of constraints

1.6 Example

In this section we give a not-so-small example of a database scheme. We will use this example on different occasions.

Example 1.10 Consider a database scheme *HOTELDB* = (SRS, DM, SDC) that represents the information concerning a hotel. We have SRS = {*ROOMS*, *ROOMMAIDS*, *VISITORS*, *STAYS*, *PHONE-BILLS*, *EMPLOYEES*} where:

ROOMS = $(\Omega_R, \Delta_R, dom_R, M_R, SC_R)$ with

- Ω_R = {*ROOM-NUMBER*, *NUMBER-OF-BEDS*, *BATH?*, *FLOOR*, *RATE*};
- Δ_R = {set of room numbers, set of positive integers, {*true*, *false*}, set of floor numbers};
- dom_R is straightforward. Note that the set of integers is associated with both *NUMBER-OF-BEDS* and *RATE*;
- the meaning M_R of this relation scheme is obvious;
- SC_R can include different conditions such as:
  - every room has a different room number,
  - there are only 8 floors and the first digit of the room number indicates the floor,
  - every room on floor 2 has a bath,
  - a room with a bath costs over 150,
  - no floor has more than 20 rooms,
  - the average number of beds per room is at least 1.60;

ROOMMAIDS = $(\Omega_C, \Delta_C, dom_C, M_C, SC_C)$ with

- Ω_C = {*ROOMMAID-NUMBER*, *ROOM-NUMBER*};
- Δ_C = {set of employee numbers, set of room numbers};

- dom_C is obvious;
- M_C indicates that every tuple denotes the employee number of a roommaid together with a room she is responsible for;
- the only two relation constraints in SC_C are that every roommaid is responsible for four rooms and that no two different roommaids can be responsible for the same room;

VISITORS $= (\Omega_V, \Delta_V, dom_V, M_V, SC_V)$ with
- Ω_V={*VIS-NUMBER*, *VIS-NAME*, *VIS-STREET*, *VIS-CITY*, *VIS-COUNTRY*};
- Δ_V and dom_V are obvious;
- M_V indicates the visitors with their visitor number, their name and the street, the city and the country they are living in;
- SC_V contains two relation constraints, expressing that every visitor has a different number and that if two visitors live in the same city, then they also live in the same country;

STAYS $= (\Omega_S, \Delta_S, dom_S, M_S, SC_S)$ with
- Ω_S={*VIS-NUMBER*, *ARRIV-DATE*, *LEAV-DATE*, *ROOM-STAY*, *NUMBER-OF-ACCOMP-PERSONS*, *BILL*};
- Δ_S and dom_S are obvious;
- M_S indicates stays of visitors with their arrival date, departure date, the room they occupied, the number of accompanying persons and the bill they had to pay. If a stay is not finished yet, then its *LEAV-DATE*-value is *unknown*;
- SC_S contains two relation constraints indicating that:
  - a visitor leaves on a later date than his arrival date,
  - a visitor cannot arrive a second time, while he stays in the hotel;

PHONE-BILLS $= (\Omega_P, \Delta_P, dom_P, M_P, SC_P)$ with
- Ω_P = {*ROOM-NB*, *TIME*, *DATE*, *DESTINATION*, *PHBILL*, *PAID?*};
- Δ_P and dom_P are obvious;
- M_P indicates phone calls from a specified room number, at a given time and date to a given destination, together with the bill, being paid or not;
- SC_P only contains one relation constraint claiming that no two different tuples are equal on the three components *ROOM-NUMBER*, *TIME* and *DATE* together;

EMPLOYEES $= (\Omega_E, \Delta_E, dom_E, M_E, SC_E)$ with
- Ω_E = {*EMPLOYEE-NUMBER*, *EMPLOYEE-NAME*, *JOB*, *SALARY*};
- Δ_E and dom_E are obvious;
- M_E indicates the employees of the hotel with their number, their name, their job and their salary;
- SC_E only contains one relation constraint claiming that all employees have a different number.

DM indicates that all the relations involved in the database contain information concerning the same hotel.

SDC is a set containing five constraints. We describe them in English. The boolean functions which represent them are left as an exercise.

- There is just one roommaid responsible for each room in the hotel;
- the rooms where visitors stay are rooms of the hotel;
- the room numbers which occur in the instance of *PHONE-BILLS* are room numbers of the hotel;
- if there is a phone call from a room then that room was occupied that date;
- each roommaid in the instance of *ROOMMAIDS* is an employee in the instance of *EMPLOYEES*, whose job is roommaid.

Consider now the dynamic database scheme

$$DYHOTELDB = (DS, SDYDC)$$

with $DS = HOTELDB$ as defined above. The set *SDYDC* of dynamic database constraints consists of four constraints:

- no visitor may be deleted if there is still some information about him in the instance of *STAYS*;
- all the phone bills of a visitor have to be paid when he leaves the hotel;
- a bath must not be removed from a room; rooms however may be annulled;
- only the stay with the oldest *LEAV-DATE* may be removed from the instance of *STAYS*.

1.7 Exercises

1.1 Give a formal definition for the boolean functions associated with the relation constraints in Example 1.5.

1.2 Give a formal definition for the boolean functions associated with the relation constraints in Example 1.6.

1.3 Give a formal definition of the boolean function *noremove* of Example 1.7.

1.4 Give a formal definition of the boolean functions which represent the dynamic database constraints in *SDYDC* in Example 1.8.

1.5 Describe the functions dom_R, dom_C, dom_V, dom_S, dom_P and dom_E in Example 1.10.

1.6 Give a formal definition for the boolean functions which represent the constraints in SC_R, SC_C, SC_V, SC_S, SC_P, SC_E, *SDC* and *SDYDC* of Example 1.10.

1.7 Some constraints are consequences of other constraints or of sets of other constraints. In Example 1.2 for instance the constraint "Every room on floor 2 costs over 150" is a consequence of the set *SC*. Prove that the constraints that are consequences of a set of tuple constraints are tuple constraints. Prove the analogous result for relation constraints and for dynamic relation constraints.

1.8 Give a database scheme with two relation schemes and two database constraints (that are not equivalent to relation constraints) and a relation constraint that is a non-trivial consequence of the two given database constraints.

1.9 Give a dynamic relation scheme with two dynamic relation constraints (that are not equivalent to relation constraints) and a relation constraint that is a non-trivial consequence of the two given dynamic relation constraints.

1.10 Let Δ consist of a set of bars, a set of beers and a set of persons and consider the database scheme

$$THIRSTY = (SRS, DM, SDC)$$

with

$$SRS = \{LIKES, VISITS, SERVES\}$$

where

$LIKES = (\Omega_L, \Delta, dom_L, M_L, SC_L)$;
$VISITS = (\Omega_V, \Delta, dom_V, M_V, SC_V)$;
$SERVES = (\Omega_S, \Delta, dom_S, M_S, SC_S)$;

with

$\Omega_L = \{L\text{-}DRINKER, L\text{-}BEER\}$;
$\Omega_V = \{V\text{-}DRINKER, V\text{-}BAR\}$;
$\Omega_S = \{S\text{-}BAR, S\text{-}BEER\}$;
$dom_L, dom_V, dom_S, M_L, M_V$ and M_S are obvious.

DM is obvious to.

The constraints of SC_L, SC_V, SC_S and SDC are:

- Every drinker visits only bars where some beers he likes are served;
- each bar serves at least one beer;
- each bar has at least one visitor;
- each bar only serves beers that are liked by some of their visitors;
- if two drinkers visit the same bar, there is some beer they both like and that is served at the bar;
- if a drinker does not visit a bar, there is at least one beer served at the bar he does not like;
- if d is a drinker who likes some beer served in a bar visited by the drinker d', then d and d' visit a common bar.

Describe the boolean functions associated to these constraints and say for each of them to which set SC_L, SC_V, SC_S or SDC they belong.

1.11 Recall Exercise 1.10. Find out which constraints are consequences of which others.

1.12 Construct a dynamic relation scheme for the following information. We consider a set of quadrilaterals in one plane. They are identified by a label and we know the cartesian coordinates of their four vertices. The position of their vertices is regularly updated. The following conditions hold (describe the boolean functions representing them):

- the quadrilaterals are convex;
- they do not intersect;
- each update only changes one vertex of one quadrilateral;
- the surface of the updated quadrilateral cannot become smaller;
- the convex hull of the eight vertices of two different quadrilaterals intersect at least one third different quadrilateral;
- the surface of each quadrilateral has to be positive;
- the quadrilateral with the greatest surface also has the greatest circumference.

Chapter 2

Query Systems

In this chapter we discuss three different systems for expressing a question or a query: the relational algebra, the tuple calculus and SQL.

We consider a database scheme $DS = (PDS, DM, SDC)$ as defined in Definition 1.6 in Chapter 1.

In Section 2.1 we define the relational algebra. This is a set of operations defined on relation schemes and on relation instances. By writing an expression in the relational algebra we describe the answer to a query. Section 2.2 handles the relational tuple calculus. In this calculus a query is expressed by a set of tuples which fulfill some condition expressed by a formula in the first order logic. The next section describes a part of the database language SQL, the Structured Query Language [27, 34, 74, 104]. This is one of the most widespread relational database languages at this moment. We do not give a full description of SQL, since this is beyond the scope of this book. Only a subset equivalent to the relational algebra is discussed.

In the next three sections we construct a way to transform an expression in the tuple calculus to the relational algebra, an expression in the relational algebra to SQL and a query in SQL to the tuple calculus respectively. We prove that the three systems we describe are in some sense equivalent, namely that they can express the same queries. This is a generalization of the classical result of Codd [31].

2.1 The Relational Algebra

Consider the database scheme $HOTELDB = (SRS, DM, SDC)$ of Example 1.10. We focus our attention on the two relation schemes *ROOMS* and *ROOMMAIDS* of SRS. The two tables in Figure 2.1 represent two instances *rooms* and *roommaids*.

The relational algebra is the first tool we present to express queries for a relational database. Actually, an expression in the relational algebra represents the answer to the query.

rooms

ROOM-NUMBER	*NUMBER-OF-BEDS*	*BATH?*	*FLOOR*	*RATE*
205	3	*true*	2	300
206	2	*true*	2	200
301	1	*true*	3	160
302	3	*false*	3	150
303	3	*true*	3	300
304	3	*true*	3	300
305	1	*true*	3	160
306	3	*true*	3	300

roommaids

ROOMMAID-NUMBER	*ROOM-NUMBER*
*M*1	205
*M*2	206
*M*1	301
*M*1	302
*M*1	303
*M*2	304
*M*2	305
*M*2	306

Figure 2.1: Database instance for *HOTELDB*.

2.1.1 Informal Description

Before giving the exact definition of the syntax and the semantics of the relational algebra, we give an informal introduction, illustrated by some examples.

Example 2.1 Suppose we are interested in all the room-numbers together with their rates, but without bothering about the values of the other three attributes of the instance *rooms*. This information can be represented by the table in Figure 2.2. This table is called the projection of the relation instance *rooms* on the set of attributes $\{ROOM\text{-}NUMBER, RATE\}$. It is denoted by $\Pi(rooms; ROOM\text{-}NUMBER, RATE)$.

Hence, informally, we could say that the projection of a relation instance on a set of attributes is the table constructed by deleting all the other attributes. Since all the tuples of this table have to be different, it is possible that the table that represents the result has fewer tuples than the original one. The projection is an operator of the relational algebra.

□

The result of any operator on relation instances is called a view instance. (View instances will be discussed in full detail in Section 2.1.4.) Clearly the operators of the relational algebra can also be applied to view instances.

ROOM-NUMBER	*RATE*
205	300
206	200
301	160
302	150
303	300
304	300
305	160
306	300

Figure 2.2: $\Pi(rooms; \mathit{ROOM\text{-}NUMBER}, \mathit{RATE})$.

Example 2.2 The second operator we introduce is the selection. Now we want to know all the available information in *rooms* only for those rooms with a rate lower than 200. The answer to this query is represented in Figure 2.3. It is called the selection on *rooms* where $\mathit{RATE} < 200$. It is written as $\sigma(rooms; \mathit{RATE} < 200)$.

ROOM-NUMBER	*NUMBER-OF-BEDS*	*BATH?*	*FLOOR*	*RATE*
301	1	*true*	3	160
302	3	*false*	3	150
305	1	*true*	3	160

Figure 2.3: $\sigma(rooms; \mathit{RATE} < 200)$

The selection of a relation instance for some condition only contains those tuples that fulfill that condition.

The condition $\mathit{RATE} < 200$ is one example of a condition that uses the operator $<$. Other possible operators are $>$, $=$, $\leq$, $\geq$ and $\neq$. Instead of a condition like $\mathit{RATE} < 200$ we may write an arbitrary computable boolean function, the arguments of which are attributes. We will discuss this later on. □

Example 2.3 The next operator is the join. The join represents all the information in two relation instances. If we want for instance for every room its room number, its number of beds, the information about a bath, its floor, its rate and finally the number of the roommaid who cleans it, then all this information is represented by the table of Figure 2.4. This join of the relation instances *rooms* and *roommaids* is denoted by $rooms \bowtie roommaids$. It is represented by a table that has one attribute for each attribute in *rooms* or in *roommaids*. (Note that the attribute *ROOM-NUMBER* only appears once.) The tuples of the join are the combinations of those tuples in *rooms* and *roommaids* that have the same value on the common attribute *ROOM-NUMBER*.

In general the table that represents the join has more tuples than the original tables. This is illustrated by Figure 2.5.

ROOM-NUMBER	*NUMBER-OF-BEDS*	*BATH?*	*FLOOR*	*RATE*	*ROOMMAID-NUMBER*
205	3	*true*	2	300	$M1$
206	2	*true*	2	200	$M2$
301	1	*true*	3	160	$M1$
302	3	*false*	3	150	$M1$
303	3	*true*	3	300	$M1$
304	3	*true*	3	300	$M2$
305	1	*true*	3	160	$M2$
306	3	*true*	3	300	$M2$

Figure 2.4: *rooms* $\bowtie$ *roommaids*

r

A	B
a	1
a	2
b	2

s

A	C
a	4
a	5
b	4
b	6

$r \bowtie s$

A	B	C
a	1	4
a	2	4
a	1	5
a	2	5
b	2	4
b	2	6

Figure 2.5: $r \bowtie s$ has more tuples than r and s.

When two instances r and s, with disjoint sets of attributes, are joined, we also call this the *cartesian product* of r and s, and we denote it $r \times s$.

□

Example 2.4 Occasionally, we want to rename the attributes of a relation, without altering its contents. Suppose we want to rename the attributes of *roommaids* by *RMN* and *RN* respectively. The result, which is represented in Figure 2.6, is called the renaming of the relation instance *roommaids* by the function f, for which $f(\textit{ROOMMAID-NUMBER}) = \textit{RMN}$ and $f(\textit{ROOM-NUMBER}) = \textit{RN}$ It is written as $\rho(\textit{roommaids}; f)$. The view instance of Figure 2.6 is also written as $\rho(\textit{roommaids}; \textit{ROOMMAID-NUMBER} \rightarrow \textit{RMN}, \textit{ROOM-NUMBER} \rightarrow \textit{RN})$.

RMN	*RN*
$M1$	205
$M2$	206
$M1$	301
$M1$	302
$M1$	303
$M2$	304
$M2$	305
$M2$	306

Figure 2.6: $\rho(\textit{roommaids}; f)$

□

Example 2.5 We know that a relation instance or a view instance is a set of tuples. As such, the set-theoretical operators union, intersection and difference are also defined on some relation instances. They have the traditional well-known meaning. Note that the two operands of such operators should have the same set of attributes. Otherwise these operators are not defined. Figure 2.7 shows a second instance *rooms1* of the scheme *ROOMS*, together with the union, the difference and the intersection of *rooms* and *rooms1*.

□

Example 2.6 The last operator we introduce is the division. This is a more complicated and ad hoc operator: suppose we have two schemes R and S, with $\Omega_S \subset \Omega_R$. The division $r \div s$, with r and s instances of R and S respectively is represented by a table, the attributes of which are those attributes of R that are not attributes of S. The tuples in this table are those subtuples of r that, together with every tuple in s, form a tuple in r.

An example can clarify this operator. Figure 2.8 shows two abstract relation instances r and s together with their division $r \div s$.

□

rooms1

ROOM-NUMBER	*NUMBER-OF-BEDS*	*BATH?*	*FLOOR*	*RATE*
205	3	*true*	2	300
207	2	*true*	2	250
301	1	*true*	3	160
302	2	*true*	3	160

rooms ∪ *rooms1*

ROOM-NUMBER	*NUMBER-OF-BEDS*	*BATH?*	*FLOOR*	*RATE*
205	3	*true*	2	300
206	2	*true*	2	200
207	2	*true*	2	250
301	1	*true*	3	160
302	3	*false*	3	150
302	2	*true*	3	160
303	3	*true*	3	300
304	3	*true*	3	300
305	1	*true*	3	160
306	3	*true*	3	300

rooms − *rooms1*

ROOM-NUMBER	*NUMBER-OF-BEDS*	*BATH?*	*FLOOR*	*RATE*
206	2	*true*	2	200
302	3	*false*	3	150
303	3	*true*	3	300
304	3	*true*	3	300
305	1	*true*	3	160
306	3	*true*	3	300

rooms ∩ *rooms1*

ROOM-NUMBER	*NUMBER-OF-BEDS*	*BATH?*	*FLOOR*	*RATE*
205	3	*true*	2	300
301	1	*true*	3	160

Figure 2.7: Union, difference and intersection.

r

A	B	C	D
a	a	1	1
b	b	1	2
a	a	2	1
a	b	1	1
a	b	1	2
b	a	1	2
b	a	1	1

s

A	B
b	a
a	a
a	b

$r \div s$

C	D
1	1

Figure 2.8: The division of two abstract instances.

We have introduced all the operators of the relational algebra now. We still have to handle the operands. A first kind of operand are clearly the names of relation instances r, as we saw in previous examples. A second kind are the domains of Δ. If A is an attribute then we write $DOM(A)$ for the domain of A. This is then considered as a relation instance with only one attribute, A, and containing every value of the domain of A. By Definition 1.6 we know that A is associated to only one domain, even if it is an attribute of more than one relation in the database.

Next we have operands of the form $[A > B]$ where A and B are attributes, the domains of which are comparable with $>$. They are called comparative instances. Such an operand is considered to be a two dimensional relation instance with two attributes, A and B, containing all the pairs (a, b), where $a \in dom(A), b \in dom(B)$ and $a > b$.

Other comparative instances are $[A = B]$, $[A < B]$, $[A \leq B]$, $[A \neq B]$ and $[A \geq B]$. Also $[A > a]$ is a comparative instance. It has only one attribute A, and contains every value of $dom(A)$ that is greater than the value a, the latter also belonging to the domain of A. Some operands of the same class are $[a \leq A]$ and $[a = A]$, the last one containing only one tuple.

Finally we discuss a last class of operands, the so-called computable instances, of which the former two classes are special cases. Suppose we want a table with two attributes, N and M, containing all the pairs (n, m) of integers such that n divides m. We write this table as $\{n\colon N; m\colon M \mid divisible(n, m)\}$ where *divisible* is a computable boolean function that indicates whether n divides m.

Consider as a second example an instance with two attributes A and B, where $dom(A)$ is the set of character strings and $dom(B)$ the set of integers. Let *length* be the computable boolean function with two arguments, a string s

and an integer i, such that $length(s, i)$ indicates whether i is the length of s. The table $\{s: A; i: B \mid length(s, i)\}$ contains all the pairs (s, i), where i is the length of the string s. It is very important here that the functions we use, *divisible* and *length*, are computable functions.

So much for the informal description of the relational algebra. All the operations in the algebra can be combined such that we can handle long and complex algebraic instance expressions. These expressions describe the answer to a query on the database.

Example 2.7 Recall Figure 2.1 and consider the following queries:

1. Give the number of each roommaid that is responsible for some rooms with bath, on floor 3;
2. Give the room numbers of the rooms that cost more than 500 or that are on floor 2.

They are represented in the relational algebra by respectively:

1. $\Pi(\sigma(\sigma(rooms \bowtie roommaids; BATH? = true); FLOOR = 3); ROOMMAID\text{-}NUMBER)$;
2. $\Pi(\sigma(rooms; RATE > 500); ROOM\text{-}NUMBER) \cup \Pi(\sigma(rooms; FLOOR = 2); ROOM\text{-}NUMBER)$.

□

2.1.2 Syntax of the Relational Algebra

In this small section we want to give an exact definition of the syntax of the expressions in the relational algebra. The most elegant way to do this is defining the syntax using syntax diagrams, that are regularly used to describe the syntax of programming languages such as Pascal.

Figure 2.9 gives the syntax diagrams of the algebraic expressions. The use of these diagrams is obvious. The reader is asked to verify these diagrams carefully and to make sure he is aware of all algebraic expressions that are syntactically correct. Also, the informal meaning of the expressions should be clear, though we will discuss the meaning later on. Note that everything on the diagram has been informally discussed, except for scheme identifiers.

2.1.3 Generating Part of the Relational Algebra

The attentive reader has noticed that we can express some operators using other operators. For instance, we can express the intersection using the difference since $r \cap s = r - (r - s)$. This means that there is a part of the relational algebra that has enough power to express also the other operators and operands. Such a part is called a *generating part.* Note that a generating part is not unique. The generating part we propose contains the identifiers of the relation instances, the projection, the renaming, the join, the union, the difference, the computable

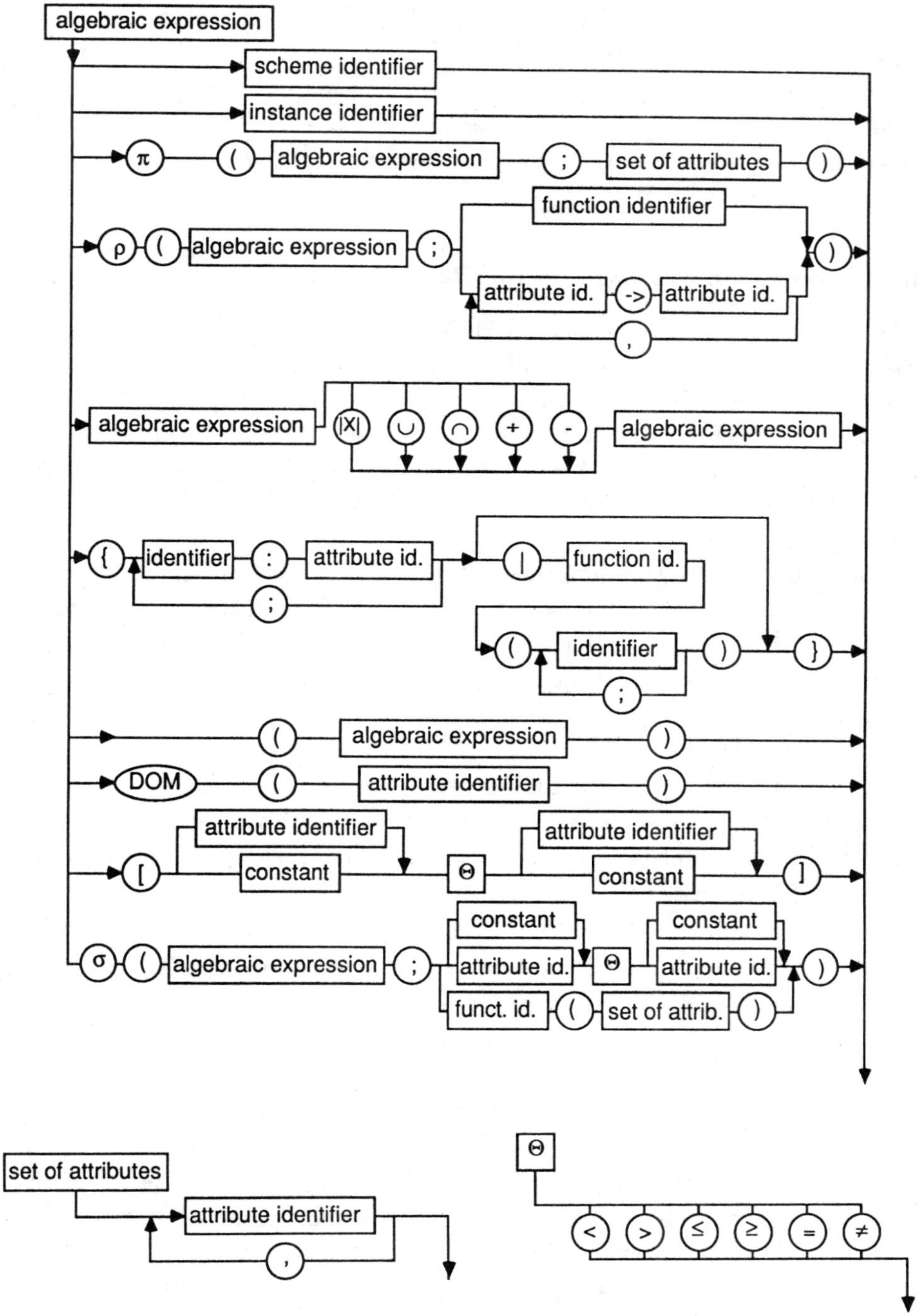

Figure 2.9: Syntax diagrams of the Relational Algebra.

instances and the algebraic expressions between brackets. As we will see in Section 2.1.5 the rest of the relational algebra (i. e., the domain, the comparative instance, the intersection, the selection and the division) can be expressed by this generating part. This implies that the generating part has the same expressive power as the whole algebra. The operands and operators that are not in the generating part only help the user in the sense that their use can simplify the algebraic expressions.

2.1.4 Views Represented by the Relational Algebra

In Section 2.1.2 we have defined an algebraic expression, as an expression that was constructed according to the diagrams in Figure 2.9. Algebraic expressions can be considered either on scheme or instance level. If all operands are scheme identifiers, such an expression is called an *algebraic scheme expression*; if all the operands are instance identifiers, it is called an *algebraic instance expression.* Obviously, an algebraic expression cannot contain both instance and scheme identifiers.

The value of an algebraic instance expression can be represented by a table. We could consider this value as an instance (of a new relation scheme). This instance, nor this scheme are part of the database. Therefore we call the value of an algebraic instance expression, a *view instance.* The scheme of this view instance (which is the value of the corresponding algebraic scheme expression) is called a *view scheme.*

Hence, in other words, the difference between a relation scheme and a view scheme is that the former is an element of the database scheme, while the latter is not. Instances of relation schemes are relation instances and instances of view schemes are view instances.

We now define the view schemes and the view instances represented by algebraic expressions of the generating part. It is left as an exercise to the reader to give analogous definitions for the rest of the relational algebra.

Suppose that V and V' are view schemes or relation schemes with

$$V = (\Omega, \Delta, dom, M, SC)$$

and

$$V' = (\Omega', \Delta', dom', M', SC')$$

Consider v and v' to be instances of V and V' respectively. Let Ω_1 be a subset of Ω. If t is a tuple over Ω then we write $t[\Omega_1]$ for $t|_{\Omega_1}$, i. e. for the function that is defined on Ω_1 and is equal to t on Ω_1, and we write $t(\Omega_1)$ for the set $\{t(A) \mid A \in \Omega_1\}$.

We have

$$\Pi(V; \Omega_1) = (\Omega_1, dom(\Omega_1), dom|_{\Omega_1}, M_1, SC_1)$$

and

$$\Pi(v;\Omega_1) = \{t[\Omega_1] \mid t \in v\}$$

where SC_1 only contains the constraint that specifies those sets of tuples that can be written as $\Pi(v;\Omega_1)$, where v is an instance of V and M_1 is the meaning that is expressed in a human language and explains the projection.

In general this constraint is not recursive. In the implementation of $\Pi(V;\Omega_1)$ we use for SC_1 a set of constraints that are satisfied by all the $\Pi(v;\Omega_1)$, where v satisfies all the constraints of SC.

Note that we write here $\Pi(v;\{\ldots\})$ instead of $\Pi(v;\ldots)$. We will do the same for other operators later on.

We now discuss the renaming. Suppose that Ω_1 is an abstract set not necessary disjoint with Ω. Let f be a one to one function from Ω to Ω_1, and suppose that $dom(A) = dom(f(A))$ if dom is already defined in the database for $f(A)$. We define dom on Ω_1 to be $dom \circ f^{-1}$, where "$\circ$" denotes function composition.

$$\rho(V;f) = (\Omega_1, \Delta, dom \circ f^{-1}, M_1, SC_1)$$

and

$$\rho(v;f) = \{t \circ f^{-1} \mid t \in v\}$$

where SC_1 only contains the constraint that specifies those sets of tuples that can be written as $\rho(v;f)$, where v is an instance of V. The meaning M_1 is obvious.

Let us now discuss the join. Consider again V and V' and suppose that $dom(A) = dom'(A)$ for every attribute $A \in \Omega \cap \Omega'$. We can extend dom to $\Omega \cup \Omega'$:

$$V \bowtie V' = (\Omega \cup \Omega', \Delta \cup Delta', dom, M_1, SC_1)$$

and

$$v \bowtie v' = \{t \mid t[\Omega] \in v \land t[\Omega'] \in v'\}$$

where SC_1 only contains the constraint that specifies those sets of tuples that can be written as $v \bowtie v'$, where v and v' are instances of V and V' respectively. The meaning M_1 is obvious.

We go on with the union and the difference. Suppose that $\Omega = \Omega'$, $\Delta = \Delta'$ and that $dom = dom'$.

$$V \cup V' = (\Omega, \Delta, dom, M_1, SC_1)$$

and

$$V - V' = (\Omega, \Delta, dom, M_2, SC_2)$$

where $v \cup v'$ and $v - v'$ denote the set theoretical union and difference respectively. The description of M_1, M_2, SC_1 and SC_2 is left to the reader.

Finally we discuss the computable schemes and instances. They are denoted as:

$$\{(x_1{:}\,A_1;\ldots;x_n{:}\,A_n) \mid f(x_1,\ldots,x_n)\} = (\{A_1,\ldots,A_n\},\{dom(A_1),\ldots,dom(A_n)\}, dom, M, SC)$$

where the x_i are identifiers, the A_i are different attribute names, and f is a Turing-computable boolean function, that does not use an actual relation or view instance of the database. Furthermore *dom* is deduced in the obvious way from the other schemes of the database. SC only contains the constraint that specifies only that instance that contains all the tuples t for which $f(t(A_1), \ldots, t(A_n)) = \mathit{true}$. Obviously f must be defined on $dom(A_1) \times \cdots \times dom(A_n)$.

In this way we defined the schemes and instances for the generating part. The order of the evaluation of the binary operators in an algebraic expression is $\bowtie$, $\cup$ and $-$.

2.1.5 Expressive Power of the Generating Part

In Section 2.1.3 we claimed that the identifiers of the relation instances, the projection, the renaming, the join, the union, the difference, the computable instances and the algebraic expressions between brackets form a generating part of the relational algebra. In the present section we prove that all the other operands and operators can be expressed by that generating part.

In the sequel we suppose that r and s are relation instances of the relation schemes R and S respectively.

We start with the domain, which is expressed using computable instances: $DOM(A) = \{x{:}\,A\}$ The comparative instances are also expressed using computable instances. Suppose that *smaller*(x,y) verifies whether $x < y$, and that *smaller-than-a*(x) verifies whether $x < a$ for a given a of $dom(A)$. Thus we have

$$[A < B] = \{x{:}\, A; y{:}\, B \mid \mathit{smaller}(x,y)\}$$

and

$$[A < a] = \{x{:}\, A \mid \mathit{smaller\text{-}than\text{-}a}(x)\}$$

The intersection is expressed using the difference: $r \cap r' = r - (r - r')$

The selection has three forms. They are all expressed using the join and computable or comparative instances:

$$\sigma(r; A < B) = r \bowtie [A < B]$$
$$\sigma(r; A < a) = r \bowtie [A < a]$$
$$\sigma(r; f(A_1, A_2, \ldots, A_n)) = r \bowtie \{x_1{:}\, A_1; x_2{:}\, A_2; \ldots; x_n{:}\, A_n \mid f(x_1, x_2, \ldots, x_n)\}$$

Finally, we discuss a more complicated operator: the division. Suppose that R has the attributes $A_1, \ldots, A_p, \ldots, A_q$ and that S has the attributes $A_p, \ldots, A_q$. The reader is invited to reformulate the division in order to get an insight in the following equality:

$$r \div s = \Pi(r; A_1, \ldots, A_{p-1}) - \Pi((\Pi(r; A_1, \ldots, A_{p-1}) \bowtie s) - r; A_1, \ldots, A_{p-1})$$

The above expressions also hold when we replace the instances r and s by algebraic instance expressions, or by view instances. They also hold when the operands are relation schemes, view schemes or algebraic scheme expressions.

2.2 The Tuple Calculus

In this section we describe a second method to express queries for a relational database. This method, called the tuple calculus, specifies the answer to a query as a set of tuples that satisfy some condition.

2.2.1 Informal Description

We give an informal description of the calculus instance expressions. The general form of such an expression is

$$\{t(\ldots, A_i, \ldots, A_j\colon B_j, \ldots) \mid < \textit{condition} >\}$$

Example 2.8 Suppose, for instance, we want all the tuples in *rooms* for those rooms on floor 2. We write:

$$\{t(\textit{ROOM-NUMBER}, \textit{NUMBER-OF-BEDS}, \textit{BATH?}, \textit{FLOOR}, \textit{RATE}) \mid \\ \textit{rooms}(t) \wedge t(\textit{FLOOR}) = 2\}$$

This expression indicates the set of all tuples over the attributes

$$\{\textit{ROOM-NUMBER}, \textit{NUMBER-OF-BEDS}, \textit{BATH?}, \textit{FLOOR}, \textit{RATE}\}$$

that belong to the relation instance *rooms* and that have their *FLOOR*-component equal to 2.

□

Example 2.9 Consider the next query: Give all the room numbers for which the rate divided by its number of beds is smaller than 100:

$$\{t(\textit{RN}\colon \textit{ROOM-NUMBER}) \mid \\ \exists t_1(\textit{ROOM-NUMBER}, \textit{NUMBER-OF-BEDS}, \textit{BATH?}, \textit{FLOOR}, \textit{RATE}) \\ (\textit{rooms}(t_1) \wedge t(\textit{RN}) = t_1(\textit{ROOM-NUMBER}) \wedge \\ \textit{average-smaller-than-100}(t_1(\textit{RATE}), t_1(\textit{NUMBER-OF-BEDS})))\}$$

where $\textit{average-smaller-than-100}(a, b)$ is *true* iff $a/b < 100$. This expression indicates the set of all tuples t over $\{\textit{RN}\}$, for which there is a tuple t_1 over

$$\{\textit{ROOM-NUMBER}, \textit{NUMBER-OF-BEDS}, \textit{BATH?}, \textit{FLOOR}, \textit{RATE}\}$$

in *rooms* with $t(\textit{RN}) = t_1(\textit{ROOM-NUMBER})$ and with

$$t_1(\textit{RATE})/t_1(\textit{NUMBER-OF-BEDS}) < 100.$$

□

Example 2.10 Finally, we are searching for the cheapest room with a bath:

$$\{t(\textit{ROOM-NUMBER}) \mid \\ \exists t_1(\textit{ROOM-NUMBER}, \textit{NUMBER-OF-BEDS}, \textit{BATH?}, \textit{FLOOR}, \textit{RATE}) \\ (\textit{rooms}(t_1) \wedge t_1(\textit{BATH?}) = \textit{true} \wedge \\ t(\textit{ROOM-NUMBER}) = t_1(\textit{ROOM-NUMBER}) \wedge \\ \forall t_2(\textit{ROOM-NUMBER}, \textit{NUMBER-OF-BEDS}, \textit{BATH?}, \textit{FLOOR}, \textit{RATE}) \\ ((\textit{rooms}(t_2) \wedge t_2(\textit{BATH?}) = \textit{true}) \Rightarrow t_2(\textit{RATE}) \geq t_1(\textit{RATE})))\}.$$

□

As the reader can see, the condition that the tuples have to satisfy is expressed by a first-order-logic-like formula. In the next sections we define the syntax and the meaning of this condition exactly.

2.2.2 Syntax of the Tuple Calculus

In Figure 2.10 we give the syntax diagram for the calculus expressions. $t(A_1, \ldots, A_i, \ldots, A_j\colon B_j, \ldots, A_n)$, where t is a tuple identifier and the As and Bs are attribute identifiers, indicates a tuple over the attributes $A_1, \ldots, A_n$ where in each occurrence of $A_j\colon B_j$, A_j has the same domain as B_j. This is explained in further detail in Section 2.2.4. The expressions that only use scheme identifiers are called *calculus scheme expressions* and those that only use instance identifiers are called *calculus instance expressions.*

2.2.3 Generating Part of the Tuple Calculus

Some operators, quantifiers and atoms are expressible using the remaining part of the calculus. The operators that are redundant are the conjunction $\wedge$ and the implication $\Rightarrow$. The universal quantifier $\forall$ is also redundant. The use of a constant identifier in a function call within an atom is redundant. Finally, the θ-comparison in an atom is also redundant. The rest of the tuple calculus is called the *generating part of the tuple calculus.* We explain in Section 2.2.5 how we can express the whole calculus using only the generating part.

2.2.4 Views Represented by the Tuple Calculus

We first give some additional restrictions for calculus expressions. Then we define view instances represented by a calculus instance expression in a formal way. Finally we give the definition of the view scheme represented by a calculus scheme expression. We only consider the generating part of the tuple calculus. The discussion for the non-generating part is left as an exercise.

First, for every condition C in the syntax diagram we define its set of free variables, denoted by *free*(C):

- $\mathit{free}(r(t)) = \{t\}$;
- $\mathit{free}(f(t_1(A_1), \ldots, t_n(A_n))) = \{t_1, \ldots, t_n\}$;
- $\mathit{free}(\neg C) = \mathit{free}(C)$;
- $\mathit{free}(C_1 \vee C_2) = \mathit{free}(C_1) \cup \mathit{free}(C_2)$;
- $\mathit{free}(\exists t(\ldots, A_i, \ldots, A_j\colon B_j, \ldots)C) = \mathit{free}(C) - \{t\}$;
- $\mathit{free}((C)) = \mathit{free}(C)$.

Next we state some additional restrictions for the calculus expressions:

- for every $t(\ldots, A_i, \ldots, A_j\colon B_j, \ldots)$, that occurs in a calculus expression, holds that all the As are distinct. They are called the attributes of t. Each A must

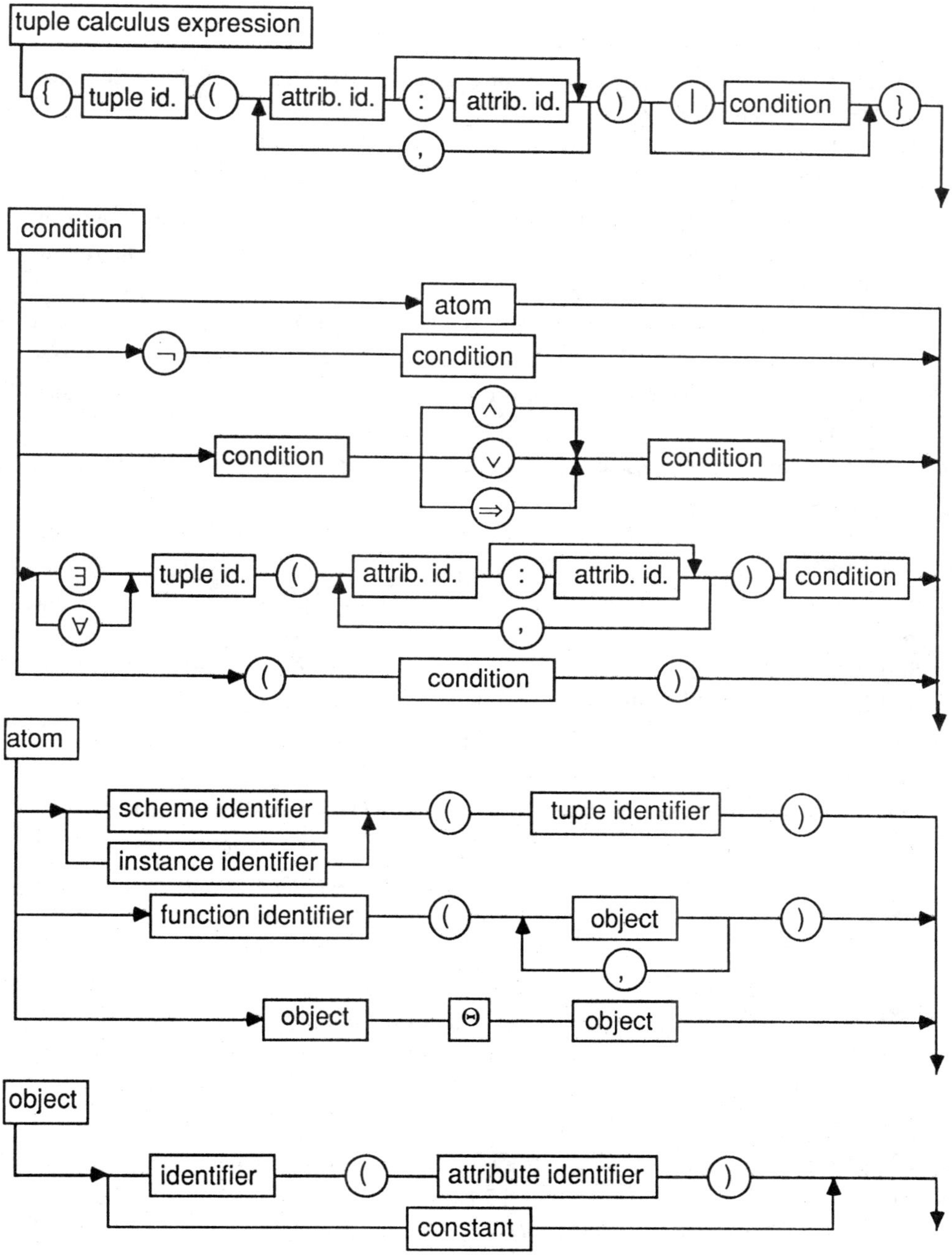

Figure 2.10: Syntax of the Tuple Calculus.

be either an attribute of the database or must be followed by a $:B$, B being an attribute of the database;

- if $t(A)$ occurs in a condition then A is an attribute of t;
- for every $t(\ldots, A_i, \ldots, A_j\colon B_j, \ldots)$ in a calculus expression we have that for each occurrence of $A_j\colon B_j$:
  - A_j belongs to the attributes of the database scheme; in this case we must have $dom(A_j) = dom(B_j)$;
  - A_j does not belong to the attributes of the database scheme and it is the only occurrence of A_j in the condition; in this case we define $dom(A_j) = dom(B_j)$;
  - A_j does not belong to the attributes of the database scheme and there are more occurrences of A_j in the condition; in this case we define $dom(A_j) = dom(B_j)$; furthermore the $dom(A_j)$ must be equal for all the occurrences of A_j;
- for every calculus expression $\{t(\ldots, A_i, \ldots, A_j\colon B_j, \ldots) \mid C\}$ we must have $free(C) \subseteq \{t\}$;
- if $\exists t(\ldots, A_i, \ldots, A_j\colon B_j, \ldots)C$ occurs in a condition and t occurs in C, then $t \in free(C)$;
- if $r(t)$ occurs in a condition, then the set of attributes of r is equal to the set of attributes of t;
- if $f(t_1(A_1), \ldots, t_n(A_n))$ occurs in a condition, then f is a boolean function, the domain of which includes $DOM(A_1) \bowtie \ldots \bowtie DOM(A_n)$.

From now on we suppose that the calculus expressions satisfy these additional restrictions.

If C has a free variable t, we use the notation $C(t/t_0)$ to indicate the condition obtained by substituting every occurrence of t in C by the tuple t_0 (we say that a condition is evaluated *true* or *false* for a specified database instance, or that it is evaluated *true* or *false*, when the database instance follows from the context). Let us now define the value of a condition C with $free(C)$ empty:

- $r(t)(t/t_0)$ is evaluated *true* iff the tuple t_0 is in r;
- $f(t_1(A_1), \ldots, t_n(A_n))(t_1/t_{1_0}) \ldots (t_n/t_{n_0})$ is evaluated *true* iff $f(t_{1_0}(A_1), \ldots, t_{n_0}(A_n)) = true$. f is a computable function in the sense of Section 2.1.4;
- $\neg C$ is evaluated *true* iff C is evaluated *false*;
- $C_1 \vee C_2$ is evaluated *true* iff C_1 is evaluated *true* or C_2 is evaluated *true*;
- $\exists t(A_1, \ldots, A_n)C$ is evaluated *true* iff there exists a tuple t_0 over $DOM(A_1) \bowtie \ldots \bowtie DOM(A_n)$ such that $C(t/t_0)$ is evaluated *true*;
- (C) is evaluated *true* iff C is evaluated *true*.

The calculus instance expression $\{t(\ldots, A_i, \ldots, A_j\colon B_j, \ldots) \mid C\}$ represents the view instance containing those tuples t_0 over $(\ldots \bowtie DOM(A_i) \bowtie \ldots \bowtie DOM(A_j) \bowtie \ldots)$ such that $C(t/t_0)$ is evaluated *true*.

Finally the view scheme represented by the calculus scheme expression $\{t(\ldots, A_i, \ldots, A_j: B_j, \ldots) \mid C\}$ is $(\Omega, \Delta, dom, M, SC)$ with

- $\Omega = \{A_1, \ldots, A_n\}$;
- $\Delta = \{dom(A_1), \ldots, dom(A_n)\}$;
- SC is the constraint that specifies all the sets of tuples that satisfy C.

2.2.5 Expressive Power of the Generating Part

In Section 2.2.3 we defined the generating part. It is obvious that the use of a constant identifier in a function call within an atom, and the use of the θ-comparison in an atom are both expressible by a call of a computable function. Taking into account the following equalities, we deduce that the generating part generates the whole calculus:

- $\forall t(\ldots, A_i, \ldots, A_j: B_j, \ldots)C = \neg\exists t(\ldots, A_i, \ldots, A_j: B_j, \ldots)(\neg C)$;
- $C_1 \wedge C_2 = \neg((\neg C_1) \vee (\neg C_2))$;
- $C_1 \Rightarrow C_2 = (\neg C_1) \vee C_2$.

2.3 SQL: Structured Query Language

SQL is a widespread commercial relational database language. It was developed by the research center of IBM in San Jose. It is based on the tuple calculus in the sense that the basic idea for a query is to select tuples from one or more relations. Only those tuples are selected that satisfy some condition. Within such a condition we can use other queries.

We do not give a general description of SQL. Only a subset of SQL equivalent to the relational algebra is discussed. A full description of SQL can be found in [27].

2.3.1 Informal Description

We give an informal description of the structured query language SQL. The general form of an instance query in SQL is an elementary query or the union, difference or intersection of elementary queries. An elementary query has the form

Select $\ldots, A_i, \ldots, t.A_j, \ldots$
From $\ldots, r_i, \ldots, r_j\ t, \ldots$
Where C

Example 2.11 Recall Example 2.8: We want all the tuples in *rooms* for those rooms that are on floor 2. We translate it in SQL to give an intuitive introduction. We write in SQL:

Select *ROOM-NUMBER*, *NUMBER-OF-BEDS*, *BATH?*, *FLOOR*, *RATE*
From *rooms*
Where $FLOOR = 2$

This query must be read as "Select from the instance *rooms* all the tuples t with $t(FLOOR) = 2$ and project them on the attribute set {*ROOM-NUMBER*, *NUMBER-OF-BEDS*, *BATH?*, *FLOOR*, *RATE*}"; this projection has no effect in this example, but the general form forces us to write it this way.

□

Example 2.12 Recall Example 2.9: Give all the room numbers for which the rate divided by its number of beds is smaller than 100:

Select *ROOM-NUMBER*
From *rooms*
Where *average-smaller-than-100*(*RATE*, *NUMBER-OF-BEDS*)

This query has to be read as "Select from the instance *rooms* all the tuples t for which *average-smaller-than-100*(t(*RATE*), t(*NUMBER-OF-BEDS*)) = *true* and consider only their *ROOM-NUMBER*-projection".

□

Example 2.13 Recall Example 2.10 where we were searching for the cheapest room with a bath:

Select *t.ROOM-NUMBER*
From *rooms t*
Where $t.BATH? = true \wedge$
(**Select** *x.ROOM-NUMBER*
From *rooms x*
Where $x.RATE < t.RATE \wedge x.BATH? = true) = \emptyset$

This query has to be read as "Select from the instance *rooms* all the tuples t that satisfy the condition after the **Where** and consider only their *ROOM-NUMBER* projection"; The condition after the **Where** says that the *BATH?* component of t must be *true* and that the set of tuples x from *rooms* whose *BATH?* component is *true* and whose *RATE*-component is smaller than the *RATE*-component of the tuple t must be empty. Note that we used t and x to distinguish between the two instances *rooms*.

□

These examples illustrate that the general form of an instance query in SQL

Select $\ldots, A_i, \ldots, t.A_j, \ldots$
From $\ldots, r_i, \ldots, r_j\ t, \ldots$
Where C

can be read as "Select from the instances $\ldots, r_i, \ldots, r_j\ t, \ldots$ all the tuples that satisfy C and consider their $\ldots, A_i, \ldots, t.A_j, \ldots$-projection".

2.3.2 Syntax of SQL

In Figure 2.11 we give the syntax diagram for an SQL-query. The meaning of this diagram is intuitively clear. Note that in the relation list, after **From** also $DOM(A)$ can occur; $DOM(A)$ is then considered as a relation instance with one attribute A, the tuples of which are the values of $dom(A)$.

Those queries that use scheme identifiers in their relation list are called SQL scheme queries and those that use instance identifiers are called SQL instance queries.

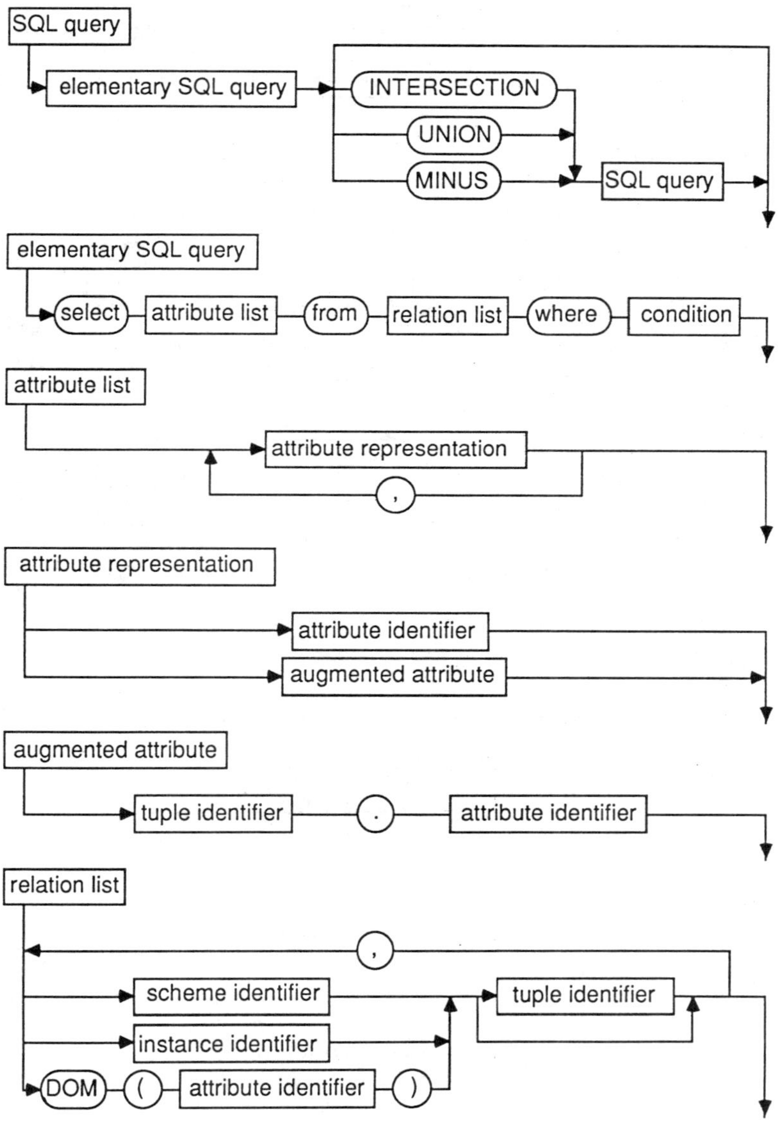

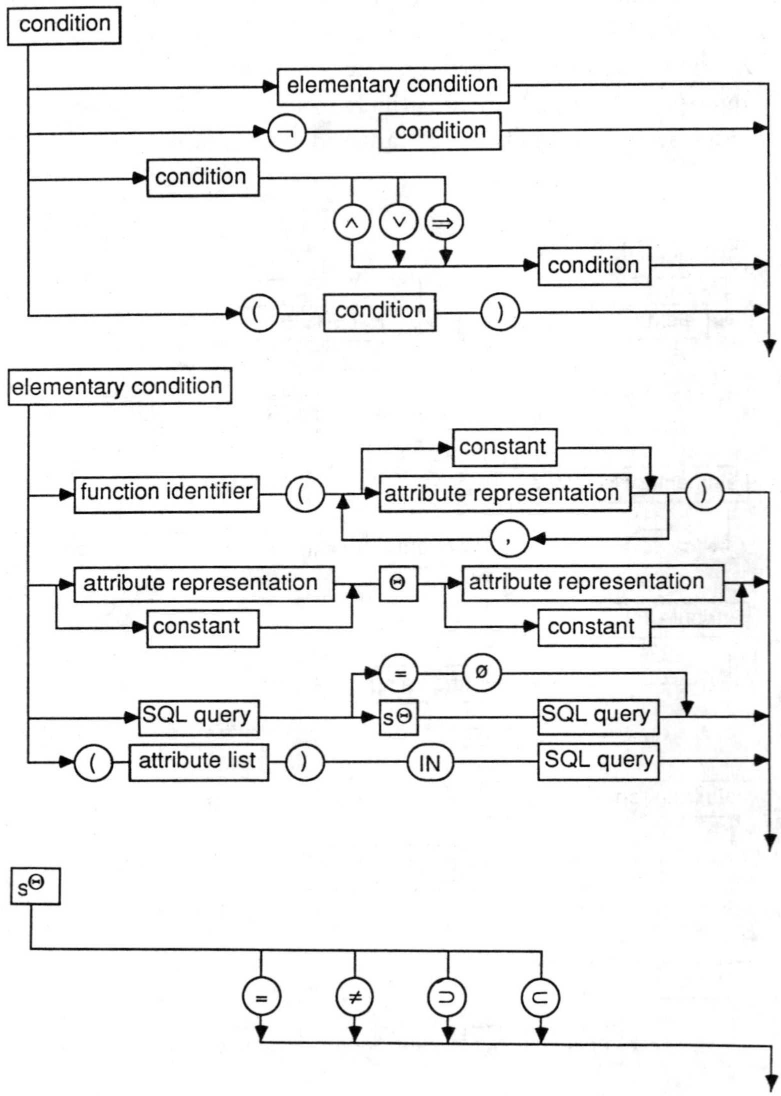

Figure 2.11: Syntax of SQL

2.3.3 Generating Part of SQL

In Figure 2.12 we give the syntax diagram of the generating part of SQL. This diagram is a subdiagram of the one of Figure 2.11. The features that are in the non-generating part are the union, the difference and the intersection of an elementary SQL-query and an SQL-query, the $\Rightarrow$ and $\wedge$, the constant identifiers, the comparisons θ, the set-comparisons $s\theta$, and the operator *IN*.

In Section 2.3.5 we express the non-generating part in terms of the generating part.

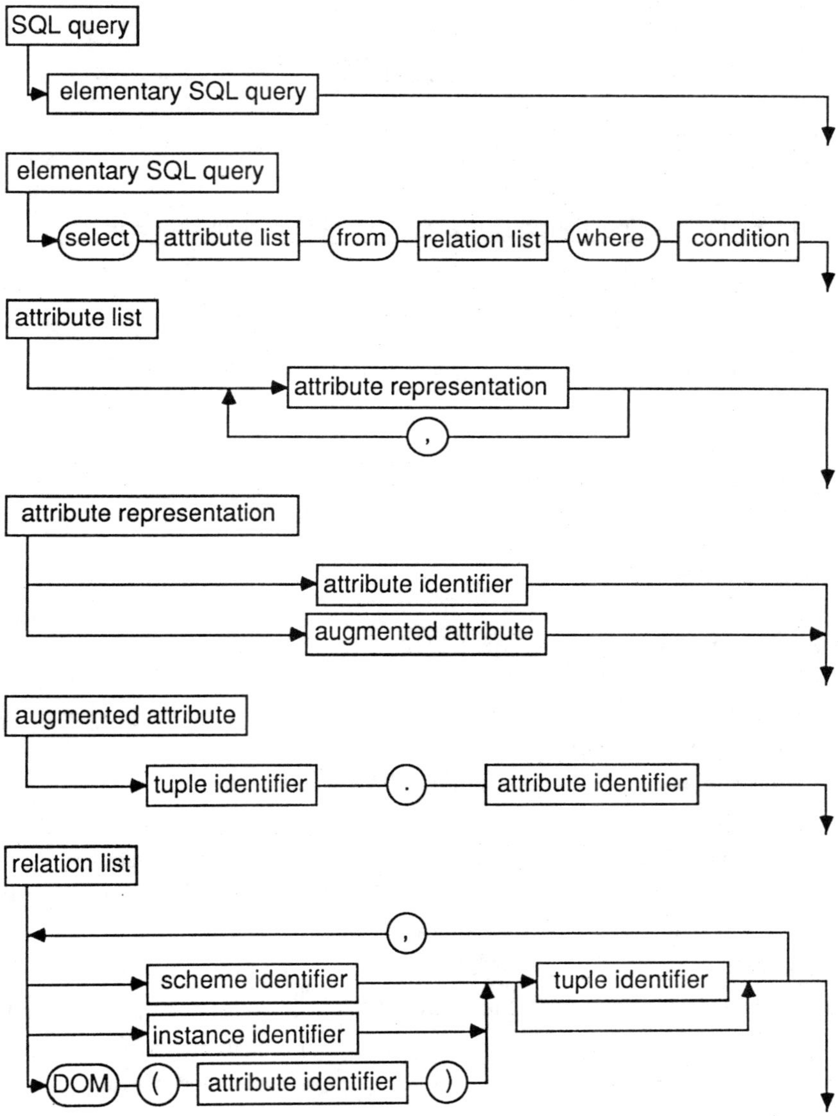

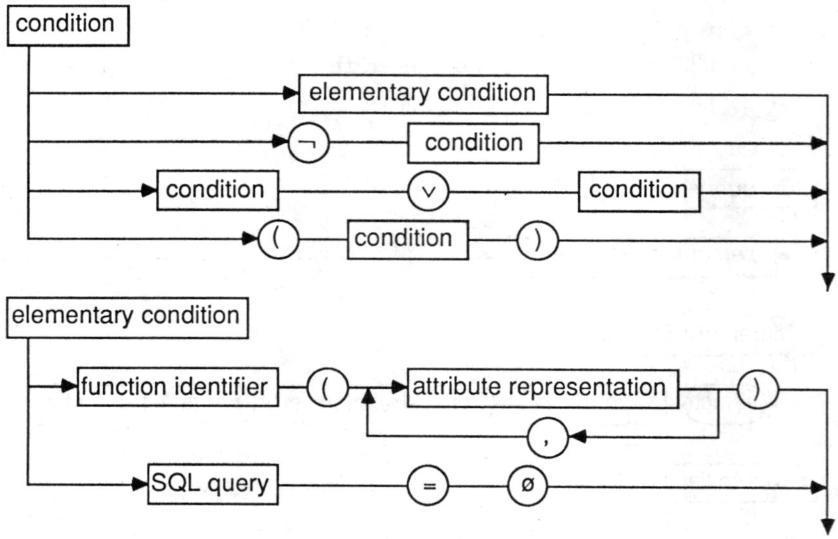

Figure 2.12: Generating part of SQL.

2.3.4 Views Represented by SQL

It is our aim to define formally the view instance represented by an SQL instance query and the view scheme represented by an SQL scheme query. Therefore we first define the attributes, the augmented attributes, the active relations and the type of an SQL query. We also state some additional restrictions on SQL queries. Finally we define the view scheme and the view instance represented by an SQL query. We restrict ourselves to the generating part of SQL. The discussion for the non-generating part is left as an exercise.

The active relations of an SQL query α are the relations (possibly together with their tuple identifier) of the relation list just behind **From** together with, if α is in the condition of another SQL query, the active relations of the latter. Hence informally the active relations of an SQL query are those relations that can be used in the SQL query.

The first additional restriction says that every attribute A that appears in an SQL query is an attribute of just one active relation and for every augmented attribute $a.A$ that appears in an SQL query there is just one active relation r a with A an attribute of R. In this way we can associate with every attribute and augmented attribute a domain, being $dom(A)$ in the corresponding relation. This domain is called the type of the attribute or the augmented attribute.

The second additional restriction says that the operands of the set operators *UNION*, *DIFFERENCE* and *INTERSECTION* must have equal attribute lists behind their **Select**. The result has the same attributes and augmented attributes as this list.

The type of an attribute list is the list of the types of the attributes and of the augmented attributes of the attribute list. The type of an SQL query is the type of the attribute list just behind its **Select**, which is in turn a list; note the importance of the order in this list.

The third additional restriction says that the type of the operands of *IN* must be equal.

Finally, the last additional restriction says that product of the types of the attributes or augmented attributes of the attribute list that is the argument of a computable function f, must be a subset of the domain of f. The function f is a computable function in the sense of Section 2.1.4. From now on we suppose that SQL queries satisfy these additional restrictions.

We now define the view instance represented in six different cases. These constructions can be combined in an obvious way in order to define the view instance of an arbitrary SQL query. Let < *relat. list* > be a list of instance identifiers, and let < *ALL attr. of relat. in* < *relat. list* >> be the set of all the attributes of the relations of < *relat. list* >.

The view instance represented by

Select < *ALL attr. of relat. in* < *relat. list* >>
From < *relat. list* >
Where $f(\ldots, A_i, \ldots, a_j.A_j, \ldots)$

is the instance containing the concatenation of tuples of the instances of the relations of the list < *relat. list* >, for which f is satisfied.

The view instance represented by

Select < *ALL attr. of relat. in* < *relat. list* >>
From < *relat. list* >
Where $\neg$
  (**Select** < *ALL attr. of relat. in* < *relat. list* >$'$>
  From < *relat. list* >$'$
  Where $C) = \emptyset$

is equal to the view instance represented by

Select < *ALL attr. of relat. in* < *relat. list* >>
From < *relat. list* >, < *relat. list* >'
Where C

The view instance represented by

Select < *ALL attr. of relat. in* < *relat. list* >>
From < *relat. list* >
Where $\neg C$

is equal to the difference of the view instances represented by

Select < *ALL attr. of relat. in* < *relat. list* >>
From < *relat. list* >

and

Select < *ALL attr. of relat. in* < *relat. list* >>
From < *relat. list* >
Where C

The view instance represented by

Select < *ALL attr. of relat. in* < *relat. list* >>
From < *relat. list* >
Where $C_1 \vee C_2$

is equal to the union of the view instances represented by

Select < *ALL attr. of relat. in* < *relat. list* >>
From < *relat. list* >
Where C_1

and

Select < *ALL attr. of relat. in* < *relat. list* >>
From < *relat. list* >
Where C_2

The view instance represented by

Select < *ALL attr. of relat. in* < *relat. list* >>
From < *relat. list* >
Where (C)

is equal to the view instance represented by

Select < *ALL attr. of relat. in* < *relat. list* >>
From < *relat. list* >
Where C

The view instance represented by

Select $\ldots, A_i, \ldots, a_j.A_j, \ldots$
From < *relat. list* >
Where C

is equal to the projection on $\ldots, A_i, \ldots, a_j.A_j, \ldots$ of the view instance represented by

Select $<$ *ALL attr. of relat. in* $<$ *relat. list* $>>$
From $<$ *relat. list* $>$
Where C

Finally we define the view scheme represented by an SQL scheme query:

Select $\ldots, A_i, \ldots, a_j.A_j, \ldots$
From $<$ *relat. list* $>$
Where C

This SQL scheme query represents the view scheme $(\Omega, \Delta, dom, M, SC)$ with

- $\Omega = \{\ldots, A_i, \ldots, A_j, \ldots\}$;
- $\Delta = dom(\Omega)$;
- dom is as defined in the database;
- the meaning M cannot be defined formally;
- SC only contains the constraint that says that the view instances are represented by the associated SQL instance query, where the relation instances in the relation list fulfill the constraints in the database.

Example 2.14 As an illustration of SQL we give in this example four different SQL instance queries of the English question: Give the roommaid-number of the roommaids that are responsible for at least one room, together with those floors where there is no room they are responsible for. Suppose that on each floor there is at least one room:

- **Select** *ROOMMAID-NUMBER, FLOOR*
  From *rooms, roommaids*
  Where $\neg$(*ROOMMAID-NUMBER, FLOOR*) *IN*
      Select *y.ROOMMAID-NUMBER, x.FLOOR*
      From *rooms x, roommaids y*
      Where *x.ROOM-NUMBER* = *y.ROOM-NUMBER*;
- **Select** *y.ROOMMAID-NUMBER, x.FLOOR*
  From *rooms x, roommaids y*
      MINUS
  Select *y.ROOMMAID-NUMBER, x.FLOOR*
  From *rooms x, roommaids y*
  Where *x.ROOM-NUMBER* = *y.ROOM-NUMBER*;
- **Select** *ROOMMAID-NUMBER, FLOOR*
  From *rooms, roommaids*
  Where $\neg$(*ROOMMAID-NUMBER*) *IN*
      Select *y.ROOMMAID-NUMBER*
      From *rooms x, roommaids y*
      Where *x.ROOM-NUMBER* = *y.ROOM-NUMBER*$\wedge$
          x.FLOOR = *FLOOR*;

- **Select** *ROOMMAID-NUMBER*, *FLOOR*
  From *rooms*, *roommaids*
  Where $\neg$(*FLOOR*) *IN*
    Select *x.FLOOR*
    From *rooms x*, *roommaids y*
    Where *x.ROOM-NUMBER* = *y.ROOM-NUMBER* $\wedge$
      y.ROOMMAID-NUMBER = *ROOMMAID-NUMBER*.

□

2.3.5 Expressive Power of the Generating Part

In Section 2.3.3 we defined the generating part of SQL. We now prove that we can express the non-generating part of SQL in terms of its generating part.

First some trivial remarks. The $\Rightarrow$ and the $\wedge$ can be expressed using the $\neg$ and the $\vee$. Furthermore the constants and the θ- comparisons can be expressed by the boolean functions of the form $f(\ldots, A_i, \ldots, a_j.A_j, \ldots)$, where $a_j.A_j$ are augmented attributes. The syntax of the latter is illustrated in Figure 2.11. Finally the set comparisons $s\theta$ can be expressed using $\neg$, $\wedge$, $\vee$, the set difference and the emptiness test of an SQL query. The proof of all these remarks is left as an exercise.

We still have to express the operator *IN* and the set operations: *UNION*, *INTERSECTION* and *MINUS*.

IN:

$(A_1, \ldots, a_j.A_j, \ldots, A_n)$ *IN*
  Select $B_1, \ldots, b_l.B_l, \ldots, B_n$
  From $r_1, \ldots, r_l\ b_l, \ldots, r_k$
  Where C

can be replaced by

$\neg$ (**Select** $B_1, \ldots, b_l.B_l, \ldots, B_n$
  From $r_1, \ldots, r_l\ b_l, \ldots, r_k$
  Where $C \wedge (A_1 = B_1) \wedge \ldots \wedge (A_n = B_n)) = \emptyset$

UNION:

We suppose that the relation lists in both queries are equal. The construction, when they are not equal is made by using augmented attributes and putting $DOM(A)$s in the relation list. This is left as an exercise.

Select $A_1, \ldots, a_j.A_j, \ldots, A_n$
From $r_1, \ldots, r_j\ a_j, \ldots, r_k$
Where C_1
  UNION
Select $A_1, \ldots, a_j.A_j, \ldots, A_n$
From $r_1, \ldots, r_j\ a_j, \ldots, r_k$
Where C_2

can be replaced by

Select $A_1, \ldots, a_j.A_j, \ldots, A_n$
From $r_1, \ldots, r_j\ a_j, \ldots, r_k$
Where $C_1 \vee C_2$

MINUS:

Select $A_1, \ldots, a_j.A_j, \ldots, A_n$
From $r_1, \ldots, r_j\ a_j, \ldots, r_k$
Where C_1
MINUS
Select $A_1, \ldots, a_j.A_j, \ldots, A_n$
From $s_1, \ldots, s_j\ a_j, \ldots, s_l$
Where C_2

can be replaced by

Select $A_1, \ldots, a_j.A_j, \ldots, A_n$
From $r_1, \ldots, r_j\ a_j, \ldots, r_k$
Where $C_1 \wedge \neg((A_1, \ldots, a_j.A_j, \ldots, A_n)$ *IN*
Select $x_{i_1}.A_1, \ldots, x_{i_n}.A_n$
From $s_1\ x_1, \ldots, s_l\ x_l$
Where $C_2)$

INTERSECTION:

α *INTERSECTION* β

can be replaced by

α *MINUS* (α *MINUS* β)

where α and β are SQL queries.

An interesting final remark is that we really need the possibility to test the emptiness of an SQL query in the where-condition of SQL scheme queries. More exactly, the expressive power of the generating part without the queries that have an SQL query in their where-condition, is strictly less than the expressive power of SQL. Take, for instance, the relation scheme R with only two attributes A and B; we ask for those A-values that are associated to every B-value in R; in the relational scheme algebra we express this by

$$R \div \Pi(R; B)$$

Suppose that we can represent this query by:

Select A
From $R\ x_1, \ldots, R\ x_p$
Where C

where C contains no SQL query. Hence, C only tests the tuples delivered by the relation list after **From**, and hence C only depends on the tuple actually tested, without being influenced by the rest of the relation.

Consider now the relation instance of R that only contains one tuple (a, b). The answer is a. So the condition has to evaluate $(a, b, a, b, \ldots, a, b)$ as *true*.

Consider now another relation instance of R that contains just two tuples (a, b) and (a_1, b_1) with $a \neq a_1$ and $b \neq b_1$. The answer is now empty. But the SQL query above returns an answer that contains at least a since it evaluates 2^p tuples, one of them is $(a, b, \ldots, a, b)$, which returns *true* and creates a in the result.

2.4 Reduction of the Tuple Calculus to the Algebra

In this section, we reduce the tuple calculus to the relational algebra. This implies that every question that can be represented by the tuple calculus can also be represented by the relational algebra. This induces that the expressive power of the relational algebra is at least that of the tuple calculus.
In Section 2.4.1 we give a method to construct an expression in the relational algebra that represents the same query as a given expression of the tuple calculus, by first reducing the latter to an expression of the generating part of the tuple calculus.

2.4.1 Method

In Section 2.2.3 we introduced a generating part of the tuple calculus. We use this generating part in our reduction method. This method only handles calculus scheme expressions. The construction for calculus instance expressions is identical except for Step 3.1 where we have to consider relation instances instead of relation schemes. The method consists of four steps:

- Step 1: given a calculus scheme expression; transform it to a calculus scheme expression of the generating part, using the techniques described in Section 2.2.5;
- Step 2: replace all the tuple identifiers by t_i, with different indices; replace the attributes of each t_i by $A_i^1, \ldots, A_i^k$;
- Step 3: let $\{t_j(A_j^1, \ldots, A_j^l) \mid C\}$ be the result of Step 2; construct an expression in the relational algebra for C, using recursively one of the Steps 3.1 to 3.6:
  - Step 3.1: $R(t_i)$ is reduced to $\rho(R; f)$ where f renames the attributes of R to A_i^ms according to Step 2;
  - Step 3.2: $f(\ldots, t_i(A_i^m), \ldots)$ is reduced to $\{\ldots; x_n\colon A_i^m; \ldots \mid f(\ldots, x_n, \ldots)\}$;
  - Step 3.3: let the condition C_1 be reduced to the relational expression E_1, the attributes of which are $B_1, \ldots, B_p$; then $\neg C_1$ is reduced to $DOM(B_1) \bowtie \ldots \bowtie DOM(B_p) - E_1$;
  - Step 3.4: let the conditions C_1 and C_2 be reduced to the relational expressions E_1 and E_2 respectively; then $C_1 \vee C_2$ is reduced to $E_1 \bowtie DOM(B_1) \bowtie \ldots \bowtie DOM(B_p) \cup E_2 \bowtie DOM(D_1) \bowtie \ldots \bowtie DOM(D_q)$, where $B_1, \ldots, B_p$ are the attributes of E_2 not in E_1 and $D_1, \ldots, D_q$ the attributes of E_1 not in E_2;

- Step 3.5: let the condition C_1 be reduced to the relational expression E_1; then $\exists t_i(A_i^1, \ldots, A_i^k)C_1$ is reduced to $\Pi(E_1; B_1, \ldots, B_p)$, where $B_1, \ldots, B_p$ are the attributes of E_1 that are not attributes of t_i;
- Step 3.6: the conditions C_1 and (C_1) are reduced to the same relational expression

;

- Step 4: t_j is the only free tuple of the condition C; apply the renaming that transforms the attributes $A_j^1, \ldots, A_j^l$ back to their original form. The result is an algebraic scheme expression that represents the same query as the given calculus scheme expression.

2.4.2 Example

We now give an example of the method above. The result of the reduction is generally rather complex. Using the reduction method for the non-generating part, results in a more simple solution. In the next example however we use the reduction method for the generating part.

Example 2.15 The relation scheme R has two attributes A and B.
Consider the next calculus scheme expression:

$$\{t(C{:}\, A) \mid \exists s(A, B)(R(s) \land t(C) = s(A))\}$$

By Step 1 this is transformed to

$$\{t(C{:}\, A) \mid \exists s(A, B)(\neg(\neg R(s) \lor \neg \mathit{equal}(t(C), s(A))))\}$$

Step 2 induces

$$\{t_1(A_1^1) \mid \exists t_2(A_2^1, A_2^2)(\neg(\neg R(t_2) \lor \neg \mathit{equal}(t_1(A_1^1), t_2(A_2^1))))\}$$

By Step 3.1 $R(t_2)$ is reduced to

$$\rho(R; A \to A_2^1, B \to A_2^2)$$

By Step 3.2 $\mathit{equal}(t_1(A_1^1), t_2(A_2^1))$ is reduced to

$$\{x_1{:}\, A_1^1; x_2{:}\, A_2^1 \mid \mathit{equal}(x_1, x_2)\}$$

By Step 3.3 $\neg R(t_2)$ is reduced to

$$\mathit{DOM}(A_2^1) \bowtie \mathit{DOM}(A_2^2) - \rho(R; A \to A_2^1, B \to A_2^2)$$

By Step 3.3 $\neg \mathit{equal}(t_1(A_1^1), t_2(A_2^1))$ is reduced to

$$\mathit{DOM}(A_1^1) \bowtie \mathit{DOM}(A_2^1) - \{x_1{:}\, A_1^1; x_2{:}\, A_2^1 \mid \mathit{equal}(x_1, x_2)\}$$

By Step 3.4 $\neg R(t_2) \lor \neg \mathit{equal}(t_1(A_1^1), t_2(A_2^1))$ is reduced to

$$\mathit{DOM}(A_1^1) \bowtie (\mathit{DOM}(A_2^1) \bowtie \mathit{DOM}(A_2^2) - \rho(R; A \to A_2^1, B \to A_2^2)) \cup$$
$$(\mathit{DOM}(A_1^1) \bowtie \mathit{DOM}(A_2^1) - \{x_1{:}\, A_1^1; x_2{:}\, A_2^1 \mid \mathit{equal}(x_1, x_2)\}) \bowtie \mathit{DOM}(A_2^2)$$

By Step 3.3 $\neg(\neg R(t_2) \lor \neg \mathit{equal}(t_1(A_1^1), t_2(A_2^1)))$ is reduced to

$$\mathit{DOM}(A_1^1) \bowtie \mathit{DOM}(A_2^1) \bowtie \mathit{DOM}(A_2^2) -$$
$$(\mathit{DOM}(A_1^1) \bowtie (\mathit{DOM}(A_2^1) \bowtie \mathit{DOM}(A_2^2) - \rho(R; A \to A_2^1, B \to A_2^2)) \cup$$
$$(\mathit{DOM}(A_1^1) \bowtie \mathit{DOM}(A_2^1) - \{x_1{:}\, A_1^1; x_2{:}\, A_2^1 \mid \mathit{equal}(x_1, x_2)\}) \bowtie \mathit{DOM}(A_2^2))$$

By Step 3.5 $\exists t_2(A_2^1, A_2^2)(\neg(\neg R(t_2) \vee \neg equal(t_1(A_1^1), t_2(A_2^1))))$ is reduced to

$$\Pi(DOM(A_1^1) \bowtie DOM(A_2^1) \bowtie DOM(A_2^2)- \\ (DOM(A_1^1) \bowtie (DOM(A_2^1) \bowtie DOM(A_2^2) - \rho(R; A \rightarrow A_2^1, B \rightarrow A_2^2)) \cup \\ (DOM(A_1^1) \bowtie DOM(A_2^1) - \{x_1: A_1^1; x_2: A_2^1 \mid equal(x_1, x_2)\}) \bowtie DOM(A_2^2)); A_1^1)$$

Finally Step 4 terminates the reduction:

$$\rho(\Pi(DOM(A_1^1) \bowtie DOM(A_2^1) \bowtie DOM(A_2^2)- \\ (DOM(A_1^1) \bowtie (DOM(A_2^1) \bowtie DOM(A_2^2) - \rho(R; A \rightarrow A_2^1, B \rightarrow A_2^2)) \cup \\ (DOM(A_1^1) \bowtie DOM(A_2^1) - \{x_1: A_1^1; x_2: A_2^1 \mid equal(x_1, x_2)\}) \bowtie \\ DOM(A_2^2)); A_1^1); A_1^1 \rightarrow C)$$

□

2.5 Reduction of the Algebra to SQL

In this section we reduce the relational algebra to SQL. This implies that every question that can be represented by the relational algebra can also be represented by SQL. This implies that the expressive power of SQL is at least that of the relational algebra.

In Section 2.5.1 we give a method to construct an expression in SQL that represents the same query as a given expression of the relational algebra, by first reducing the latter to an expression of the generating part of the relational algebra.

2.5.1 Method

In Section 2.1.3 we introduced a generating part of the relational algebra. We use this generating part in our reduction method. This method only handles algebraic scheme expressions. The construction for algebraic instance expressions is identical except for Step 2.1 where we have to consider relation instances instead of relation schemes.

- Step 1: in this step we reduce the given relational scheme expression to the generating part of the relational algebra. This was explained in Section 2.1.5;
- Step 2: reduction of the operands to SQL:
  - Step 2.1: let R be an identifier of a relation scheme the attributes of which are $A_1, \ldots, A_n$. It is reduced to:

    Select $A_1, \ldots, A_n$
    From R
  - Step 2.2: $\{x_1: A_1; \ldots; x_n: A_n \mid f(x_1, \ldots, x_n)\}$ is reduced to:

    Select $A_1, \ldots, A_n$
    From $DOM(A_1), \ldots, DOM(A_n)$
    Where $f(A_1, \ldots, A_n)$

- Step 3: reduction of the operations (in Steps 3.1 to 3.5 we only consider attributes of the form A_i in the attribute list of E, E_1 and E_2; a generalization for the augmented attributes of the form $a_i.A_i$ is left as an exercise; in Step 3.3 we only consider one relation in the relation list of E_1 and E_2; the generalization for more relations is also left as an exercise):
  - Step 3.1: let the algebraic scheme expression E be reduced to

    Select $A_1, \ldots, A_n$
    From $<$ *relat. list* $>$
    Where $<$ *condition* $>$

    the projection $\Pi(E; A_i, \ldots, A_j)$ is reduced to

    Select $A_i, \ldots, A_j$
    From $<$ *relat. list* $>$
    Where $<$ *condition* $>$

  - Step 3.2: let the algebraic scheme expression E be reduced to

    Select $A_1, \ldots, A_n$
    From $<$ *relat. list* $>$
    Where $<$ *condition* $>$

    if $f(A_i) = B_i$ for all $1 \leq i \leq n$ then the renaming $\rho(R; f)$ is reduced to:

    Select $B_1, \ldots, B_n$
    From $DOM(B_1), \ldots, DOM(B_n)$
    Where $(B_1, \ldots, B_n)$ *IN*
        Select $A_1, \ldots, A_n$
        From $<$ *relat. list* $>$
        Where $<$ *condition* $>$

  - Step 3.3: let the algebraic expressions E_1 and E_2 be respectively reduced to

    Select $A_1, \ldots, A_k, \ldots, A_n$
    From R_1
    Where $<$ *condition-1* $>$

    and

    Select $A_k, \ldots, A_n, \ldots, A_p$
    From R_2
    Where $<$ *condition-2* $>$

    the join $E_1 \bowtie E_2$ is reduced to

    Select $A_1, \ldots, A_k, \ldots, A_n, \ldots, A_p$
    From $DOM(A_1), \ldots, DOM(A_k), \ldots, DOM(A_n), \ldots, DOM(A_p)$
    Where $(A_1, \ldots, A_k, \ldots, A_n, \ldots, A_p)$ *IN*
        Select $x.A_1, \ldots, x.A_k, \ldots, x.A_n, \ldots, y.A_p$
        From $R_1\ x, R_2\ y$
        Where $<$ *condition-1* $> \wedge <$ *condition-2* $>$
            $\wedge x.A_k = y.A_k \wedge \ldots \wedge x.A_n = y.A_n$

– Step 3.4: let the algebraic expressions E_1 and E_2 be respectively reduced to:

Select $A_1, \ldots, A_n$
From < *relat. list-1* >
Where < *condition-1* >

and

Select $A_1, \ldots, A_n$
From < *relat. list-2* >
Where < *condition-2* >

the union $E_1 \cup E_2$ is reduced to

Select $A_1, \ldots, A_n$
From < *relat. list-1* >
Where < *condition-1* >
UNION
Select $A_1, \ldots, A_n$
From < *relat. list-2* >
Where < *condition-2* >

– Step 3.5: under the same assumptions as in Step 3.4, the difference $E_1 - E_2$ is reduced to:

Select $A_1, \ldots, A_n$
From < *relat. list-1* >
Where < *condition-1* >
MINUS
Select $A_1, \ldots, A_n$
From < *relat. list-2* >
Where < *condition-2* >

2.5.2 Example

Example 2.16 illustrates the above method.

Example 2.16 Let R be a relation scheme with two attributes A and B satisfying the condition $dom(A) = dom(B)$.

Now consider the algebraic scheme expression

$$\Pi(\sigma(R; A < B); A) \cup \rho(\Pi(R; B); B \rightarrow A)$$

Step 1 reduces this expression to

$$\Pi(R \bowtie \{x_1 \colon A; x_2 \colon B \mid lower(x_1, x_2)\}; A) \cup \rho(\Pi(R; B); B \rightarrow A)$$

Step 2.1 reduces R to

Select A, B
From R

Step 2.2 reduces $\{x_1 : A, x_2 : B \mid lower(x_1, x_2)\}$ to

Select A, B
From $DOM(A), DOM(B)$
Where $lower(A, B)$

Step 3.3 reduces $R \bowtie \{x_1{:}\, A; x_2{:}\, B \mid lower(x_1, x_2)\}$ to

Select A, B
From $DOM(A), DOM(B)$
Where (A, B) *IN*
  Select $x.A, x.B$
  From $R\ x, DOM(A)\ y, DOM(B)\ z$
  Where $lower(y.A, z.B) \wedge x.A = y.A \wedge x.B = z.B$

Step 3.1 reduces $\Pi(R \bowtie \{x_1{:}\, A; x_2{:}\, B \mid lower(x_1, x_2)\}; A)$ to

Select A
From $DOM(A), DOM(B)$
Where (A, B) *IN*
  Select $x.A, x.B$
  From $R\ x, DOM(A)\ y, DOM(B)\ z$
  Where $lower(y.A, z.B) \wedge x.A = y.A \wedge x.B = z.B$

Step 3.1 reduces $\Pi(R; B)$ to

Select B
From R

Step 3.2 reduces $\rho(\Pi(R; B); B \rightarrow A)$ to

Select A
From $DOM(A)$
Where A *IN*
  Select B
  From R

Finally Step 3.4 reduces the expression obtained in Step 1 to

Select A
From $DOM(A), DOM(B)$
Where (A, B) *IN*
  Select $x.A, x.B$
  From $R\ x, DOM(A)\ y, DOM(B)\ z$
  Where $lower(y.A, z.B) \wedge x.A = y.A \wedge x.B = z.B$
  UNION
Select A
From $DOM(A)$
Where A *IN*
  Select B
  From R

□

2.6 Reduction of SQL to the Tuple Calculus

In this section we reduce SQL to the tuple calculus. This implies that the expressive power of the tuple calculus is at least that of SQL.

In Section 2.6.1 we give a method to construct an expression in the tuple calculus that represents the same query as a given expression in SQL, by first reducing the latter to an expression of the generating part of SQL.

2.6.1 Method

In Section 2.3.3 we introduced a generating part of SQL. We use this generating part in our reduction method. This method only handles SQL scheme queries. The construction for SQL instance queries is identical except that relation instances are used instead of relation schemes. We use the following notation:

$$ace(< \textit{relat. list} >; < \textit{condition} >)$$

indicates the so-called *auxiliary calculus expression.*

Informally, this notation indicates those tuples of the join of the relations in the list $< \textit{relat. list} >$ that fulfill the $< \textit{condition} >$.

Formally $ace(< \textit{relat. list} >; < \textit{condition} >)$ is
$\{t(< \textit{ALL the attr. of } < \textit{relat. list} >>) \mid$
$\exists t_1(< \textit{ALL the attr. of } R_1 >)(\ldots \exists t_k(< \textit{ALL the attr. of } R_k >)$
$(R_1(t_1) \wedge \ldots \wedge R_k(t_k) \wedge \ldots \wedge t(A_{i_j}) = t_i(A_{i_j}) \wedge \ldots \wedge < \textit{condition} >) \ldots)\}$
where the $< \textit{relat. list} >$ is $(R_1, \ldots, R_k)$ and the $< \textit{ALL the attr. of } R_i >$ is $\{A_{i_1}, A_{i_2}, \ldots\}$. $< \textit{condition} >$ is an arbitrary condition of a tuple calculus expression. If some R_i is a $DOM(A)$ then $R_i(t_i)$ is replaced by *true* in the auxiliary calculus expression. Finally if $k = 1$ we have

$$ace(R; < \textit{condition} >)$$

indicates the tuple calculus expression

$$\{t(< \textit{ALL the attr. of } R >) \mid R(t) \wedge < \textit{condition} >\}$$

We propose the following reduction method:

- Step 1: Reduce the given SQL query to the generating part of SQL, as described in Section 2.3.5;
- Step 2: reduce the SQL query by recursively applying Steps 2.1 to 2.6:
  - Step 2.1: reduce

    Select $< \textit{ALL the attr. of the relat. in } < \textit{relat. list} >>$
    From $< \textit{relat. list} >$
    Where $f(A_1, \ldots, A_n)$

    to the tuple calculus expression

    $ace(< \textit{relat. list} >; f(t(A_1), \ldots, t(A_n)))$

– Step 2.2: the SQL query

Select < *ALL the attr. of the relat. in* < *relat. list* >>
From < *relat. list* >
Where $\neg$
(**Select** < *SOME attr. of relat. in* < *relat. list1* >>
From < *relat. list1* >
Where $C) = \emptyset$

is reduced to the same tuple calculus expression as the SQL query

Select < *ALL the attr. of the relat. in* < *relat. list* >>
From < *relat. list* >, < *relat. list1* >
Where C

– Step 2.3: if the SQL query

Select < *ALL the attr. of the relat. in* < *relat. list* >>
From < *relat. list* >
Where C

is reduced to the tuple calculus expression

{*t*(< *ALL the attr. of the relat. in* < *relat. list* >>) |
< *condition* >}

then the SQL query

Select < *ALL the attr. of the relat. in* < *relat. list* >>
From < *relat. list* >
Where $\neg C$

is reduced to the tuple calculus expression

ace(< *ALL the attr. of the relat. in* < *relat. list* >>;
$\neg$ < *condition* >)

– Step 2.4: let the SQL query

Select < *ALL the attr. of the relat. in* < *relat. list* >>
From < *relat. list* >
Where $C1$

be reduced to the tuple calculus expression

{*t*(< *ALL the attr. of the relat. in* < *relat. list* >>) |
< *condition1* >}

and let the SQL query

Select < *ALL the attr. of the relat. in* < *relat. list* >>
From < *relat. list* >
Where $C2$

be reduced to the tuple calculus expression

{*t*(< *ALL the attr. of the relat. in* < *relat. list* >>) |
< *condition2* >}

then

Select < *ALL the attr. of the relat. in* < *relat. list* >>
From < *relat. list* >
Where $C1 \vee C2$

is reduced to the tuple calculus expression

{*t*(< *ALL the attr. of the relat. in* < *relat. list* >>) |
< *condition1* > ∨ < *condition2* >}

The case that the < *relat. list* >s in the SQL queries are different is left as an exercise.

- Step 2.5: the following SQL queries

  Select < *ALL the attr. of the relat. in* < *relat. list* >>
  From < *relat. list* >
  Where (C)

  and

  Select < *ALL the attr. of the relat. in* < *relat. list* >>
  From < *relat. list* >
  Where C

  are reduced to the same tuple calculus expression

- Step 2.6: if the following SQL query

  Select < *ALL the attr. of the relat. in* < *relat. list* >>
  From < *relat. list* >
  Where C

  is reduced to

  {*t*(< *ALL the attr. of the relat. in* < *relat. list* >>) |
  < *condition* >}

  then

  Select < *SOME attr. of relat. in* < *relat. list* >>
  From < *relat. list* >
  Where C

  is reduced to

  {*t′*(< *SOME attr. of relat. in* < *relat. list* >>) |
  ∃*t*(< *ALL the attr. of the relat. in* < *relat. list* >>)
  $(t'(A_1) = t(A_1) \ldots \wedge t'(A_n) = t(A_n) \wedge$ < *condition* >)},

  with < *SOME attr. of relat. in* < *relat. list* >>= $\{A_1, \ldots, A_n\}$

Remark the use of < *ALL the attr. of the relat. in* < *relat. list* >> that contains all the attributes of the relations in the relation list.

In our discussion, we did not consider augmented attributes of the form $a.A$. The generalization of the method above to augmented attributes is left as an exercise to the reader.

2.6.2 Example

In Example 2.17 below, we illustrate the method discussed in the previous section to reduce a given SQL query to a tuple calculus expression.

Example 2.17 In some cases, it may be not straightforward how Steps 2.1 to 2.6 have to be applied on a given SQL query. First, we have to decompose the SQL query in a top down way until we can apply Step 2.1. Then, we have to work bottom up again and construct calculus expressions according to Steps 2.2 to 2.6.

Let R and S be two relation schemes, each of which consists of two attributes. The attributes of R are called A and B, and the attributes of S are called C and D. Suppose furthermore that $dom(B) = dom(C)$.

The following SQL scheme query is given:

Select A
From R
Where $B < 5 \vee$
    (**Select** C
    From S
    Where $B = C) = \emptyset$

Step 1 reduces this query to query $Q1$

Select A
From R
Where *smaller-than-5*$(B) \vee$
    (**Select** C
    From S
    Where *equal*$(B, C)) = \emptyset$

In order to reduce $Q1$ we will use Step 2.6 and query $Q2$

Select A, B
From R
Where *smaller-than-5*$(B) \vee$
    (**Select** C
    From S
    Where *equal*$(B, C)) = \emptyset$

In order to reduce $Q2$ we will use Step 2.4 and queries $Q3$

Select A, B
From R
Where *smaller-than-5*(B)

and $Q4$

Select A, B
From R
Where
(**Select** C
From S
Where $equal(B, C)) = \emptyset$

In order to reduce $Q4$ we will use Step 2.3 and query $Q5$

Select A, B
From R
Where $\neg$
(**Select** C
From S
Where $equal(B, C)) = \emptyset$

In order to reduce $Q5$ we will use Step 2.2 and query $Q6$

Select A, B
From R, S
Where $equal(B, C)$

In order to reduce $Q6$ we will use Step 2.6 and query $Q7$

Select A, B, C, D
From R, S
Where $equal(B, C)$

Query $Q3$ is reduced by Step 2.1 to

$$\{t(A, B) \mid R(t) \wedge \textit{smaller-than-5}(t(B))\}$$

Query $Q7$ is reduced by Step 2.1 to

$$\{t(A, B, C, D) \mid \exists t_1(A, B)(\exists t_2(C, D)(R(t_1) \\ \wedge S(t_2) \wedge t(A) = t_1(A) \wedge t(B) = t_1(B) \wedge t(C) = t_2(C) \\ \wedge t(D) = t_2(D) \wedge equal(t(B), t(C))))\}$$

Query $Q6$ is reduced by Step 2.6 to

$$\{t'(A, B) \mid \exists t(A, B, C, D)(t(A) = t'(A) \wedge t(B) = t'(B) \wedge \\ \exists t_1(A, B)(\exists t_2(C, D)(R(t_1) \wedge \\ S(t_2) \wedge t(A) = t_1(A) \wedge t(B) = t_1(B) \wedge t(C) = t_2(C) \wedge \\ t(D) = t_2(D) \wedge equal(t(B), t(C)))))\}$$

Query $Q5$ is reduced by Step 2.2 to the same calculus expression.

Query $Q4$ is reduced by Step 2.3 to

$$\{t'(A, B) \mid R(t') \wedge \neg(\exists t(A, B, C, D)(t(A) = t'(A) \wedge t(B) = t'(B) \wedge \\ \exists t_1(A, B)(\exists t_2(C, D)(R(t_1) \wedge \\ S(t_2) \wedge t(A) = t_1(A) \wedge t(B) = t_1(B) \wedge t(C) = t_2(C) \wedge \\ t(D) = t_2(D) \wedge equal(t(B), t(C))))))\}$$

Query $Q2$ is reduced by Step 2.4 to

$$\{t'(A,B) \mid (R(t') \wedge \textit{smaller-than-5}(t'(B))) \vee (R(t')$$
$$\wedge\neg(\exists t(A,B,C,D)(t(A) = t'(A) \wedge t(B) = t'(B)\wedge$$
$$\exists t_1(A,B)(\exists t_2(C,D)(R(t_1)\wedge$$
$$S(t_2) \wedge t(A) = t_1(A) \wedge t(B) = t_1(B) \wedge t(C) = t_2(C)\wedge$$
$$t(D) = t_2(D) \wedge \textit{equal}(t(B), t(C)))))))\}$$

Finally query $Q1$ is reduced by Step 2.6 to

$$\{tt(A) \mid \exists t'(A,B)(R(t') \wedge t'(A) = tt(A) \wedge (R(t') \wedge \textit{smaller-than-5}(t'(B)))$$
$$\vee(R(t') \wedge \neg(\exists t(A,B,C,D)(t(A) = t'(A) \wedge t(B) = t'(B)\wedge$$
$$\exists t_1(A,B)(\exists t_2(C,D)(R(t_1)\wedge$$
$$S(t_2) \wedge t(A) = t_1(A) \wedge t(B) = t_1(B) \wedge t(C) = t_2(C)\wedge$$
$$t(D) = t_2(D) \wedge \textit{equal}(t(B), t(C))))))))\}$$

□

2.7 Exercises

2.1 Define the view schemes for the domain, the comparative instances, the intersection, the selections and the division.

2.2 Let r and s be two relation instances with attributes $\{A, B, C, D\}$. Prove or disprove:

- $\Pi(r \cap s; A, B) = \Pi(r; A, B) \cap \Pi(s; A, B)$
- $\Pi(r - s; A, B) = \Pi(r; A, B) - \Pi(s; A, B)$
- $\Pi(\sigma(r; A = a); A, B) = \sigma(\Pi(r; A, B); A = a)$
- $\sigma(r - s; A > a) = \sigma(r; A > a) - \sigma(s; A > a)$
- $\sigma(r \bowtie \Pi(s; B); A = a) = \sigma(r; A = a) \bowtie \Pi(s; B)$
- $(r \div \Pi(s; C, D)) \bowtie \Pi(s; C, D) = r$
- $(r \cup s) \div \Pi(s; A, B) = (r \div \Pi(s; A, B)) \cup (s \div \Pi(s; A, B))$
- $(r - s) \div \Pi(s; A, B) = (r \div \Pi(s; A, B)) - (s \div \Pi(s; A, B))$
- $r \div (\Pi(r; B, C, D)) = \Pi(r; A, B) \div (\Pi(r; B, C) \div (\Pi(r; C, D) \div \Pi(r; D)))$

2.3 Let r and s be two relation instances with attributes $\{A, B, C, D\}$. Reduce the following expressions using the proposed generating set:

- $\sigma(r \cap s; A = B)$
- $r \div [A < B]$
- $r \div (\Pi(r; B, C, D) \div \Pi(r; C, D))$
- $\sigma(\sigma(r; B > C); A < B)$

2.4 Recall Example 1.10 of Section 1.6. Express the following English queries by an algebraic scheme expression:

- give the roommaid-numbers together with those floors where they are responsible for all the rooms;
- give the name of those visitors who never stayed for more than three days;

- give for every phone bill that has not yet been paid, the room number, the date, the name and the address of the visitor
- give the name of the visitors who only stayed once in the hotel;
- give the salary of the roommaids who are responsible for those rooms on the first floor where some Belgian visitor stayed on January 1, who did not pay his phone bill;
- give all the rooms where some Italian visitor ever stayed.

2.5 Recall Example 1.10 of Section 1.6. Express the following algebraic scheme expressions by an English query:

- $\Pi(ROOMS; ROOM\text{-}NUMBER, FLOOR) \div \rho(\Pi(\sigma(PHONE\text{-}BILLS; PAID? = false); ROOM\text{-}NB); ROOM\text{-}NB \to ROOM\text{-}NUMBER)$
- Let V be $\Pi(ROOMS \bowtie ROOMMAIDS \bowtie \rho(STAYS; ROOM\text{-}STAY \to ROOM\text{-}NUMBER) \bowtie VISITORS; ROOMMAID\text{-}NUMBER, FLOOR, VIS\text{-}COUNTRY)$.
  Describe $\Pi(V; ROOMMAID\text{-}NUMBER, FLOOR) \div ((\Pi(V; FLOOR, VIS\text{-}COUNTRY)) \div \Pi(V; VIS\text{-}COUNTRY))$
- $\Pi(EMPLOYEES; JOB, SALARY) \div (\Pi(EMPLOYEES; JOB, SALARY) \div \Pi(EMPLOYEES; JOB))$
- $\sigma(\rho(STAYS; ROOM\text{-}STAY \to ROOM\text{-}NUMBER) \bowtie ROOMS; NUMBER\text{-}OF\text{-}BEDS < NUMBER\text{-}OF\text{-}ACCOMP\text{-}PERSONS)$
- $\Pi(\sigma(\sigma(\sigma(\rho(STAYS; ROOM\text{-}STAY \to ROOM\text{-}NUMBER) \bowtie PHONE\text{-}BILLS; ARRIV\text{-}DATE < DATE); DATE < LEAV\text{-}DATE); PAID? = false); VIS\text{-}NUMBER)$

2.6 Express the English queries in Exercise 2.4 by a tuple calculus scheme expression.

2.7 Express the following tuple calculus scheme expressions in English:

- $\{t(VIS\text{-}COUNTRY) \mid \exists t_1(VIS\text{-}NUMBER, VIS\text{-}NAME, VIS\text{-}STREET, VIS\text{-}CITY, VIS\text{-}COUNTRY)(VISITOR(t_1) \wedge (t(VIS\text{-}COUNTRY) = t_1(VIS\text{-}COUNTRY)) \wedge (t_1(VIS\text{-}NUMBER) = 3451))\}$
- $\{t(FLOOR, ROOM\text{-}NUMBER, ROOMMAID\text{-}NUMBER, ROOM\text{-}NUMBER_1, FLOOR_1) \mid$
  $\exists t_1(ROOMMAID\text{-}NUMBER, ROOM\text{-}NUMBER),$
  $\exists t_2(ROOMMAID\text{-}NUMBER, ROOM\text{-}NUMBER),$
  $\exists t_3(ROOM\text{-}NUMBER, NUMBER\text{-}OF\text{-}BEDS, BATH?, FLOOR, RATE)$
  $\exists t_4(ROOM\text{-}NUMBER, NUMBER\text{-}OF\text{-}BEDS, BATH?, FLOOR, RATE)$
  $(ROOMMAIDS(t_1) \wedge ROOMMAIDS(t_2) \wedge$
  $ROOMS(t_3) \wedge ROOMS(t_4) \wedge (t_1(ROOMMAID\text{-}NUMBER) = t(ROOMMAID\text{-}NUMBER)) \wedge (t_1(ROOM\text{-}NUMBER) = t(ROOM\text{-}NUMBER)) \wedge$
  $(t_2(ROOMMAID\text{-}NUMBER) = t(ROOMMAID\text{-}NUMBER)) \wedge$

$(t_2(ROOM\text{-}NUMBER) = t(ROOM\text{-}NUMBER_1))\wedge$
$(t_3(ROOM\text{-}NUMBER) = t(ROOM\text{-}NUMBER_1))\wedge$
$(t_3(FLOOR) = t(FLOOR_1))\wedge$
$(t_4(ROOM\text{-}NUMBER) = t(ROOM\text{-}NUMBER))\wedge$
$(t_4(FLOOR) = t(FLOOR)))\}$

- $\{t(RN) \mid \forall t_1(ROOM\text{-}NB, TIME,$
  $DATE, DESTINATION, PHBILL, PAID?)$
  $(PHONE\text{-}BILLS(t_1) \Rightarrow (\neg(t(RN) = t_1(ROOM\text{-}NB))$
  $\vee(t_1(PAID? = false))))\}$

2.8 Complete Section 2.2.4 for the non-generating part of the tuple calculus.

2.9 Translate the English questions of Exercise 2.4 in SQL.

2.10 Translate the English questions, that are the result of Exercise 2.5 in SQL. Do the same thing for Exercise 2.7.

2.11 Express the $\Rightarrow$ and $\wedge$, the constant identifiers, the comparisons θ and the set-comparison $s\theta$ in terms of the generating part of SQL.

2.12 Express the *UNION* in term of the generating part, if the relation lists of the operand queries are different.

2.13 Prove that the following SQL instance query is not a good translation for the English query in Section 2.3.4:

Select $y.ROOMMAID\text{-}NUMBER, x.FLOOR$
From $rooms.x, roommaids.y$
Where $x.ROOM\text{-}NUMBER \neq y.ROOM\text{-}NUMBER$

Give an English translation of this query.

2.14 Reduce the following calculus scheme expressions to the relational algebra, using the method of Section 2.4.1.
Suppose that R has only two attributes C and D. Furthermore $dom(C) = dom(D)$.

- $\{t(C, D) \mid R(t) \wedge t(C) = t(D)\}$
- $\{s(A{:}\,C) \mid \exists t(C, D)(R(t) \wedge t(C) = s(A))\}$
- $\{s(C) \mid \exists t(C, D)(R(t)\wedge s(C) = t(C))\wedge\neg(\exists t(C, D)(R(t)\wedge s(C) = t(D)))\}$
- $\{s(C) \mid \exists t(C, D)(R(t) \wedge s(C) = t(C) \wedge s(C) \neq t(D))\}$
- $\{s(C, D) \mid \forall t(C, D)((t(C) = s(C)) \Rightarrow (t(D) = s(D)))\}$

2.15 Reduce the calculus scheme expressions of Exercise 2.7 to the relational algebra, using the method of Section 2.4.1.

2.16 Give a method for directly reducing the non-generating part of the tuple calculus to the relational algebra.

2.17 Reduce the following algebraic scheme expressions to SQL, using the method of Section 2.5.1. Suppose that R has only two attributes C and D. Furthermore $dom(C) = dom(D)$.

- $R \div \Pi(R; D)$
- $\sigma(R; D < d)$

- $\Pi(R; D) \bowtie \Pi(R; C)$
- $\rho(R; C \to C_1) \bowtie R$
- $\sigma(R; C < c) \bowtie \sigma(R; D > d)$

2.18 Reduce the algebraic scheme expressions of Exercise 2.5 to SQL, using the method of Section 2.5.1

2.19 Give a method for directly reducing the non-generating part of the relational algebra to SQL.

2.20 In Steps 3.1 to 3.5 of the method of Section 2.5 we only considered attributes of the form A_i in the attribute list of E, E_1 and E_2. Give a generalization for the augmented attributes of the form $a_i.A_i$.

2.21 In Step 3.3 of the method of Section 2.5 we only considered one relation in the relation list of E_1 and E_2. Give the generalization for more relations.

2.22 Reduce the following SQL scheme queries to tuple calculus, using the method of Section 2.6.1. Suppose that R has only two attributes C and D. Furthermore $dom(C) = dom(D) = \{integer\}$.

Select C
From R
Where $C = D$

Select $x.D$
From $R\ x$
Where $\neg(x.C)$ *IN*
  Select C
  From R
  Where $D > C$

Select $x.C, y.D$
From $R\ x$, $R\ y$
Where $x.D < y.C$

2.23 Give a method for directly reducing the non-generating part of SQL to the tuple calculus.

2.24 Generalize Step 2.4 of the reduction method of Section 2.6, for the case that the SQL queries have different relation lists.

2.25 Generalize the reduction method of Section 2.6 such that also augmented attributes of the form $a.A$ are taken into account.

Chapter 3

Constraints

As we saw in Chapter 1, we need to specify constraints in the description of a database in order to ensure that the instances we might obtain are meaningful. We distinguished relation constraints, database constraints, dynamic relation constraints and dynamic database constraints. In this chapter, we restrict ourselves to "static" relation constraints. Database constraints will not be discussed in detail; however we do urge the reader to convince himself that there exist database constraints which cannot be expressed by constraints on the relations contained in the database (see Exercise 1.8). Dynamic constraints will be discussed in Chapter 8. Section 3.1 is devoted to some general terminology concerning constraints. In Sections 3.2 till 3.6, we discuss some important types of relation constraints.

3.1 Some Terminology

We recall from Section 1 that a constraint is represented by a boolean function that associates *true* or *false* to the possible relation instances of some primitive relation scheme. Let $PRS = (\Omega, \Delta, dom)$ be such a primitive relation scheme. We denote by $\mathcal{SC}(PRS)$ the set of all constraints that can be defined over PRS. Obviously, a set of constraints SC of a relation scheme $RS = (PRS, M, SC)$ is a subset of $\mathcal{SC}(PRS)$.

Before we introduce more terminology, we first have a look to an example.

Example 3.1 Reconsider the relation scheme $FRIENDS = (\Omega, \Delta, dom, M, SC)$ introduced in Example 1.1. We recall that the following table represents a relation instance of *FRIENDS*:

LAST-NAME	*FIRST-NAME*	*TOWN-WHERE-LIVING*	*COUNTRY-WHERE-LIVING*	*PHONE-NUMBER*
Tillery	*Tom*	*Paris*	*France*	33-1-876-55-89
Johannes	*Jeff*	*Amsterdam*	*Holland*	31-20-822-56-78
Picavillo	*Pietro*	*Torino*	*Italy*	39-11-678-41-72

We defined SC as the set containing the following two constraints:

- sc_1: the town in which a friend lives is in the country he lives in.
- sc_2: the prefix of the phone number of a friend agrees with the town he lives in.

We now consider the constraint:

- sc_3: the prefix of the phone number of a friend agrees with the country he lives in.

Obviously, the constraint sc_3 must also be satisfied by each instance of *FRIENDS*. More in particular, the constraint sc_3 is *logically implied* by the constraints sc_1 and sc_2. In other words, each instance of *FRIENDS* satisfying both sc_1 and sc_2 also satisfies sc_3. Hence we might replace SC in *FRIENDS* by $SC' = \{sc_1, sc_2, sc_3\}$, without changing the set of relation instances of *FRIENDS*. Since the prefix of a phone-number always begins with the country code, it follows that the constraint sc_1 is logically implied by sc_2 and sc_3. Hence SC could also be replaced by $SC'' = \{sc_2, sc_3\}$. So we see that different sets of constraints can describe the same database. Therefore, given a relation scheme, it is an interesting question to verify whether the set of constraints of that relation scheme cannot be "optimized" in order to make constraint-checking more efficient each time an update is performed.

□

We are now ready to formalize the notion of logical implication of constraints.

Definition 3.1 Let $PRS = (\Omega, \Delta, dom)$ be a primitive relation scheme and let SC_1 and SC_2 be subsets of $\mathcal{SC}(PRS)$.

- SC_1 *implies* SC_2, denoted $SC_1 \models SC_2$, if each possible instance of *PRS* satisfying SC_1 also satisfies SC_2.
- SC_1 *is equivalent to* SC_2, denoted $SC_1 \Leftrightarrow SC_2$, if $SC_1 \models SC_2$ and $SC_2 \models SC_1$.

□

If the set SC_2 consists of a single constraint sc_2, we shall often write $SC_1 \models sc_2$ instead of $SC_1 \models \{sc_2\}$.

Example 3.2 Reconsider the constraints in Example 3.1. Obviously, we have:

$$\begin{array}{rcl} \{sc_1, sc_2\} & \models & sc_3 \\ \{sc_2, sc_3\} & \models & sc_1 \\ \{sc_1, sc_2\} & \Leftrightarrow & \{sc_2, sc_3\} \end{array}$$

□

In the following sections, we shall study some types of constraints. Formally we define a type of constraint as follows:

Definition 3.2 A *type of constraint* is a set of pairs (PRS, T) where *PRS* is a possible relation scheme and T is a subset of $\mathcal{SC}(PRS)$.

□

Example 3.3 In Example 1.3, we mentioned the notion of a *key dependency*. In general, given a primitive relation scheme $PRS = (\Omega, \Delta, dom)$, a key dependency $keydep(X)$, with $X \subseteq \Omega$, is a constraint that is satisfied by some possible relation instance, if the contents of each tuple is uniquely determined by its projection onto X. Key dependencies are clearly a type of constraint.

□

For the types of constraints we are going to discuss, we shall try to answer the following question: is it possible to decide efficiently whether a given constraint is implied by a given set of constraints. This is called the *implication problem:*

Definition 3.3 Let $\mathcal{T}$ be a type of constraint. The *implication problem of type* $\mathcal{T}$ is: *Is it decidable for arbitrary* $(PRS, T) \in \mathcal{T}$ *and for arbitrary* $SC \subseteq T$ *and* $sc \in T$ *whether* $SC \models sc$*?*

□

In order to solve the implication problem for a given type $\mathcal{T}$ of constraint, we need some tool to compute the set of all consequences of type $\mathcal{T}$ of any arbitrary set of constraints SC of type $\mathcal{T}$. We first explain this on our example of key dependencies.

Example 3.4 Reconsider all the key dependencies $keydep(X)$ of a given primitive relation scheme $PRS = (\Omega, \Delta, dom)$, with $X \subseteq \Omega$. Suppose SC is an arbitrary set of such key dependencies. Obviously, we have that the trivial key dependency $keydep(\Omega)$ is always implied by SC. Furthermore, whenever $keydep(X)$ is implied by SC then so is $keydep(Y)$ for all $Y \supseteq X$. These "rules" for the inference of key dependencies can be summarized as follows:

$$\begin{array}{ll} \emptyset \vdash keydep(\Omega) & (K1) \\ \{keydep(X)\} \vdash keydep(XZ) & (K2) \end{array}$$

Such a set of rules is called an axiom system for the implication of key dependencies. In the axioms above, Ω should be interpreted as the set of all attributes and X and Z as arbitrary subsets of Ω.

□

Informally, an *axiom system* for the implication or inference of constraints is a set of rules which tell you how "new" constraints can be derived from already "existing" ones. A formal definition of an axiom system is outside the scope of this book; we briefly come back to this issue at the end of this chapter.

Now, let $\mathcal{A}$ be a set of axioms for the inference of constraints of type $\mathcal{T}$. Let PRS be a primitive relation scheme and let $SC \cup \{sc\} \subseteq SC(PRS)$. We denote by $SC \overset{\mathcal{A}}{\vdash} sc$ the fact that sc can be derived from SC using the rules of $\mathcal{A}$. Of course, we would like $SC \overset{\mathcal{A}}{\vdash} sc$ to be equivalent to $SC \models sc$. Therefore, we introduce the following terminology:

Definition 3.4 Let $\mathcal{T}$ be a type of constraint. Let $\mathcal{A}$ be a set of axioms for the implication of constraints of type $\mathcal{T}$.

- Let $(PRS, T) \in \mathcal{T}$ and let $SC \subseteq T$. We denote:

$$SC^*_{\mathcal{T}} = \{sc \in T \mid SC \models sc\}$$
$$SC^+_{\mathcal{T},\mathcal{A}} = \{sc \in T \mid SC \overset{\mathcal{A}}{\vdash} sc\}$$

- $\mathcal{A}$ is called *sound* if for all $(PRS, T) \in \mathcal{T}$ and $SC \subseteq T$: $SC^+_{\mathcal{T},\mathcal{A}} \subseteq SC^*_{\mathcal{T}}$;
- $\mathcal{A}$ is called *complete* if for all $(PRS, T) \in \mathcal{T}$ and $SC \subseteq T$: $SC^*_{\mathcal{T}} \subseteq SC^+_{\mathcal{T},\mathcal{A}}$;
- $\mathcal{A}$ is called *non-redundant* if for all $\mathcal{B} \subseteq \mathcal{A}$: $SC^+_{\mathcal{T},\mathcal{A}} = SC^+_{\mathcal{T},\mathcal{B}}$ implies $\mathcal{B} = \mathcal{A}$. □

If it is clear which type of constraints and which systems of axioms are under consideration, we shall omit the subscripts in the above notations.

In our previous example, $\{(K1), (K2)\}$ is a sound, complete and non-re dundant set of axioms for the implication of key dependencies. We leave it as an exercise to the reader to check this. Key dependencies are actually a special case of *functional dependencies.* This is the first type of constraint we shall discuss in detail.

3.2 Functional Dependencies

Historically, the study of constraints in relational databases started with the introduction of functional dependencies by E. F. Codd [29] in 1970. Before defining these dependencies formally, we give an example.

Example 3.5 Consider the relation scheme

$$VISITORS = (\Omega_V, \Delta_V, dom_V, M_V, SC_V)$$

of Example 1.10. We recall that:

- $\Omega_V = \{$ *VIS-NUMBER, VIS-NAME, VIS-STREET, VIS-CITY, VIS-COUNTRY*$\}$;
- SC_V contains two constraints:
  - sc_1: every visitor has a different number;
  - sc_2: if two visitors live in the same city, they also live in the same country.

sc_1 can be rephrased as follows: two tuples of *VISITORS* that agree on *VIS-NUMBER* agree on all the other attributes (and hence are equal, in this case). So, two different tuples of *VISITORS* necessarily have different values for *VIS-NUMBER*. In other words, the value for *VIS-NUMBER* in a tuple of a relation instance over *VISITORS* uniquely determines the values for the other attributes in that tuple.

We can express sc_2 in a similar way: the value of *VIS-CITY* in a tuple of a relation instance over *VISITORS* uniquely determines the value of *VIS-COUNTRY* in that tuple.

Constraints that can be expressed in such a way are called *functional dependencies* because for sc_1, in each tuple the value of *VIS-NUMBER functionally determines* the values of *VIS-NAME*, *VIS-STREET*, *VIS-CITY* and *VIS-COUNTRY* and, for sc_2, the value of *VIS-CITY functionally determines* the value of *VIS-COUNTRY*. The functional dependency sc_1 is therefore denoted as *VIS-NUMBER* $\rightarrow$ {*VIS-NAME*, *VIS-STREET*, *VIS-CITY*, *VIS-COUNTRY*} whereas sc_2 is written as *VIS-CITY* $\rightarrow$ *VIS-COUNTRY*. Note that no distinction is made between a single attribute and the set containing that attribute.

□

Example 3.6 Recall our examples on key dependencies in the previous section. Clearly, the key dependency $keydep(X)$ is equivalent to the functional dependency $X \rightarrow \Omega$.

□

We are now ready to define a functional dependency in a formal way.

Definition 3.5 Let $PRS = (\Omega, \Delta, dom)$ be a primitive relation scheme. Let $X, Y \subseteq \Omega$. A *functional dependency (fd)* $X \rightarrow Y$ over PRS is a constraint that is satisfied by a possible relation instance prs if and only if for all $t_1, t_2 \in prs$: $t_1[X] = t_2[X]$ implies $t_1[Y] = t_2[Y]$.

□

It is now time to consider a more abstract example.

Example 3.7 Consider a relation scheme $RS = (\Omega, \Delta, dom, M, SC)$ where $\Omega = \{A, B, C, D\}$ and[1] $SC = \{A \rightarrow B, B \rightarrow C, AC \rightarrow D\}$. Now, in any instance of RS, we know that in any tuple of that instance, the value of A uniquely determines the value of B (since $A \rightarrow B$ holds) and also that the value of B uniquely determines the value of C (since $B \rightarrow C$ holds). Combining these facts, we get that the value of A uniquely determines the value of C. Hence $A \rightarrow C$ also holds. It can easily be verified that each relation instance of RS furthermore satisfies the other fds below:

$$\begin{array}{rcl} A & \rightarrow & C \\ A & \rightarrow & AC \\ A & \rightarrow & D \\ A & \rightarrow & ABCD \\ CD & \rightarrow & D \end{array}$$

and many others.

□

[1]From now on, we make no distinction between the attribute A and the set $\{A\}$. Also, for sets of attributes X and Y we denote the union $X \cup Y$ by XY. Hence AC denotes the set $\{A, C\}$.

Let us now try to find an axiom system for the implication of fds, of which we can examine its soundness, its completeness and its non-redundancy. (Historicaly, such an axiom system was first found by Armstrong [7].) Note first that some functional dependencies are always satisfied. This is the case for the functional dependencies:[2]

$$X \rightarrow Y \ \textit{with} \ Y \subseteq X \tag{F1}$$

Such dependencies are called *trivial functional dependencies*. From Example 3.7, we can deduce some rules that allow to derive new fds from a given set of fds. We can easily see that the following rule is correct:

$$X \rightarrow Y \vdash X \rightarrow XY \tag{F2}$$

An application of this rule is called *augmentation*. Clearly *transitivity* is also valid in general:

$$\{X \rightarrow Y, Y \rightarrow Z\} \vdash X \rightarrow Z \tag{F3}$$

It seems that all the fds we can derive from SC in Example 3.7 can be derived with the above rules. Before we show that $\{(F1), (F2), (F3)\}$ is indeed a non-redundant, sound and complete set of axioms for the inference of fds, we first present a number of other rules which can be derived from axioms $(F1)$–$(F3)$ above, and which will turn out to be useful in proofs and derivations, e. g. in the completeness proof we just announced.

Theorem 3.1 *Let $\mathcal{F}$ be the following system of axioms:*

$\emptyset \vdash X \rightarrow Y$ *if* $Y \subseteq X$ (trivial fds) $(F1)$
$X \rightarrow Y \vdash X \rightarrow XY$ (augmentation) $(F2)$
$\{X \rightarrow Y, Y \rightarrow Z\} \vdash X \rightarrow Z$ (transitivity) $(F3)$

The following rules can be derived from $\mathcal{F}$:

$\{X \rightarrow Y, X \rightarrow Z\} \vdash X \rightarrow YZ$ (union) $(F4)$
$\{X \rightarrow Y, X \rightarrow Z\} \vdash X \rightarrow Y \cap Z$ (intersection) $(F5)$
$X \rightarrow Y \vdash X \rightarrow Y - X$ (reduction) $(F6)$
$X \rightarrow Y \vdash U \rightarrow V$ *if* $X \subseteq U$ *and* $V \subseteq XY$ (generalized augmentation) $(F7)$
$X \rightarrow Y \vdash X \rightarrow A$ *if* $A \in Y$ (fragmentation) $(F8)$
$\{X \rightarrow Y, U \rightarrow V\} \vdash W \rightarrow Z$ *if* $U \subseteq XY$, $X \subseteq W$ *and* $Z \subseteq VW$
(generalized transitivity) $(F9)$

Proof We show $(F4)$. So $X \rightarrow Y$ and $X \rightarrow Z$ are given. By augmentation $(F2)$, we can deduce $X \rightarrow XY$. From $(F1)$ we can derive $XY \rightarrow X$. This fd together with $X \rightarrow Z$ imply $XY \rightarrow Z$ by $(F3)$. Another application of $(F3)$ then yields the desired fd $X \rightarrow Z$. We leave the rest of the proof as an exercise to the reader.

□

[2] From now on, we assume that a primitive relation scheme $PRS = (\Omega, \Delta, dom)$ is given and hence that the sets of attributes under consideration are subsets of Ω.

We now show:

Theorem 3.2 *$\mathcal{F}$ is a non-redundant, sound and complete system of axioms system for the implication of fds.*

Proof Let $PRS = (\Omega, \Delta, dom)$ be a primitive relation scheme.

- *sound:* We first have to show that $\mathcal{F}$ is sound. For the correctness of $(F1)$, we refer to Exercise 3.4. We show e. g. that $(F2)$ is correct. Let prs be a possible relation instance satisfying $X \rightarrow Y$. We show that prs satisfies $X \rightarrow XY$. Therefore, let t_1 and t_2 be two arbitrary tuples of prs with $t_1[X] = t_2[X]$. Since prs satisfies $X \rightarrow Y$ it follows that $t_1[Y] = t_2[Y]$. Hence also $t_1[XY] = t_2[XY]$. By Definition 3.5, prs satisfies $X \rightarrow XY$. The proof of the correctness of $(F3)$ is equally straightforward and left to the reader.
- *complete:* Let $\mathcal{FD}$ be the set of all fds of PRS. Let $SC \subseteq \mathcal{FD}$. We have to prove that $SC^* \subseteq SC^+$, or, alternatively, that $\mathcal{FD} - SC^+ \subseteq \mathcal{FD} - SC^*$. To this end, consider an fd $X \rightarrow Y \in \mathcal{FD} - SC^+$. Then there exists $A \in Y$ such that $X \rightarrow A \in \mathcal{FD} - SC^+$ (Indeed, if $X \rightarrow A \in SC^+$ for all $A \in Y$, then also $X \rightarrow Y \in SC^+$ by the union rule, a contradiction.) We are now going to show that $X \rightarrow A \in \mathcal{FD} - SC^*$ from which it can easily be deduced ex absurdo that $X \rightarrow Y \in \mathcal{FD} - SC^*$. In order to do so, we first define:

$$\overline{X} = \{A \in \Omega \mid X \rightarrow A \in SC^+\}.$$

Clearly, $X \rightarrow U \in SC^+$ if and only if $U \subseteq \overline{X}$. Consider the possible relation instance $r = \{t_1, t_2\}$ consisting of two tuples defined by:

$$\begin{aligned} t_1(a) &= 0 \textit{ for all } A \in \Omega \\ t_2(a) &= 0 \textit{ for all } A \in \overline{X} \\ t_2(a) &= 1 \textit{ for all } A \in \Omega - \overline{X} \end{aligned}$$

We can visualize r as follows:

$\overline{X}$	$\Omega - \overline{X}$
0 . . . 0	0 . . . 0
0 . . . 0	1 . . . 1

First, we remark that r does not satisfy $X \rightarrow A$. Let us now show that r satisfies all the fds of SC. Therefore, let $U \rightarrow V \in SC$. If $U \not\subseteq \overline{X}$, then $t_1[U] \neq t_2[U]$, and hence $U \rightarrow V$ is trivially satisfied by r. If on the other hand $U \subseteq \overline{X}$ we have that $X \rightarrow U \in SC^+$ and $t_1[U] = t_2[U]$. By transitivity, it follows that $X \rightarrow V \in SC^+$. Hence $V \subseteq \overline{X}$ and $t_1[V] = t_2[V]$. So, by Definition 3.5, r satisfies all the fds of SC. As a consequence, r also satisfies each fd of SC^*, whence $X \rightarrow A \in \mathcal{FD} - SC^*$.

- *non-redundant:* To show that $\mathcal{F}$ is non-redundant, it suffices to show that from two rules of $\mathcal{F}$ the third one cannot be derived. We show that $(F2)$ and $(F3)$ do not imply $(F1)$. Therefore, choose $A \in \Omega$ arbitrary and let $SC = \{A \rightarrow \emptyset\}$. Then $SC^+_{\{(F2),(F3)\}} = \{A \rightarrow \emptyset, A \rightarrow A\}$, whereas $SC^+_{\mathcal{F}} = \{X \rightarrow Y \mid Y \subseteq X \text{ and } X, Y \subseteq \Omega\}$. In particular, $SC^+_{\mathcal{F}}$ always contains the fd $\emptyset \rightarrow \emptyset$ which is not contained in $(SC)^+_{\{(F2),(F3)\}}$. It is left as an exercise to the reader to show that axioms $(F2)$ and $(F3)$ are not superfluous in $\mathcal{F}$.

□

How can we actually decide whether a given functional dependency $X \rightarrow Y$ is implied by some set SC of fds? To answer this question we recall from the proof of Theorem 3.2 that $SC \models X \rightarrow Y$ if and only if $Y \subseteq \overline{X}$ where $\overline{X} = \{A \in \Omega \mid X \rightarrow A \in SC^+\} = \{A \in \Omega \mid X \rightarrow A \in SC^*\}$. $\overline{X}$ is called the *fd-closure* of X. Hence the problem is reduced to finding an algorithm that, given $X \subseteq \Omega$ and SC, computes $\overline{X}$:

Algorithm 3.1 *Attributeset Closure*

Input: $X \subseteq \Omega$ and SC, a set of fds of the primitive relation scheme $PRS = (\Omega, \Delta, dom)$.

Output: $\overline{X}$

Method:

```
var OLDX, NEWX, XPLUS : set of attributes;
NEWX := X;
repeat
    OLDX := NEWX;
    for each U → Z in SC do
        if U ⊆ NEWX
            then
                NEWX := NEWX ∪ Z
    od
until NEWX = OLDX;
XPLUS := NEWX;
return(XPLUS)
```

□

Theorem 3.3 *Algorithm 3.1 is correct.*

Proof We have to show that the output $XPLUS$ of the execution of Algorithm 3.1 equals $\overline{X}$.

We first show that $XPLUS \subseteq \overline{X}$. Therefore we have to prove that $NEWX \subseteq \overline{X}$ is an invariant of the repeat loop. This results from the fact that by rule (F9), $X \rightarrow NEWX$, $U \subseteq X \subseteq NEWX$ and $U \rightarrow Z$ imply $X \rightarrow NEWX \cup Z$.

We now show $\overline{X} \subseteq XPLUS$. Since $SC^* = SC^+$, we can construct SC^* from SC using axioms $(F1)$, $(F2)$ and $(F3)$. We first show by induction that for any intermediate set $\subseteq \mathcal{G} \subseteq SC^*$ obtained during this construction, we have:

$$\textit{if } Y \rightarrow Z \in \mathcal{G} \textit{ and } Y \subseteq XPLUS \textit{ then } Z \subseteq XPLUS. \qquad (1)$$

Note that if $Y \rightarrow Z \in SC$, then the above assertion follows immediately. Hence the basis of our induction is sound. Now suppose that $\mathcal{G}$, an intermediate set of fds obtained during the construction of SC^+, satisfies condition (1). Let $\mathcal{G}'$ be obtained from $\mathcal{G}$ by one application of an axiom. We have to show that:

$$\textit{if } Y \rightarrow Z \in \mathcal{G}' \textit{ and } Y \subseteq XPLUS \textit{ then } Z \subseteq XPLUS. \qquad (1')$$

Let $Y \rightarrow Z$ be in $\mathcal{G}'$ and suppose $Y \subseteq XPLUS$. If $Y \rightarrow Z$ is also in $\mathcal{G}$ then $(1')$ is obviously satisfied. Therefore suppose $Y \rightarrow Z$ is not in $\mathcal{G}$. Then there are three possibilities:

1. $Y \rightarrow Z$ is obtained by an application of axiom $(F1)$, i.e. $Y \rightarrow Z$ is a trivial fd. Then $(1')$ is trivially satisfied.
2. $Y \rightarrow Z$ is obtained from $\mathcal{G}$ by augmentation, i.e. there exists $Y \rightarrow Z' \in \mathcal{G}$ with $YZ' = Z$. By induction, $Z' \subseteq XPLUS$ since $Y \subseteq XPLUS$ and hence $Z \subseteq XPLUS$, whence $(1')$ for this case.
3. $Y \rightarrow Z$ is obtained from $\mathcal{G}$ by transitivity. Hence there exist $Y \rightarrow U$ and $U \rightarrow Z$ in $\mathcal{G}$. Since $Y \subseteq XPLUS$, it follows by induction that $U \subseteq XPLUS$. Since $U \subseteq XPLUS$, again by induction, it follows that $Z \subseteq XPLUS$. Hence condition $(1')$ is satisfied.

In particular, we have:

$$\textit{if } Y \rightarrow Z \in SC^* \textit{ and } Y \subseteq XPLUS \textit{ then } Z \subseteq XPLUS. \qquad (1'')$$

Finally, substitution of $X \rightarrow \overline{X}$ for $Y \rightarrow Z$ in $(1'')$ yields the inclusion that had to be shown, which completes the proof.

□

Example 3.8 Reconsider the relation scheme $RS = (\Omega, \Delta, dom, M, SC)$ of Example 3.7 with $\Omega = \{A, B, C, D\}$ and $SC = \{A \rightarrow B, B \rightarrow C, AC \rightarrow D\}$. Let us compute A^+ using Algorithm 3.1. Initially, we put $X = A$ and $XPLUS = A$. Since $A \rightarrow B \in SC$, we add B to $XPLUS$. Since the left-hand side of $B \rightarrow C$ is now included in $XPLUS$, we can also add C. Finally, the presence of $AC \rightarrow D$ allows us to add D, whence $\overline{X} = \Omega$. So, we may conclude that SC implies $X \rightarrow \Omega$, which is equivalent to the key dependency $keydep(X)$.

□

Let us now investigate the time complexity of Algorithm 3.1. Let n be the number of attributes in Ω and let p be the number of fds in SC. Checking the inclusion and performing the union in the if-statement takes $O(n)$ time. Hence the execution of one cycle of the repeat-loop takes $O(np)$ time. The repeat loop can be executed at most $n+1$ times before no more changes occur since in each cycle except for the last one at least one attribute is added to $NEWX$. On the other hand, each fd in SC can be effectually applied at most once during the execution of Algorithm 3.1. Hence we also have that the repeat-loop can be executed at most $p+1$ times. Hence we have shown:

Theorem 3.4 *The time complexity of Algorithm 3.1 is $O(np \min\{n,p\})$ where n is the number of attributes in Ω and p is the number of fds in SC.*

□

The time complexity of the above algorithm can still be improved. Indeed, as mentioned above, each fd of SC can be used at most once. Hence we may remove an fd from SC immediately after its application. Furthermore, there is a better way to check whether the left-hand side of an fd in SC is included in the current value of *XPLUS*.

The algorithm we are going to propose now works as follows. For each fd $U \rightarrow Z$ in SC we count the number of attributes of U not in *XPLUS*. This number is called $NOTIN[U \rightarrow Z]$. Since *XPLUS* is going to be initialized as the empty set, $NOTIN[U \rightarrow Z]$ is at first simply the number of attributes in U. Then, *XPLUS* will be built up attribute by attribute. Therefore, we use a set *XWAIT* that keeps track of the attributes that still have to be added to *XPLUS*. The initial contents of *XWAIT* are of course the attributes of X. During each cycle of the algorithm, an attribute A is deleted from *XWAIT* and added to $\overline{X}$. $NOTIN[U \rightarrow Z]$ will be decremented by one for each fd $U \rightarrow Z$ with $A \in U$, in accordance with the meaning of $NOTIN[U \rightarrow Z]$. In order to do this, we must keep track of the fds in SC that have a given attribute in their left-hand side. Therefore, we make an array $INLFD[A]$ for each attribute A that contains each fd with A in its left-hand side. If at a certain time during the execution of the algorithm, $NOTIN[U \rightarrow Z]$ becomes 0, we know that from that moment on, U is contained in the current value of *XPLUS*. Then Z will be added to *XWAIT*. The algorithm stops when $XWAIT = \emptyset$ since no more attributes can be added to *XPLUS*. We now describe the algorithm formally.

Algorithm 3.2 *Optimized Attributeset Closure*

Input: $X \subseteq \Omega$ and SC, a set of fds of the primitive relation scheme $PRS = (\Omega, \Delta, dom)$.

Output: $\overline{X}$

Method:

var *XPLUS*, *XWAIT* : set of attributes;
    NOTIN : array[SC] of integer;
    INLFD : array[Ω] of set of fds;
XPLUS := $\emptyset$;
XWAIT := X;
for each $U \rightarrow Z$ **in** SC **do**
    $NOTIN[U \rightarrow Z] := |U|$; (1)

```
    if U = Ø                                              (2)
        then
            XWAIT := XWAIT ∪ Z;                           (3)
    for each A in U do
        INLFD[A] := INLFD[A] ∪ {U → Z}                    (4)
    od
od;
while XWAIT ≠ Ø do
    choose A in XWAIT;                                    (5)
    XWAIT := XWAIT − {A};                                 (6)
    XPLUS := XPLUS ∪ {A};                                 (7)
    for each U → Z in INLFD[A] do
        NOTIN[U → Z] := NOTIN[U → Z] − 1;                 (8)
        if NOTIN[U → Z] = 0                               (9)
            then
                XWAIT := XWAIT ∪ (Z − XPLUS)              (10)
    od
od;
return(XPLUS)
```

□

Obviously, the above algorithm does essentially the same as Algorithm 3.1. Therefore we leave the proof of the following theorem as an exercise to the reader:

Theorem 3.5 *Algorithm 3.2 is correct.*

□

We are now going to compute the time complexity of Algorithm 3.2:

Theorem 3.6 *The time complexity of Algorithm 3.2 is $O(np)$ where n is the number of attributes in Ω and p is the number of fds in SC.*

Proof Clearly, the time complexity of Algorithm 3.2 is determined by the time complexities of the labeled statements and the number of times they are executed.

Statements (1), (2) and (3) are executed p times; their time complexities are $O(n)$, 1 and $O(n)$ respectively. Hence these statements all together take $O(np)$ time. Statement (4) is executed $O(np)$ times. Since adding an fd $U \to Z$ to $INLFD[A]$ can be done in constant time if $INLFD[A]$ is represented in an appropriate way as a list, we may conclude that the initialization on the whole takes $O(np)$ time.

Let us now have a look to the actual computation. Since each attribute is considered at most once, statements (5), (6) and (7) are executed $O(p)$ times. Since these statements can be done in constant time, they do not contribute to the time complexity of the entire algorithm. Because of the additional for-loop, statements (8) and (9) are executed $O(np)$ times. Since these statements take constant time too, their contribution to the time complexity of Algorithm 3.2

is also $O(np)$. It only remains now to consider statement (10). Clearly, if $NOTIN[U \rightarrow Z] = 0$, then all the attributes of U have been considered and $U \rightarrow Z$ cannot occur any further in the algorithm. Hence the if-test evaluates to *true* at most p times. Since one union-operation on $XWAIT$ takes $O(n)$ time, it follows that this statement takes on the whole also $O(np)$ time. Hence the algorithm has time complexity $O(np)$.

□

In the literature, $O(np)$ is usually considered as the order of the input. From this point of view, Algorithm 3.2 is a linear time algorithm for the computation of the closure of a set of attributes and also the main part of a linear time algorithm for the implication problem for fds, as can be easily seen.

We shall now discuss an important application of the above algorithm. As explained in Chapter 1, the specification of constraints in the description of a database is needed to make sure that the instances we can obtain are meaningful. In order to prevent illegal changes, it is necessary to check after each update if the constraints are not violated. This is called *integrity checking.* The time integrity checking takes usually depends on the size of the set of constraints that is involved. Therefore it is of major interest to keep that set as small as possible. Let us illustrate our argument with an example.

Example 3.9 Reconsider the constraints in Example 3.1. From Example 3.2 it follows that

$$\{sc_1, sc_2\} \Leftrightarrow \{sc_1, sc_2, sc_3\}.$$

If these are the constraints used to specify a relation scheme, we obviously represent them by the first set and not by the second one.

□

In general, given a set of constraints, we shall look for the smallest subset which is still equivalent with the original one and use this subset to represent the relation scheme. A set of constraints obtained in such a way is called *non-redundant.* More formally, we define:

Definition 3.6 *Let $PRS = (\Omega, \Delta, dom)$ be a primitive relation scheme and let $SC \subset SC(PRS)$. SC is said to be non-redundant if no proper subset of SC is equivalent to SC itself.*

□

A set of constraints equivalent to a given set of constraints and satisfying certain conditions is called a *cover* for that given set. Of course, it is possible to define many types of covers. $\{sc_1, sc_2\}$ in Example 3.9 is called a *non-redundant cover* for $\{sc_1, sc_2, sc_3\}$. non-redundant covers for a set of constraints SC can be constructed by checking if each constraint of SC is not already implied by the other constraints of SC. If so, the constraint has to be removed from SC. In the case where only fds are involved, one can use Algorithm 3.2 to test the implications.

Other possible criteria to define covers could be:

- minimize the number of constraints;
- minimize the number of symbols needed to represent the constraints;
- allow only constraints of a certain subtype.

A rather exhaustive overview of covers for sets of fds can be found in [74].

We now end this more general discussion in order to get back to the fds. We shall only discuss one type of covers for fds, namely *canonical covers* introduced by Paredaens [84].

Definition 3.7 Let $PRS = (\Omega, \Delta, dom)$ be a primitive relation scheme and let SC be a set of fds of PRS. A set SC' of fds of PRS is a *canonical cover* for SC if:

1. $SC, \Leftrightarrow SC$;
2. the right-hand side of each fd in SC' consists of only one attribute;
3. SC' is non-redundant;
4. for each fd $X \rightarrow A$ in SC' and for each $B \in X$, $(SC - \{X \rightarrow A\}) \cup \{(X - B) \rightarrow A\}$ is not equivalent to SC.

□

In other words, in a canonical cover, no fd is superfluous, each fd has only one attribute in its right-hand side and no attributes can be removed from the left-hand side of any fd. The conditions a canonical cover must satisfy are intended to optimize the set of fds needed for the description of a relation scheme. For conditions 3 and 4 this is obvious; that condition 2 is not merely a normalization condition but also an optimization condition is illustrated by Exercise 3.15. Definition 3.7 immediately suggests a way to compute canonical covers. We illustrate this by the following example:

Example 3.10 Consider the following set of fds of a primitive relation scheme $PRS = (\Omega, \Delta, dom)$ with $\Omega = \{A, B, C, D, E, F\}$.

$$\begin{array}{ccc} AD \rightarrow C & B \rightarrow E & CF \rightarrow BD \\ C \rightarrow A & B \rightarrow F & CE \rightarrow AF \\ CD \rightarrow B & BE \rightarrow C & BC \rightarrow D \end{array}$$

To enforce condition 2 of Definition 3.7, we replace each fd $X \rightarrow Y$ by the set $\{X \rightarrow A \mid A \in Y\}$. By the union rule, the set of fds thus obtained is equivalent to the original one. In our example, we get:

$$\begin{array}{cccc} AD \rightarrow C & B \rightarrow E & CF \rightarrow B & CF \rightarrow D \\ C \rightarrow A & B \rightarrow F & CE \rightarrow A & CE \rightarrow F \\ CD \rightarrow B & BE \rightarrow C & BC \rightarrow D & \end{array}$$

In the next step we check for each of the above fds if it is not already implied by the other ones. If so, we remove that fd. $AD \rightarrow C$ and $B \rightarrow E$ are not implied by the other fds, but $CF \rightarrow B$ is (by $CF \rightarrow D$ and $CD \rightarrow B$). Hence $CF \rightarrow B$ is removed. The next fds to be removed are $CE \rightarrow A$ and $BC \rightarrow D$. $CE \rightarrow A$ is implied by $C \rightarrow A$ and $BC \rightarrow D$ is implied by $B \rightarrow F$ and $CF \rightarrow D$. Eventually we get:

$$\begin{array}{llll} AD \rightarrow C & B \rightarrow E & CF \rightarrow D & C \rightarrow A \\ B \rightarrow F & CE \rightarrow F & CD \rightarrow B & BE \rightarrow C \end{array}$$

Note that the result depends on the order in which the fds were checked. The set of fds we obtained is clearly still equivalent with the original one, is also non-redundant and of course each fd in it still has only one attribute in its right-hand side.

Finally, we are going to check if it is possible to remove attributes from the left-hand sides of these fds. We can replace $BE \rightarrow C$ by $B \rightarrow C$. ($B \rightarrow C$ is implied by $B \rightarrow E$ and $BE \rightarrow C$.) This replacement does neither violate the equivalence with the original set of fds nor the non-redundancy. Hence we obtain the following canonical cover:

$$\begin{array}{llll} AB \rightarrow C & B \rightarrow E & CF \rightarrow D & C \rightarrow A \\ B \rightarrow F & CE \rightarrow F & CD \rightarrow B & B \rightarrow C \end{array}$$

□

Until now, we have been mainly concerned with those aspects of fds related to integrity checking. The presence of fds however can also have implications with regard to the structure of our database, as was already seen by Codd, who introduced the functional dependencies [29, 30] as a part of the relational database model. Before proceeding to formal theory, let us explain this by an example.

Example 3.11 Let us consider again the relation scheme *FRIENDS*. Of course, we continuously make new friends. So we may expect the relation instance of Example 3.1 to grow to the instance of *FRIENDS* in the first table of Figure 3.1.

As you can see, there is a lot of redundant information in this instance. This is caused by the presence of the fd *TOWN-WHERE-LIVING* $\rightarrow$ *COUNTRY-WHERE-LIVING*. The information that Amsterdam is in Holland is contained three times in the above instance and the information that Paris lies in France twice. Repetition of information is not only undesirable for the redundancy itself, but also for the risk on *update anomalies* when the repeated information is changed in some tuples but not in all of them. We can eliminate this redundancy by representing the above relation by a database consisting of two schemes *ADDRESSES* and *TOWNS* with the instances, shown in Figure 3.1.

We can always recover the original instance by performing the join *addresses* $\bowtie$*towns*. Representing a relation scheme by a database consisting of several subschemes is called *decomposing a relation scheme*. The database resulting from a decomposition is called a *(lossless join) decomposition* of the given relation scheme provided of course that the instance of the original relation scheme can always be recovered from the database instance performing the join.

□

friends

LAST-NAME	*FIRST-NAME*	*TOWN-WHERE-LIVING*	*COUNTRY-WHERE-LIVING*	*PHONE-NUMBER*
Tillery	*Tom*	*Paris*	*France*	33-1-876-55-89
Pelletier	*François*	*Paris*	*France*	31-1-533-64-32
Johannes	*Jeff*	*Amsterdam*	*Holland*	31-20-822-56-78
Jansma	*Koos*	*Amsterdam*	*Holland*	31-20-678-44-13
Janssens	*Tim*	*Amsterdam*	*Holland*	31-20-145-28-66
Picavillo	*Pietro*	*Torino*	*Italy*	39-11-678-41-72
Bellini	*Marco*	*Rome*	*Italy*	39-6-512-13-34

addresses

LAST-NAME	*FIRST-NAME*	*TOWN-WHERE-LIVING*	*PHONE-NUMBER*
Tillery	*Tom*	*Paris*	33-1-876-55-89
Pelletier	*François*	*Paris*	31-1-533-64-32
Johannes	*Jeff*	*Amsterdam*	31-20-822-56-78
Jansma	*Koos*	*Amsterdam*	31-20-678-44-13
Janssens	*Tim*	*Amsterdam*	31-20-145-28-66
Picavillo	*Pietro*	*Torino*	39-11-678-41-72
Bellini	*Marco*	*Rome*	39-6-512-13-34

towns

TOWN-WHERE-LIVING	*COUNTRY-WHERE-LIVING*
Paris	*France*
Amsterdam	*Holland*
Torino	*Italy*
Rome	*Italy*

Figure 3.1: A decomposition of *friends*.

It is clear that the above example is only a special case of a more general fact:

Theorem 3.7 *Let $RS = (\Omega, \Delta, dom, M, SC)$ be a relation scheme and let $X \to Y$ be an fd in SC. Let r be a relation instance of RS. Then $r = \Pi(r, XY) \bowtie \Pi(r, X(\Omega - Y))$.*

Proof By definition of join and projection, the inclusion $r \subseteq \Pi(r, XY) \bowtie \Pi(r, X(\Omega - Y))$ always holds, regardless of the presence of some constraint. Let us therefore focus our attention to the other inclusion. In order to show that $\Pi(r, XY) \bowtie \Pi(r, X(\Omega - Y)) \subseteq r$, let t be a tuple of $\Pi(r, XY) \bowtie \Pi(r, X(\Omega - Y))$. By definition, there exist tuples u and v in r such that $u[XY] = t[XY]$ and $v[X(\Omega - Y)] = t[X(\Omega - Y)]$. In particular, it follows that $u[X] = v[X] = t[X]$. Since r satisfies the fd $X \to Y$, it follows that $u[Y] = v[Y]$. Since also $u[Y] = t[Y]$, we have that $v[Y] = t[Y]$.Together with $v[X(\Omega - Y)] = t[X(\Omega - Y)]$ this implies that $v = t$ and hence that t is in r. Thus the inclusion we wanted to prove holds. □

In the next chapter, which deals with vertical decompositions, we shall make extensive use of the above result. For now, we end our discussion on functional dependencies and proceed to other types of constraints that were introduced and studied subsequently. In the next section we show how Theorem 3.7 has played a crucial role in devising some of these constraint types.

3.3 Multivalued Dependencies

Let us first have another look at Theorem 3.7. Informally, this theorem says that whenever a functional dependency must hold in a relation, this relation can be decomposed in such a way that the original relation can always be recovered by performing a join. A natural question indeed is to ask whether also the converse of Theorem 3.7 holds. We can prove:

Theorem 3.8 *Let $RS = (\Omega, \Delta, dom, M, SC)$ be a relation scheme in which SC is a set of fds. Let $X, Y \subseteq \Omega$ and suppose that for each relation instance r of RS we have that $r = \Pi(r, XY) \bowtie \Pi(r, X(\Omega - Y))$. Then $X \to Y \in SC^*$ or $X \to \Omega - Y \in SC^*$.*

Proof Suppose that neither $X \to Y$ nor $X \to \Omega - Y$ hold. Consider the relation instance r already encountered in the proof of Theorem 3.2:

$\overline{X}$	$\Omega - \overline{X}$
$0 \ldots 0$	$0 \ldots 0$
$0 \ldots 0$	$1 \ldots 1$

Projection of r onto XY and $X(\Omega - Y)$ then gives:

$\overline{X} \cap XY$	$Y - \overline{X}$
$0 \ldots 0$	$0 \ldots 0$
$0 \ldots 0$	$1 \ldots 1$

$\overline{X} \cap X(\Omega - Y)$	$\Omega - \overline{X}Y$
$0 \ldots 0$	$0 \ldots 0$
$0 \ldots 0$	$1 \ldots 1$

Note that, because of the assumption, $Y - \overline{X}$ and $\Omega - \overline{X}Y$ are both nonempty. If we take the join of these two relation instances we get:

$\overline{X}$	$Y - \overline{X}$	$\Omega - \overline{X}Y$
$0 \ldots 0$	$0 \ldots 0$	$0 \ldots 0$
$0 \ldots 0$	$0 \ldots 0$	$1 \ldots 1$
$0 \ldots 0$	$1 \ldots 1$	$0 \ldots 0$
$0 \ldots 0$	$1 \ldots 1$	$1 \ldots 1$

and this is not the relation instance r, a contradiction.

□

If we compare this result with Theorem 3.7 we observe two major differences:

- we only know that one out of two fds must hold;
- the set SC only contains fds.

The first observation is easy to explain. Whereas decomposition is a symmetric notion, fds are not. Hence one can associate two fds with each decomposition in two subrelations, depending on the order in which these subrelations are considered. We come back to this point later on.

The latter difference is also fundamental. This condition cannot be removed from Theorem 3.8 as is shown in the following example:

Example 3.12 Consider a relation scheme $RS = (\Omega, \Delta, dom, M, SC)$ with:

- $\Omega = \{DRINKER, BEER, BAR\}$;
- M says that every tuple in the relation indicates a person that drinks a certain beer in a certain bar;
- SC consists of one constraint sc that specifies that whenever a *DRINKER* drinks a *BEER* he drinks that *BEER* in every *BAR* where it is served.

It is obvious that due to the constraints it is possible to decompose the relation RS into its projections onto $\{DRINKER, BEER\}$ and $\{BEER, BAR\}$ without losing information. If Theorem 3.8 would hold also without the condition that SC consists only of fds, we would expect that either the fd $BEER \rightarrow DRINKER$ or $BEER \rightarrow BAR$ holds in RS. This is however not the case as is illustrated by the following instance of RS:

DRINKER	*BEER*	*BAR*
Jones	*Tuborg*	*Tivoli*
Smith	*Tuborg*	*Far West*
Jones	*Tuborg*	*Far West*
Smith	*Tuborg*	*Tivoli*

Clearly, this instance satisfies the constraint sc but neither of the fds mentioned above.

□

So we may conclude that fds are only a sufficient condition for a relation to be decomposable into two subrelations but not a necessary one. Let us have a closer look at the constraint sc in the previous example. We can express sc also in the following way: *whenever there are two tuples, say t and u in a relation instance r of RS and $t[BEER] = u[BEER]$, then there must exist a tuple v in r such that $t[DRINKER, BEER] = v[DRINKER, BEER]$ and $u[BEER, BAR] = v[BEER, BAR]$* (and vice-versa of course, as can be seen by interchanging the roles of t and u). A constraint that can be expressed in such a way is called a *multivalued dependency* [39, 116]. The multivalued dependency sc is denoted $BEER \twoheadrightarrow DRINKER$ (or, equivalently, due to the symmetry in the definition, $BEER \twoheadrightarrow BAR$). A closer examination also shows that a multivalued dependency actually expresses exactly when a relation can be decomposed into two subrelations without losing information. It is now time to be more formal:

Definition 3.8 Let $PRS = (\Omega, \Delta, dom)$ be a primitive relation scheme. Let $X, Y \subseteq \Omega$. A *multivalued dependency (mvd)* $X \twoheadrightarrow Y$ over PRS is a constraint that is satisfied by a possible relation instance prs if and only if for all $t, u \in sot$ with $t[X] = u[X]$ there exists $v \in prs$ such that $v[XY] = t[XY]$ and $v[X(\Omega - Y)] = u[X(\Omega - Y)]$.

□

As is already said earlier, an mvd expresses exactly when a relation can be decomposed into two projections of that relation. Hence we have:

Theorem 3.9 *Let $RS = (\Omega, \Delta, dom, M, SC)$ be a relation scheme. Let $X, Y \subseteq \Omega$. $SC \models X \twoheadrightarrow Y$ if and only if for each relation instance r of RS we have that $r = \Pi(r, XY) \bowtie \Pi(r, X(\Omega - Y))$.*

□

As an immediate corollary we get:

Corollary 3.1 *The following rules are sound for the implication of fds and mvds:*

$$X \twoheadrightarrow Y \vdash X \twoheadrightarrow \Omega - Y \text{ complementation}$$
$$X \rightarrow Y \vdash X \twoheadrightarrow Y \text{ mvds implied by fds}$$

Proof Follows immediately from Theorem 3.9 and Theorem 3.7.

□

Let us now consider the following abstract example:

Example 3.13 Consider a relation scheme $RS = (\Omega, \Delta, dom, M, SC)$ where

$$\Omega = \{A, B, C, D, E, F\}$$

and

$$SC = \{A \twoheadrightarrow BC, A \twoheadrightarrow CD, BC \twoheadrightarrow CE, B \rightarrow C, CD \rightarrow DF\}$$

Among others, the following constraints are also satisfied by each relation instance of RS:

$$\begin{array}{rcl} A & \twoheadrightarrow & DEF \\ A & \twoheadrightarrow & ADEF \\ A & \twoheadrightarrow & C \\ A & \twoheadrightarrow & B \\ A & \twoheadrightarrow & D \\ A & \twoheadrightarrow & BCD \\ A & \twoheadrightarrow & E \\ AEF & \twoheadrightarrow & BCE \\ B & \twoheadrightarrow & C \\ A & \rightarrow & F \end{array}$$

Actually proving that these constraints are implied by SC may often turn out to be rather difficult; therefore we defer this issue until we shall introduce an axiom system for fds and mvds. Nevertheless, we invite the reader for an attempt to prove some of the implications above, using the definition of an mvd.

□

Of course, we would like to have an axiom system for the implication of functional *and* multivalued dependencies. Hence we not only have to understand how multivalued dependencies can interact with each other, but also how multivalued dependencies can interact with functional dependencies. An axiom system for fds and mvds will certainly incorporate an axiom system for fds. We may also expect that the rules established in Corollary 3.1 must be included in such an axiom system. Also, we could look for counterparts to the augmentation and transitivity axioms for fds. Eventually we might come up with the following axiom system:

Theorem 3.10 *Let $\mathcal{M}$ be the following system of axioms:*

$\emptyset \vdash X \rightarrow Y$ *if* $Y \subseteq X$ (trivial fds) $(F1)$
$X \rightarrow Y \vdash X \rightarrow XY$ (fd-augmentation) $(F2)$
$\{X \rightarrow Y, Y \rightarrow Z\} \vdash X \rightarrow Z$ (fd-transitivity) $(F3)$
$X \twoheadrightarrow Y \vdash X \twoheadrightarrow \Omega - Y$ (mvd-complementation) $(M1)$
$X \twoheadrightarrow Y \vdash WX \twoheadrightarrow VY$ *if* $V \subseteq W$ (mvd-augmentation) $(M2)$
$\{X \twoheadrightarrow Y, Y \twoheadrightarrow Z\} \vdash X \twoheadrightarrow Z - Y$ (mvd-pseudotransitivity) $(M3)$
$X \rightarrow Y \vdash X \twoheadrightarrow Y$ (mvds implied by fds) $(FM1)$
$\{X \twoheadrightarrow Y, Y \rightarrow Z\} \vdash X \rightarrow Z - Y$ (mixed pseudotransitivity) $(FM2)$

$\mathcal{M}$ is sound for the implication of fds and mvds.

Proof The soundness of axioms $F1$–$F3$ has been dealt with in Theorem 3.2 and the soundness of $M1$ and $FM1$ was shown in Corollary 3.1. It remains to show that axioms $M2$, $M3$ and $FM2$ are sound. Let PRS be a primitive relation scheme and let prs be a possible relation instance of PRS.

- *axiom $M2$:* Assume prs satisfies $X \twoheadrightarrow Y$. Let $t, u \in prs$ with $t[WX] = u[WX]$. We have to show that there exists $v \in sot$ such that $v[WXY] = t[WXY]$ and $v[XW(\Omega - VY)] = u[XW(\Omega - VY)]$. Since prs satisfies $X \twoheadrightarrow Y$ and since, in particular, $t[X] = u[X]$, it follows that there exists $v \in prs$ such that $v[XY] = t[XY]$ and $v[X(\Omega - Y)] = u[X(\Omega - Y)]$. Furthermore, since $t[W] = u[W]$ it follows that necessarily $v[W] = t[W] = u[W]$, whence the desired result.
- *axiom $M3$:* Assume prs satisfies both $X \twoheadrightarrow Y$ and $Y \twoheadrightarrow Z$. Let $t, u \in prs$ with $t[X] = u[X]$. We prove that there exists $w \in prs$ such that $w[X(Z-Y)] = t[X(Z-Y)]$ and $w[X(\Omega-(Z-Y))] = u[X(\Omega-(Z-Y))]$. For sake of clarity, note that $\Omega - (Z - Y)$ can be rewritten as $Y(\Omega - Z)$. Hence we can rewrite the last condition as $w[XY(\Omega - Z)] = u[XY(\Omega - Z)]$. Since prs satisfies $X \twoheadrightarrow Y$ (and hence, by Corollary 3.1, also $X \twoheadrightarrow \Omega - Y$) and since in particular $t[X] = u[X]$, it follows that there exists $v \in prs$ such that $v[X(\Omega - Y)] = t[X(\Omega - Y)]$ and $v[XY] = u[XY]$. In particular, $v[Y] = u[Y]$. Since prs satisfies $Y \twoheadrightarrow Z$ it then follows that there exists $w \in sot$ such that $w[YZ] = v[YZ]$ and $w[Y(\Omega - Z)] = u[Y(\Omega - Z)]$. Let us now fit everything together in order to show that w is the desired tuple. From $v[XY] = u[XY]$ and the construction of w it follows that $w[XY] = u[XY] = v[XY]$. Hence $w[XYZ] = v[XYZ]$ and $w[XY(\Omega - Z)] = u[XY(\Omega - Z)]$. Hence the second condition that w should satisfy is fulfilled. From $w[XYZ] = v[XYZ]$ and $v[X(\Omega - Y)] = t[X(\Omega - Y)]$ it follows that w and t agree on the intersection $XYZ \cap X(\Omega - Y) = X(Z - Y)$, and this is exactly the first condition that w must satisfy.
- *axiom $FM2$*: Assume prs satisfies $X \twoheadrightarrow Y$ and $Y \rightarrow Z$. Suppose t_1 and t_2 are tuples of prs satisfying $t_1[X] = t_2[X]$. Since prs satisfies $X \twoheadrightarrow Y$ there exists $u \in sot$ such that $u[XY] = t_1[XY]$ and $u[X(\Omega - Y)] = t_2[X(\Omega - Y)]$. Since $u[Y] = t_1[Y]$ and because of $Y \rightarrow Z$, it follows that $u[Z] = t_1[Z]$. From

this last equality and from $u[\Omega - Y] = t_2[\Omega - Y]$ it then follows that t_1 and t_2 agree on the intersection $Z \cap (\Omega - Y) = Z - Y$, i. e. $t_1[Z - Y] = t_2[Z - Y]$. Hence *prs* satisfies $X \rightarrow Z - Y$.

□

The next question that arises is of course whether the above axiom system is also complete. We invite the reader to try to infer the mvds and fds listed in Example 3.13 from the given set of mvds and fds using the rules of axiom system $\mathcal{M}$. You should come to the conclusion that this axiom system does indeed allow you to derive all these constraints from the given ones. Of course this is not a proof!

In order to shed some more light on this problem, let us re-examine the proof of Theorem 3.2 in which we showed the soundness, completeness and non-redundancy of an axiom system for fds. In the part where we showed the completeness, it turned out to be important to consider for a given set of fds and a given set of attributes X, all the fds implied by that set with X as left-hand side. Therefore, we needed to define $\overline{X}$. This suggests us to examine the set of all fds and mvds implied by a given set of fds and mvds with a fixed set of attributes as left-hand side. Is it possible to give a fairly simple description of this set? Therefore we first establish some additional inference rules.

Lemma 3.1 *The following rules can be derived from the axiom system* $\mathcal{M}$ *in Theorem 3.10. (and hence are sound):*

$X \twoheadrightarrow Y \vdash X \twoheadrightarrow \Omega - Y$ (mvd-complementation) $(M1)$
$\{X \twoheadrightarrow Y, X \twoheadrightarrow Z\} \vdash X \twoheadrightarrow Y \cap Z$ (mvd-intersection) $(M4)$
$\{X \twoheadrightarrow Y, X \twoheadrightarrow Z\} \vdash X \twoheadrightarrow YZ$ (mvd-union) $(M5)$
$\{X \twoheadrightarrow Y, X \twoheadrightarrow Z\} \vdash X \twoheadrightarrow Y - Z$ (mvd-difference) $(M6)$

Proof First note that rule $M1$ is already an axiom of $\mathcal{M}$ that is only repeated here for sake of completeness. Let us consider rule $M4$. From $X \twoheadrightarrow Y$ one can deduce $X \twoheadrightarrow X(\Omega - Y)$ by applying first axiom $M1$ and then axiom $M2$. From $X \twoheadrightarrow Z$ one can derive $X(\Omega - Y) \twoheadrightarrow Z$, again by using axiom $M2$. If we now use the pseudotransitivity axiom $M3$ on $X \twoheadrightarrow X(\Omega - Y)$ and $X(\Omega - Y) \twoheadrightarrow Z$ we get $X \twoheadrightarrow Z - (X(\Omega - Y))$. Since $Z - (X(\Omega - Y))$ equals $(Y \cap Z) - X$, a final application of axiom $M2$ yields the desired result. Rules $M5$ and $M6$ can be easily derived from axiom $M1$ and rule $M4$ knowing that $YZ = \Omega - ((\Omega - Y) \cap (\Omega - Z))$ and $Y - Z = Y \cap (\Omega - Z)$ and are left as an exercise to the reader.

□

A set of sets that is closed under complementation and intersection (and, as a consequence, under union and set difference) can be described as consisting of all possible unions of members of the partition induced by that set. We are going to use this idea in order to describe the set of fds and mvds that can be derived from a given set of fds and mvds.

Theorem 3.11 *Let $PRS = (\Omega, \Delta, dom)$ be a primitive relation scheme and let $\mathcal{FD}$ and $\mathcal{MD}$ be the sets of all fds and mvds of PRS respectively. Let $SC \subseteq \mathcal{FD} \cup \mathcal{MD}$. Let $DepB(X)$ be the partition induced by $\{Y \mid X \to\to Y \in SC^+_{\mathcal{FD}\cup\mathcal{MD}}\}$*[3] *and let $\overline{X} = \{A \mid X \to A \in SC^+_{\mathcal{FD}\cup\mathcal{MD}}\}$.*[4] *Then:*

- *$X \to\to Y \in SC^+$ if and only if there exists $\mathcal{Y} \subseteq DepB(X)$ such that $Y = \bigcup \mathcal{Y}$;*
- *$X \to Y \in SC^+$ if and only if $Y \subseteq \overline{X}$;*
- *if $A \in \overline{X}$, then $\{A\} \in DepB(X)$.*

The set $DepB(X)$ is called the dependency basis of X for the set SC.

Proof Left as an exercise to the reader.

□

Example 3.14 Let us consider a primitive relation scheme *PRS* with:

- $\Omega = \{A, B, C, D, E, F, G\}$
- $SC = \{AB \to\to CDE, AB \to\to EFG\}$.

Let $X = AB$. Since SC does not contain fds, the rules of Theorem 3.10 allow only to derive trivial fds. Hence $\overline{X} = \{A, B\}$ and $\{A\}$ and $\{B\}$ certainly belong to $DepB(X)$. By rules $M1$, $M4$ and $M6$, $AB \to\to CD$, $AB \to\to E$ and $AB \to\to FG$ can also be derived from SC. The reader can check by constructing a counterexample that it is impossible to infer $AB \to\to C$, $AB \to\to D$, $AB \to\to F$ or $AB \to\to G$ from SC. Since the rules in Theorem 3.10 are sound, this mvds are not in SC^+ either. Hence $DepB(X) = \{A, B, CD, E, FG\}$. Recall that, in accordance with an earlier remark, A, B and E stand for the sets $\{A\}$, $\{B\}$ and $\{C\}$ respectively.

□

Of course, a more efficient procedure to compute $\overline{X}$ and $DepB(X)$ is needed. The algorithm we give here is based on [15].

Algorithm 3.3 *Attributeset Closure and Dependency Basis*

Input: $X \subseteq \Omega$ and SC, a set of fds and mvds of a primitive relation scheme $PRS = (\Omega, \Delta, dom)$.

Output: $\overline{X}$, $DepB(X)$

Method:

var *OLDX*, *NEWX*, *XPLUS*, *DBU*, *DBV*, *W* : set of attributes;
    OLDD, *NEWD*, *DEPBX* : set of sets of attributes;
NEWX := *X*;
NEWD := $\{\{A\} \mid A \in X\} \cup \{\Omega - X\}$;
repeat
    OLDX := *NEWX*;
    OLDD := *NEWD*;

[3] In the remainder of this section, we shall write $SC^+_{\mathcal{FD}\cup\mathcal{MD}}$ as SC^+ for short.

[4] If we suppose that $SC \subseteq \mathcal{FD}$, we get back the definition of $\overline{X}$ given in the proof of Theorem 3.2.

```
    for each U → V in SC do
        DBU := ⋃{W | W ∈ NEWD & W ∩ U ≠ ∅};
        DBV := V − DBU;
        if DBV ≠ ∅
            then
                begin
                    NEWX := NEWX ∪ DBV;
                    NEWD := {W − DBV | W ∈ NEWD & W − DBV ≠ ∅}
                                                    ∪{{A} | A ∈ DBV}
            end
    od
    for each U →→ V in SC do
        DBU := ⋃{W | W ∈ NEWD & W ∩ U ≠ ∅};
        DBV := V − DBU;
        if DBV ≠ ∅
            then
                for each W in NEWD do
                    if (W ∩ DBV ≠ ∅) and (W ∩ DBV ≠ W)
                        then
                            NEWD := (NEWD − {W})
                                                ∪{W ∩ DBV, W − DBV};
                od
    od
until (NEWX = OLDX) and (NEWD = OLDD);
XPLUS := NEWX;
DEPBX := NEWD;
return(XPLUS, DEPBX)
```

□

Theorem 3.12 *Algorithm 3.3 is correct and computes attributeset closure and dependency basis in polynomial time.*

Proof We shall only give an outline of the proof. The reader is invited to fill out the details. First, we have to show that the operations performed on *NEWX* and *OLDX* do not violate the following conditions which are trivially satisfied after initialization:

- $X \rightarrow NEWX \in SC^+$;
- for all $W \in NEWD$, $X \rightarrow\!\!\!\rightarrow W \in SC^+$.

This can be easily achieved using various axioms and the rules we derived from them. Then we have to show that $X \rightarrow\!\!\!\rightarrow W'$ is *not* in SC^+ for any proper subset W' of a set W in *DEPBX*. This can be done by showing that from the sets

$$\{X \rightarrow Y \mid Y \subseteq XPLUS\}$$

and

$$\{X \rightarrow\!\!\!\rightarrow Y \mid Y \textit{ is a union of some members of } DEPBX\}$$

no other fds and mvds can be derived using an axiom of $\mathcal{M}$ in Theorem 3.10. Finally, the time complexity of Algorithm 3.3 can be computed in a straightforward manner.

□

It is still possible to improve the time complexity of Algorithm 3.3. There exist various quadratic and even almost linear algorithms in the literature ([53, 59, 96]). We do not intend however to discuss them here. We now illustrate Algorithm 3.3 with an example.

Example 3.15 Let us consider a primitive relation scheme PRS with:

- $\Omega = \{A, B, C, D, E, F, G\}$
- $SC = \{AB \rightarrow\!\!\!\rightarrow CD, C \rightarrow\!\!\!\rightarrow F, C \rightarrow E\}$.

and calculate the dependency basis of $X = AB$ using Algorithm 3.3. Initially we have:

$$NEWX{=}AB$$
$$NEWD{=}\{A, B, CDEFG\}$$

After the application of $AB \rightarrow\!\!\!\rightarrow CD$ we get:

$$NEWX{=}AB$$
$$NEWD{=}\{A, B, CD, EFG\}$$

An application of $C \rightarrow\!\!\!\rightarrow F$ gives:

$$NEWX{=}AB$$
$$NEWD{=}\{A, B, CD, EG, F\}$$

Finally, after the use of $C \rightarrow E$ we get:

$$NEWX{=}ABE$$
$$NEWD{=}\{A, B, CD, E, F, G\}$$

It is easily seen that another pass through SC does not lead to any additional changes. Hence the algorithm gives:

$$\overline{X}{=}XPLUS = ABE$$
$$DepB(X){=}DEPBX = \{A, B, CD, E, F, G\}$$

□

In order for this algorithm to be the basis of an algorithm to decide the implication problem for fds and mvds, we have to prove the completeness of the axiom system $\mathcal{M}$ introduced in Theorem 3.10, for which we are now ready.

Theorem 3.13 *The axiom system $\mathcal{M}$ in Theorem 3.10 is sound, complete and non-redundant for the implication of fds and mvds.*

Proof First recall from Theorem 3.10 that $\mathcal{M}$ is sound. Let PRS be a primitive relation scheme. Let $\mathcal{FD}$ be the set of all fds of PRS and let $\mathcal{MD}$ be the set of all mvds of PRS. Let $SC \subseteq \mathcal{FD} \cup \mathcal{MD}$. We have to show that $SC^* \subseteq SC^+$.[5] Let $W_1, \ldots, W_k$ be those member of $DepB(X)$ that are not contained in $\overline{X}$. We now construct the following relation s:

$\overline{X}$	W_1	W_2	$\cdots$	W_k
$0\ldots0$	$0\ldots0$	$0\ldots0$	$\cdots$	$0\ldots0$
$0\ldots0$	$1\ldots1$	$0\ldots0$	$\cdots$	$0\ldots0$
$0\ldots0$	$0\ldots0$	$1\ldots1$	$\cdots$	$0\ldots0$
$0\ldots0$	$1\ldots1$	$1\ldots1$	$\cdots$	$0\ldots0$
		$\vdots$		
$0\ldots0$	$1\ldots1$	$1\ldots1$	$\cdots$	$1\ldots1$

So s contains 2^k tuples.[6] We now show that s satisfies all the fds and mvds of SC. Therefore, let $U \rightarrow V \in SC$. Let W be the union of those W_i's that intersect U. (W may be empty). Clearly, $\overline{X}W \rightarrow V \in SC^+$. Now let t_1 and t_2 be tuples of s such that $t_1[U] = t_2[U]$. Note that by construction of s it follows that $t_1[\overline{X}W] = t_2[\overline{X}W]$. By Theorem 3.11, we have that $X \twoheadrightarrow \overline{X}W$ is in SC^+. Hence by mixed pseudo-transitivity, $X \rightarrow V - \overline{X}W$ is in SC^+, whence $V - \overline{X}W \subseteq \overline{X}$. By construction of s it then follows that $t_1[V - \overline{X}W] = t_2[V - \overline{X}W]$. Since we already know that t_1 and t_2 agree on $\overline{X}W$, we get that $t_1[V] = t_2[V]$ whence satisfaction of $U \rightarrow V$ by s. Now assume that $U \twoheadrightarrow V$ is in SC. We must show that whenever there exist tuples t_1 and t_2 that agree on U, there also exists a tuple t such that $t[UV] = t_1[UV]$ and $t[U(\Omega - V)] = t_2[U(\Omega - V)]$. Let W be again the union of those W_i's that intersect U. Then it follows from the construction of s that $t_1[\overline{X}W] = t_2[\overline{X}W]$. Also, by Theorem 3.11, it follows that $X \twoheadrightarrow \overline{X}W$ is in SC^+. By mvd-augmentation, $\overline{X}W \twoheadrightarrow V$ is in SC^+. Hence, by mvd-transitivity, $X \twoheadrightarrow V - \overline{X}W$ is in SC^+. So $V - \overline{X}W$ is a union of W_i's. From the construction of s the existence of the above described tuple t now easily follows.

Now suppose that $X \rightarrow Y$ is in SC^*. Since s satisfies all the dependencies in SC, it also satisfies all those of SC^*. Hence $Y \subseteq \overline{X}$ by construction of s, which in turn implies that $X \rightarrow Y$ is in SC^+. Similarly, suppose that $X \twoheadrightarrow Y$ is in SC^*. Then again s must satisfy this mvd and this can only be the case if Y is the union of some members of $\overline{X}$, whence $X \twoheadrightarrow Y \in SC^+$. Hence $SC^* \subseteq SC^+$ as had to be shown.

It only remains to be shown that the axiom system is non-redundant. This can be done according to the principle used in the proof of Theorem 3.2 in a straightforward way. Therefore we leave this part of the proof to the reader. □

[5] SC^* of course denotes $SC^*_{\mathcal{FD}\cup\mathcal{MD}}$.

[6] Note that in case only fds are involved, $k = 1$ and $W_1 = \Omega - \overline{X}$. Hence the relation instance s constructed above then becomes the relation instance r constructed in the proof of Theorem 3.2.

From Theorem 3.12 and Theorem 3.13 it immediately follows:

Corollary 3.2 *The implication problem for fds and mvds is decidable in polynomial time.*

□

3.4 Join Dependencies

In the previous section, we presented mvds as a necessary and sufficient condition to decompose a relation into two subrelations without losing information. We shall however not end our discussion on decomposition-related constraints here, since there exist situations, as was shown by J.-M. Nicolas [81], in which a relation can be decomposed into three subrelations but not into two. We illustrate this point with an example.

Example 3.16 Consider again the relation scheme $RS = (\Omega, \Delta, dom, M, SC)$ of Example 3.12. Recall in particular that SC consists of only one constraint saying that whenever a *DRINKER* drinks a *BEER*, he drinks that *BEER* in every *BAR* where it is served. We showed that this constraint can be represented by the mvd $BEER \rightarrow\!\!\!\rightarrow DRINKER$ (or, equivalently, by $BEER \rightarrow\!\!\!\rightarrow BAR$).

In this example, we consider a relation scheme RS' obtained from RS by slightly modifying the only constraint. We now assume that *whenever a DRINKER drinks a BEER and whenever that DRINKER frequents a BAR in which that BEER is served, he drinks that BEER in that BAR.* We call this constraint sc'. Let us now consider the following instance of RS':

DRINKER	*BEER*	*BAR*
Jones	*Tuborg*	*Tivoli*
Jones	*Tuborg*	*Far West*
Jones	*Carlsberg*	*Tivoli*
Smith	*Tuborg*	*Tivoli*

It is readily verified that this instance satisfies the new constraint sc'. It is also easily seen that none of the mvds

$$\begin{aligned} BEER &\rightarrow\!\!\!\rightarrow DRINKER \\ DRINKER &\rightarrow\!\!\!\rightarrow BAR \\ BAR &\rightarrow\!\!\!\rightarrow BEER \end{aligned}$$

holds. Hence it is not possible to decompose RS' into two subschemes without losing information. It is however easy to see that there exists a lossless decomposition of RS' into *three* subschemes, namely the projections of RS' onto $\{DRINKER, BEER\}$, $\{BEER, BAR\}$ and $\{DRINKER, BAR\}$ respectively. If we apply this decomposition strategy on the above instance, we get:

DRINKER	*BEER*
Jones	*Tuborg*
Jones	*Carlsberg*
Smith	*Tuborg*

BEER	*BAR*
Tuborg	*Tivoli*
Tuborg	*Far West*
Carlsberg	*Tivoli*

DRINKER	*BAR*
Jones	*Tivoli*
Jones	*Far West*
Smith	*Tivoli*

It is easily seen that we can recover the original instance by performing a natural join on these projections. Moreover, a closer examination of the constraint sc' reveals that it actually *says* that RS' can be decomposed into the three subschemes mentioned above.

□

Nicolas [81] called a constraint such as the one we introduced in the above example, which yields a necessary and sufficient condition for a relation to be decomposable into three subrelations, a *mutual dependency.* The generalization is of course obvious [91]:

Definition 3.9 Let $PRS = (\Omega, \Delta, dom)$ be a primitive relation scheme. Let $X_1, \ldots, X_k \subseteq \Omega$ with $\bigcup_{i=1}^{k} X_i = \Omega$. A *join dependency* $X_1 \bowtie \cdots \bowtie X_k$ over PRS is a constraint that is satisfied by a possible relation instance prs if and only if for all $t_1, \ldots, t_k \in prs$ with $t_i[X_i \cap X_j] = t_j[X_i \cap X_j]$ for all $i, j = 1, \ldots, k$ there exists a tuple $t \in prs$ such that $t[X_i] = t_i[X_i]$ for all $i = 1, \ldots, k$.

□

Hence the constraint sc' in Example 3.16 is a join dependency (jd) with three components that can be denoted as

$$\{DRINKER, BEER\} \bowtie \{BEER, BAR\} \bowtie \{DRINKER, BAR\}.$$

From Definition 3.9 we can immediately derive:

Theorem 3.14 *Let* $RS = (\Omega, \Delta, dom, M, SC)$ *be a relation scheme. Let* $X_1, \ldots, X_k \subseteq \Omega$ *with* $\bigcup_{i=1}^{k} X_i = \Omega$. $SC \models X_1 \bowtie \cdots \bowtie X_k$ *if and only if for each relation instance* r *of* RS *we have that* $r = \Pi(r, X_1) \bowtie \cdots \bowtie \Pi(r, X_k)$.

□

Theorem 3.14 explains the notation we used to denote a jd. Theorem 3.14 also yields the following corollary:

Corollary 3.3 *Let* $PRS = (\Omega, \Delta, dom)$ *be a primitive relation scheme.*

- *Let* $X, Y \subseteq \Omega$. *Then* $X \twoheadrightarrow Y \Leftrightarrow XY \bowtie X(\Omega - Y)$.
- *Let* $X_1, X_2 \subseteq \Omega$ *with* $X_1 \cup X_2 = \Omega$. *Then* $X_1 \bowtie X_2 \Leftrightarrow X_1 \cap X_2 \twoheadrightarrow X_1$.[7]

Proof Follows immediately from Theorem 3.14 and Theorem 3.9.

□

[7]Instead of X_1 we might also have written X_2, $X_1 - X_2$ or $X_2 - X_1$.

Corollary 3.3 says that the mvds of a primitive relation scheme are exactly those jds that have two components. In the remainder of this section, we shall always represent an mvd in this way. At this point, the reader might wonder why we chose to introduce mvds as an extension of fds and not as a particular case of jds. The reason for this is that many desirable properties of fds, such as the existence of a sound and complete axiomatization and a polynomial algorithm to decide implication, carry over to mvds but not to jds. We come back to this problem in a little while, but first we give another example of a jd.

Example 3.17 Consider the following (simplified) example of a bank record, first introduced by [46] and represented here by the relation scheme $RS = (\Omega, \Delta, dom, M, SC)$ with:

- $\Omega = \{BANK, ACCOUNT, LOAN, CUSTOMER, CUST\text{-}ADDR\}$;
- In the domains of $ACCOUNT$ and $LOAN$ there is a so-called *null value* (see Chapter 6) which is used whenever a customer of a bank has only a loan (although unlikely!) or only an account;
- The existence of a tuple in an instance of this scheme means that a bank has issued an account and a loan to a customer, specified by his name and address. The specification of the null value as a value for the attribute $LOAN$ or the attribute $ACCOUNT$ means that the customer has at that bank no loan or no account, respectively;
- SC consists of two constraints: the fd $CUSTOMER \rightarrow CUST\text{-}ADDR$ and the jd $\{BANK, ACCOUNT\} \bowtie \{BANK, LOAN\} \bowtie \{ACCOUNT, CUSTOMER\} \bowtie \{LOAN, CUSTOMER\} \bowtie \{CUSTOMER, CUST\text{-}ADDR\}$, indicating that the relation can be decomposed into five components.

□

At this point we note that the structure of a larger jd such as the one above is not obvious. Therefore a jd is often represented by a *hypergraph*.

Definition 3.10 A *hypergraph* is an ordered pair $(\mathcal{N}, \mathcal{E})$ where $\mathcal{N}$ is a finite set of *nodes* and $\mathcal{E}$ is a set of *edges*. Each edge of $\mathcal{E}$ is a subset of $\mathcal{N}$.

□

Hence (undirected) graphs are a special case of hypergraphs, namely those hypergraphs in which all edges are pairs.

Now, a jd can be represented by a hypergraph of which the nodes are all the attributes of Ω and the edges the components of the jd.

Example 3.18 Reconsider the jd of Example 3.17. This jd can be represented by the following hypergraph:

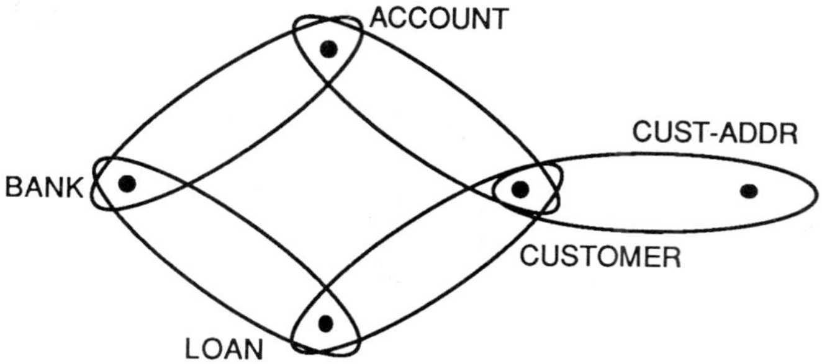

□

Let us now have a look into the implication problem for fds and jds together. (We need not specify mvds here separately, since they are contained in the class of jds.) We shall present an algorithm to decide this implication, called the *chase*, introduced by Maier, Mendelzon and Sagiv in [75]. Therefore we need to define some initial concepts.

The chase is based on the idea of a *tableau*, which was introduced in [6] and subsequently studied in various papers one of which is [5]. Here, we shall use the following variation [60] on the original definition:

Definition 3.11 Let $PRS = (\Omega, \Delta, dom)$ be a primitive relation scheme. Let $V_D = \{\alpha_A \mid A \in \Omega\}$ be a set of symbols, indexed by Ω, called *distinguished variables*. Let $V_U = \{\beta_A^1, \beta_A^2, \beta_A^3, \dots \mid A \in \Omega\}$ be a another set of symbols indexed by both Ω and the set of positive integers, called *undistinguished variables*. We assume $V_D \cap V_U = \emptyset$.

- A *row* ℓ of *PRS* is a mapping from $\Omega \to V_D \cup V_U$. If $X \subseteq \Omega$, we denote by $\ell[X]$ the restriction of ℓ to X. The set of attributes corresponding to a row ℓ, denoted $\tilde{\ell}$, is defined as $\tilde{\ell} = \{A \in \Omega \mid \ell(A) \in V_D\}$.
- A *tableau* τ of *PRS* is a set of rows of *PRS*.

□

The chase algorithm we intend to describe checks whether a given jd is implied by a given set of fds and jds. Roughly speaking, the algorithm works as follows. First, an initial tableau is constructed for the jd of which we want to know whether or not it is implied by the set of constraints under consideration. Then we modify that initial tableau by "applying" the fds and jds of the given set until no further action is possible. We shall show that the implication holds if and only if the final tableau satisfies a certain condition. First though, we define the initial tableau of a jd.

Definition 3.12 Let $PRS = (\Omega, \Delta, dom)$ be a primitive relation scheme. Let $J : X_1 \bowtie \cdots \bowtie X_k$ be a jd over *PRS* (whence $\bigcup_{i=1}^{k} X_i = \Omega$). The *initial tableau* for J, is a tableau $\tau(J) = \{\ell_1, \dots, \ell_k\}$ of *PRS* satisfying the following conditions:

1. $\forall i = 1, \dots, k; \forall A \in X_i : \ell_i(A) = \alpha_A$;
2. $\forall i = 1, \dots, k; \forall A \notin X_i : \ell_i(A) = \beta_A^i$.

□

Example 3.19 Consider a primitive relation scheme $PRS = (\Omega, \Delta, dom)$ where $\Omega = \{A, B, C, D\}$. Let J be the jd $AB \bowtie BC \bowtie CD$. The initial tableau $\tau(J)$ equals:

rnr.	A	B	C	D
1	α_A	α_B	β_C^1	β_D^1
2	β_A^2	α_B	α_C	β_D^2
3	β_A^3	β_B^3	α_C	α_D

□

The best intuitive way to look at a tableau is to imagine it as a subset of a kind of "formal" possible relation instance of PRS. The construction of the initial tableau for J reminds us of Definition 3.9. The tuples $t_1, \ldots, t_k$ correspond to the rows $\ell_1, \ldots, \ell_k$ and the relevant parts of these tuples to the distinguished variables in these rows. In this way, the tuple t in Definition 3.9 corresponds with a row consisting of distinguished variables only. The idea behind the chase algorithm is the following. Starting from the initial tableau for J we try to enforce all the fds and jds of the given set in a minimal way, by either equating variables or adding rows. J will then be implied by the given set of constraints depending on whether or not the *final tableau* contains a row consisting of distinguished variables only.

Example 3.20 Reconsider Example 3.19. Let $SC = \{C \rightarrow D, AB \bowtie BCD\}$. Let us check whether $SC \models J$ by using the chase. Since the second and third row of $\tau(J)$ have the same C-value, we have to enforce $C \rightarrow D$ by equating variables. This results in a tableau:

rnr.	A	B	C	D
1	α_A	α_B	β_C^1	β_D^1
2	β_A^2	α_B	α_C	α_D
3	β_A^3	β_B^3	α_C	α_D

If we now try to enforce $AB \bowtie BCD$ by adding the appropriate rows, we obtain:

rnr.	A	B	C	D
1	α_A	α_B	β_C^1	β_D^1
2	β_A^2	α_B	α_C	α_D
3	β_A^3	β_B^3	α_C	α_D
4	α_A	α_B	α_C	α_D
5	β_A^2	α_B	β_C^1	β_D^1

Obviously, all the constraints of SC "hold" in this tableau. Since the fourth row contains distinguished variables only, we may conclude that indeed $SC \models J$. □

We now describe the *chase algorithm* formally.

Algorithm 3.4 *Chase*

Input: A jd J and a set of fds and jds SC over a primitive relation scheme $PRS = (\Omega, \Delta, dom)$.

Output: *true* or *false*.

Method:

```
var ℓ : row;
      TAB, HELPTAB, OLDTAB : tableau;
TAB := τ(J);
repeat
    OLDTAB := TAB;
    for each Y_1 ⋈ ··· ⋈ Y_l in SC do
        HELPTAB := TAB;
        for all ℓ_1, ..., ℓ_l in TAB do
            if ∀i, j = 1, ... l : ℓ_i[Y_i ∩ Y_j] = ℓ_j[Y_i ∩ Y_j]
                then
                    begin
                        for i := 1 to l do
                            ℓ[Y_i] := ℓ_i[Y_i]
                        od;
                        if ℓ ∉ HELPTAB
                            then
                                HELPTAB := HELPTAB ∪ {ℓ}
                    end
        od;
        TAB := HELPTAB
    od;
    for each X → Y in SC do
        for each ℓ_1, ℓ_2 in TAB do
            if ℓ_1[X] = ℓ_2[X]
                then
                    for each A in Y do
                        if ℓ_1(A) ≠ ℓ_2(A)
                            then
                                begin
                                    if (ℓ_1(A) = α_A) or (ℓ_2(A) = α_A)
                                        then
                                            begin
                                                ℓ_1(A) := α_A;
                                                ℓ_2(A) := α_A;
                                            end
```

```
                                if (ℓ1(A) = β^i_A) and (ℓ2(A) = β^j_A)
                                  then
                                    begin
                                      ℓ1(A) := β_A^min(i,j);
                                      ℓ2(A) := β_A^min(i,j)
                                    end
                              end
                        od
                od
            od
        until TAB = OLDTAB;
        for each A in Ω do
            ℓ(A) := α_A
        od;
        if ℓ ∈ TAB
            then
                return(true)
            else
                return(false)
```

□

Of course it goes without saying that there is no need to continue the chase algorithm as soon as a row consisting of distinguished variables only is created.

Theorem 3.15 *Algorithm 3.4 terminates and returns the value "true" if $SC \models J$ and "false" in the other case.*

Proof First, note that nowhere in Algorithm 3.4 symbols are introduced that were not already in the initial tableau for J. Since the initial tableau for J contains exactly as many rows as there are components in J, say k, there are at most kn symbols in this table. Now with kn symbols, at most $(kn)^n$ rows can be constructed. Hence, since no new variables are added during the chase, after at most that many passes through the repeat-loop, the algorithm must end. The tableau which is obtained at the end of the algorithm is denoted $chase_{SC}(\tau(J))$ (or $chase(\tau(J))$ if no ambiguity is possible).

Let us first assume that $SC \models J : X_1 \bowtie \cdots \bowtie X_k$. Let ρ be a one-to-one mapping from the symbols in $\tau(J) = \{\ell_1, \ldots, \ell_k\}$ into $\bigcup \Delta$ such that a symbol indexed by the attribute A is mapped into a value of $dom(A)$. We extend ρ to rows and tableaux in the obvious way. This implies that ρ maps rows into tuples and tableaux into relation instances. Because of the operations performed in Algorithm 3.4, it readily follows that $\rho(chase(\tau(J))$ satisfies SC. Hence, by our assumptions, $\rho(chase(\tau(J))$ also satisfies J. Since by construction of the initial tableau, we have that for all $i, j = 1, \ldots, k : \rho(\ell_i)[X_i \cap X_j] = \rho(\ell_j)[X_i \cap X_j]$.

Hence there exists a tuple in $\rho(chase(\tau(J))$ that we can write as $\rho(\ell)$ such that for $i = 1, \ldots, k : \rho(\ell)[X_i] = \rho(\ell_i)[X_i]$. Since ρ is one-to-one, it follows that for $i = 1, \ldots, k : \ell[X_i] = \ell_i[X_i]$. Since by construction $\tilde{\ell_i} = X_i$, it follows that $\tilde{\ell} = \Omega$. Hence $\ell \in \rho(chase(\tau(J))$ contains only distinguished variables, and Algorithm 3.4 will return the value *true*.

Let us now assume that Algorithm 3.4 returns the value *true*, i.e. that $chase(\tau(J))$ contains a line ℓ that consists of distinguished variables only. We have to show that $SC \models J : X_1 \bowtie \cdots \bowtie X_k$. Therefore, let prs be a possible relation instance of the primitive scheme $PRS = (\Omega, \Delta, dom)$ and let $t_1, \ldots, t_k$ be tuples of prs satisfying the conditions of Definition 3.9. We need to prove the existence of an appropriate tuple t. Since $t_1, \ldots, t_k$ satisfy the conditions of Definition 3.9, it follows by construction that there exists a mapping ρ from variables to values (which does not have to be one-to-one) such that the rows of $\tau(J)$ are mapped onto the tuples $t_1, \ldots, t_k$ respectively. We are now going to show by induction that $\rho(\tau(J)) \subseteq prs$. Therefore let τ be any of the intermediate tableaux obtained during the chase process and suppose that $\rho(\tau) \subseteq prs$. We have to distinguish two cases:

- *τ is modified by applying an fd $X \rightarrow Y$:* In this case, there exist rows ℓ_1 and ℓ_2 such that $\ell_1[X] = \ell_2[X]$. Hence $\rho(\ell_1)[X] = \rho(\ell_2)[X]$. Since by the induction hypothesis, both tuples are in prs which satisfies SC, it follows that $\rho(\ell_1)[Y] = \rho(\ell_1)[Y]$. Now let τ' be the tableau constructed from τ by equating the respective variables of $\ell_1[Y]$ and $\ell_2[Y]$. Since equated variables are mapped by ρ to the same values, it follows that $\rho(\tau') \subseteq prs$.
- *τ is modified by applying a jd $Y_1 \bowtie \cdots \bowtie Y_l$:* Hence there exist $\ell_1, \ldots, \ell_l \in \tau$ such that for all i, j, $1 \leq i, j \leq l$, $\ell_i[Y_i \cap Y_j] = \ell_j[Y_i \cap Y_j]$. Now define ℓ' by $\ell[Y_i] = \ell_i[Y_i]$ for all $i = 1, \ldots l$ and let $\tau' = \tau \cup \{\ell'\}$. Since by the induction hypothesis, $\rho(\ell_1), \ldots, \rho(\ell_l) \in prs$ which satisfies SC, it follows that $\rho(\ell') \in prs$. Hence $\rho(\tau') \subseteq prs$.

Hence we may conclude from the inductive argument above that $\rho(chase(\tau(J))$ $\subseteq prs$. In particular, $\rho(\ell) \in prs$. Obviously, this is the tuple t we were looking for.

□

We give one more example of an application of the chase algorithm.

Example 3.21 Let $RS = (\Omega, \Delta, dom, M, SC)$ be a relation scheme with

- $\Omega = \{A, B, C, D, E, F, G\}$;
- $SC = \{ABCD \bowtie DEFG, ABDEG \bowtie ACDFG\}$.

Let J be the jd $ABD \bowtie ACD \bowtie DEG \bowtie DFG$. We show that $SC \models J$. Let us first construct the initial tableau $\tau(J)$:

rnr.	A	B	C	D	E	F	G
1	α_A	α_B	β_C^1	α_D	β_E^1	β_F^1	β_G^1
2	α_A	β_B^2	α_C	α_D	β_E^2	β_F^2	β_G^2
3	β_A^3	β_B^3	β_C^3	α_D	α_E	β_F^3	α_G
4	β_A^4	β_B^4	β_C^4	α_D	β_E^4	α_F	α_G

For convenience, we have numbered the rows. Since $\ell_1[ABCD \cap DEFG] = \ell_3[ABCD \cap DEFG]$ it follows that a row ℓ_5 can be added such that $\ell_5[ABCD] = \ell_1[ABCD]$ and $\ell_5[DEFG] = \ell_3[DEFG]$. Similarly, since $\ell_2[ABCD \cap DEFG] = \ell_4[ABCD \cap DEFG]$, we can add a row ℓ_6 with $\ell_6[ABCD] = \ell_2[ABCD]$ and $\ell_6[DEFG] = \ell_4[DEFG]$. After this addition, our tableau becomes:

rnr.	A	B	C	D	E	F	G
1	α_A	α_B	β_C^1	α_D	β_E^1	β_F^1	β_G^1
2	α_A	β_B^2	α_C	α_D	β_E^2	β_F^2	β_G^2
3	β_A^3	β_B^3	β_C^3	α_D	α_E	β_F^3	α_G
4	β_A^4	β_B^4	β_C^4	α_D	β_E^4	α_F	α_G
5	α_A	α_B	β_C^1	α_D	α_E	β_F^3	α_G
6	α_A	β_B^2	α_C	α_D	β_E^4	α_F	α_G

Since $\ell_5[ABDEG \cap ACDFG] = \ell_6[ABDEG \cap ACDFG]$ it follows that the row ℓ_7 with $\ell_7[ABDEG] = \ell_5[ABDEG]$ and $\ell_7[ACDFG] = \ell_6[ACDFG]$ can be added to the tableau. Since this row consists of distinguished variables only, it follows that $SC \models J$.

□

As an application of Theorem 3.15 we show:

Corollary 3.4 *Let $PRS = (\Omega, \Delta, dom)$ be a primitive relation scheme. Let $J : X_1 \bowtie \cdots \bowtie X_k$ and $J' : Y_1 \bowtie \cdots \bowtie Y_l$ be jds of PRS. $J \models J'$ if and only if for each $i = 1, \ldots, k$ there exists j, $1 \leq j \leq l$ such that $X_i \subseteq Y_j$.*

Proof We first show the if-part. Let $\tau(J') = \{\ell_1, \ldots, \ell_l\}$ be the initial tableau of J'. Hence $\tilde{\ell}_j = Y_j$ for all $j = 1, \ldots, l$. Now choose for each $i = 1, \ldots, k$ a number j_i such that $X_i \subseteq Y_{j_i}$. Hence $X_i \subseteq \tilde{\ell}_{j_i}$ which implies in particular that for all $s, t = 1, \ldots, k$ we have that $\ell_{j_s}[X_s \cap X_t] = \ell_{j_t}[X_s \cap X_t]$. Hence the chase algorithm guarantees that a row ℓ will be added satisfying the condition $\ell[X_i] = \ell_{j_i}[X_i]$ for all $i = 1, \ldots k$. Since $\ell_{j_i}[X_i]$ consists of distinguished variables only and since by the definition of jd, $\bigcup_{i=1}^k X_i = \Omega$, it follows that $\tilde{\ell} = \Omega$. So $J \models J'$ by Theorem 3.15.

We now show the only-if part. Therefore assume on the contrary that there exists m, $1 \leq m \leq k$ such that for all $j = 1, \ldots, l$ $X_m \not\subseteq Y_j$. Hence the projection of each row of $\tau(J')$ onto X_m contains some undistinguished variables.

We know that for each $\ell \in chase_J(\tau(J'))$ and for each $i = 1, \ldots, k$ there exists $\ell'_i \in chase_J(\tau(J'))$ such that $\ell'_i[X_i] = \ell[X_i]$. Now, let us denote by $or_i(\ell)$ the (non-empty) set of all rows $\ell'_i \in chase_J(\tau(J')$ satisfying this condition. Now define:

$$\tau = \{\ell \in chase_J(\tau(J')) \mid \forall i = 1, \ldots, k : or_i(\ell) \cap \tau(J') \neq \emptyset\}$$

Let ℓ be an arbitrary row of τ. Let ℓ'_m be an arbitrary row from $or_m(\ell) \cap \tau(J')$. Since $\ell[X_m] = \ell'_m[X_m]$ and since $\ell'_m[X_m]$ contains some undistinguished variables, ℓ too contains some undistinguished variables. Hence no row of τ consists of distinguished variables only. It now suffices to show that $\tau = chase_J(\tau(J'))$. Therefore, note that for each $\ell \in chase_J(\tau'_J))$ and for all $i = 1, \ldots, k$, $or_i(\ell)$ contains a row which was created before ℓ. Our claim now follows from the straightforward observation that for each $\ell'_i \in or_i(\ell)$, $or_i(\ell'_i) \subseteq or_i(\ell)$. □

Example 3.22 Reconsider Example 3.21. We showed already that $SC \models J$. Now, the jds (they are actually even mvds) in SC are implied by J, by Corollary 3.4. Hence SC and J are equivalent.

□

Since the number of rows that can be formed in a tableau is exponential in the number of symbols appearing in it, it follows immediately that the chase algorithm is exponential in the size of the input. Unfortunately we cannot expect better, since in [76] it is shown that (proof omitted):

Theorem 3.16 *The implication problem for (fds and) jds is NP-hard.*

□

Here we encounter one the fundamental differences between mvds and jds in general to which we already referred earlier. Whereas implication of mvds can be decided fairly quickly, this cannot be done efficiently for jds in general. Related to this problem is that whereas for the implication of mvds a rather simple axiomatization exists, it is unknown whether there is a finite sound and complete set of axioms for the inference of jds similar to those we already encountered (see also [100, 23]). So, although jds may seem an obvious choice for modeling a database, they may have some definite disadvantages. Luckily there is a way out of this dilemma. In Example 3.21 we introduced a jd which turned out to be equivalent to a set of (two) mvds. If in general we restrict ourselves to sets of jds with a fixed maximum number of components the chase algorithm becomes polynomial (See Exercise 3.33). Consider now the class of the jds equivalent to set of jds with a fixed maximum number of components. Provided it is possible to effectively construct such a set in polynomial time (which is the case), the implication problem remains polynomial if we restrict ourselves to this class of jds. This suggests to introduce the following definition:

Definition 3.13 Let $PRS = (\Omega, \Delta, dom)$ be a primitive relation scheme and let J be a jd of PRS. Let m be a positive integer. J is said to be *m-cyclic* if J is equivalent to a set of jds each of which consists of at most m components. □

We first need to explain why we use the term "cyclicity" for a notion that induces a hierarchical classification of jds according to the complexity of their "structure" or, indirectly, to the complexity of integrity checking for that class. The reason for this can be found in the structure of the hypergraph representation of these jds. However we cannot discuss this issue in further detail within the scope of this book. Let us now formalize the observation made earlier:

Theorem 3.17 *Let m be a fixed positive constant. The implication problem for fds and m-cyclic jds is decidable in polynomial time.* □

As observed earlier, this theorem can be derived from a straightforward calculation of the time-complexity of the chase algorithm provided there exists a polynomial algorithm to replace an m-cyclic jd with a set of jds all of which have at most m components. We shall make no attempt to prove this fact here and refer the interested reader to [61].

Although integrity checking is polynomial for m-cyclic jds for a fixed value of m, the complexity can be higher or lower depending on whether we fix a higher or a lower value for m. The choice of m will therefore be a compromise between syntactical richness of database modeling abilities and efficiency of integrity checking. Let us illustrate this statement with the following example.

Example 3.23 Consider again the jd introduced in Example 3.17. One can show that this jd is 4-cyclic. Observe that the hypergraph representation of this jd indeed contains a cycle with four edges, although this is not a sufficient condition for 4-cyclicity. For a more rigorous investigation into the level of cyclicity of a jd, please see Exercise 3.36.

Now suppose that we have chosen to allow only 2-cyclic jds. Then we cannot use the jd of Example 3.17 to structure our banking database. We shall have to replace it by a 2 cyclic one. Intuitively speaking, we mentioned already that the 4-cyclicity of the jd of Example 3.17 stems from the existence of a 4-cycle in its hypergraph representation. Therefore we shall try to break this cycle. A way to this is "splitting" the attribute *CUSTOMER* into two new attributes *DEPOSITOR* and *BORROWER*. If a similar operation is performed on the attribute *CUST-ADDR*, we obtain the following picture:

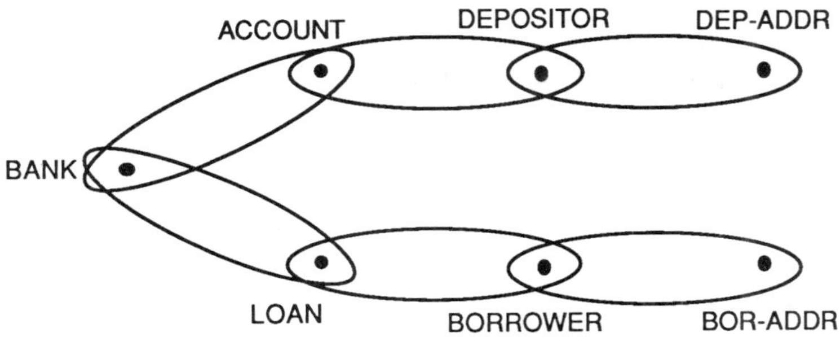

□

Later on, we shall be able to show that the jd represented by this last hypergraph is indeed 2-cyclic. The advantage of performing the above operation is that integrity checking becomes easier. The disadvantage is that it gets more difficult to check whether a borrower at a bank is also a depositor. The choice between these two alternatives has to be made by the database manager.

Now it can be readily seen that the 1-cyclic jds are the trivial jds (see also Exercise 3.36). So 2-cyclicity is the least complex class of jds with respect to integrity checking. There exist various ways to characterize 2-cyclicity. One of these characterizations which examines the hypergraph representation of the jd is responsible for the more common term *acyclicity*. Hence we may say:

Definition 3.14 A jd is *acyclic* if its equivalent to a set of mvds. A jd which is not acyclic is called *cyclic*.

□

Another question that is probably raised by Definition 3.13, Theorem 3.17 and Example 3.23 is, given m, whether it is a decidable if a jd is m-cyclic. In [61] it is shown that this question can even be decided in polynomial time (see also Exercise 3.36). Here we shall limit our ambitions, and only give an algorithm to check acyclicity, which is due to Graham [55], and independently to Yu and Özsoyoğlu ([113, 114]). Although the latter made essential contributions to the actual formulation of the algorithm and the proof of its correctness, it is generally known as the *Graham-algorithm*.

Algorithm 3.5 *Graham Algorithm*

Input: A jd $X_1 \bowtie \cdots \bowtie X_k$ of a primitive relation scheme $PRS = (\Omega, \Delta, dom)$.

Output: *true* or *false*.

Method:

var $COUNTTOT$, $COUNTOLD$, $COUNTATT$: integer;
$COUNTTOT := \sum_{i=1}^{k} |X_i|$;
repeat
$COUNTOLD := COUNTTOT$;

```
        for i := 1 to k do
            for j := 1 to k do
                if (i ≠ j) and X_i ≠ emptyset and (X_i ⊆ X_j)
                    then
                        begin
                            COUNTTOT := COUNTTOT − |X_i|;
                            X_i := ∅
                        end
            od
        od;
        for each A in Ω do
            COUNTATT := 0;
            for i := 1 to k do
                if A ∈ X_i
                    then
                        COUNTATT := COUNTATT + 1
            od;
            if COUNTATT = 1
                then
                    begin
                        COUNTTOT := COUNTTOT − 1;
                        for i := 1 to k do
                            X_i := X_i − {A}
                        od
                    od
        od
    until COUNTTOT = COUNTOLD;
    if COUNTTOT = 0
        then
            return(true);
        else
            return(false)
```

□

Let us first explain what happens. The Graham-algorithm first checks whether there are components of the given jd which are contained in another one. Such components are deleted. This process is called *reducing a jd*; the result of it is the *reduction* of the given jd (see also Exercise 3.34). After this is finished, the Graham algorithm looks for *isolated attributes*, i.e. attributes that appear only once. The algorithm disposes of all the isolated attributes. After the removal of these attributes, the algorithm tries to reduce further on; after this reduction, some attributes may have become isolated and will consequently be deleted. The algorithm continues in this way until no further action is possible. If the result of this repeated process is the removal of everything , then the original jd is acyclic. If on the other hand still something remains, the original jd is cyclic. Without proof we state:

Theorem 3.18 *Algorithm 3.5 returns the value true if the jd given as input is acyclic and false if that jd is cyclic.*

□

The Graham algorithm is only one of the many characterizations known for acyclicity. We refer to [10, 11, 9, 25, 14, 17, 18, 21, 35, 44, 45, 46, 59, 61, 56, 77, 87, 94, 95, 101, 111] for those who are interested. We conclude this section with an example on the Graham algorithm.

Example 3.24 Let J be a jd $BCD \bowtie ACE \bowtie ABF \bowtie ABC$ of a primitive relation scheme with set of attributes $\{A, B, C, D, E, F\}$. For practical convenience, we start by writing the jd row by row in a table:

$$\begin{matrix} BCD \\ ACE \\ ABF \\ ABC \end{matrix}$$

This jd is obviously reduced; however there are isolated attributes, namely D, E and F. After the removal of this attributes, we get:

$$\begin{matrix} BC \\ AC \\ AB \\ ABC \end{matrix}$$

This set of components is not reduced any more. In the next step of the Graham algorithm, the first three edges will be deleted. As a consequence, all the remaining attributes become isolated since they are only appearing in one edge, and they get deleted too. So nothing remains, which means that J is acyclic.

If on the other hand we would have considered the jd J' : $BCD \bowtie ACE \bowtie ABF$ then we would still be able to perform the first step of the Graham algorithm, but then, we would get stuck. Hence J' is cyclic. More precisely, it is 3-cyclic, since there are obviously no other alternatives.

□

3.5 Inclusion Dependencies

At this time, we want to make some reflections as to the "nature" of the constraints we introduced. The point we want to make is that there is a significant difference between fds on the one hand and mvds and jds on the other hand. Clearly fds are meaningful from a semantic point of view; they give additional information about the data in the data base; as a side effect, fds also give rise to decompositions. It is however not so clear whether mvds and jds really tell us much about the contents of the database; they rather tell us something about the way we chose to structure the database. In this respect, mvds and jds could be named "syntactic" constraints.

The constraint we shall discuss in this section is quite different from those we already encountered and is clearly of a semantic nature. Furthermore, it has nothing to do with decomposition! We introduce this constraint with an example.

Example 3.25 Consider a relation scheme $WORK = (\Omega, \Delta, dom, M, SC)$ with

- $\Omega = \{EMP\text{-}NR, EMP\text{-}NAME, MAN\text{-}NR, MAN\text{-}NAME, JOB, SALARY\}$;
- Δ and *dom* may be defined in any appropriate way, but we do assume that $dom(EMP\text{-}NR) = dom(MAN\text{-}NR)$ and $dom(EMP\text{-}NAME) = dom(MAN\text{-}NAME)$. This corresponds to the assumption that at the one hand a manager is always an employee and on the other hand that every employee potentially can become a manager;
- The meaning of this relation is obvious: each tuple represents an employee, specified by number and name, working at a job to which a certain salary is associated, under the direction of a manager also specified by a number and his name;
- *SC* contains the fds $EMP\text{-}NR \rightarrow EMP\text{-}NAME$, $MAN\text{-}NR \rightarrow MAN\text{-}NAME$ and $\{EMP\text{-}NR, JOB\} \rightarrow SALARY$ and also the condition that each manager is an employee one of whose jobs is manager.

Part of the last constraint could be formalized as follows: the projection of any relation instance of *WORK* onto *MAN-NR* must be contained in the projection of that instance onto *EMP-NR*. Such a constraint will be called an *inclusion dependency* (for obvious reasons) and we shall denote it by $[MAN\text{-}NR] \subseteq [EMP\text{-}NR]$. Inclusion dependencies can also involve more than one attribute. For example, the inclusion dependency we could denote as $[MAN\text{-}NR, MAN\text{-}NAME] \subseteq [EMP\text{-}NR, EMP\text{-}NAME]$ also holds.

□

Note that the order in which the attributes appear in an inclusion dependency is crucial. So we have to consider sequences rather than sets of attributes in the formal definition of an inclusion dependency:

Definition 3.15 Let $PRS = (\Omega, \Delta, dom)$ be a primitive relation scheme and let $A_1, \ldots, A_k$ and $B_1, \ldots, B_k$ be two sequences of *different* attributes of Ω with the same length. An *inclusion dependency* $[A_1, \ldots, A_k] \subseteq [B_1, \ldots, B_k]$ over *PRS* is a constraint which is satisfied by a possible relation instance *prs* if and only if: $\forall t \in prs\, \exists t' \in prs\, \forall i = 1, \ldots, k : t(A_i) = t'(B_i)$

□

Inclusion dependencies [26, 33, 41] were introduced by Fagin and Casanova in 1981. There exist various variations on the above definition. A slight extension of our definition redefines inclusion dependencies as database constraints. Earlier, one of the authors defined *inclusions* [85] which is a constraint quite similar to inclusion dependencies, although there exist some major differences. For both topics, we refer to the exercises.

Before we discuss the implication problem for inclusion dependencies (from now on abbreviated to ids), we need to observe that, contrary to the constraints encountered previously, ids are *untyped constraints*. Indeed, in order to check fds, mvds or jds, we never had to compare values corresponding to different attributes, so we never had to face compatibility problems. Hence the decidability as well as the complexity of the implication problem may heavily depend on the nature of the domains corresponding to the various attributes. In order to keep things tractable, we assume that the same infinite domain is associated to each attribute under consideration. We establish without proof [26]:

Theorem 3.19 *Let $\mathcal{I}$ be the following system of axioms:*

$\emptyset \vdash [A_1, \ldots, A_k] \subseteq [A_1, \ldots, A_k]$ (trivial ids) $\quad (I1)$

$[A_1, \ldots, A_k] \subseteq [B_1, \ldots, B_k] \vdash [A_{i_1}, \ldots, A_{i_l}] \subseteq [B_{i_1}, \ldots, B_{i_l}]$ for each subsequence $i_1, \ldots, i_l$ of different integers of $\{1, \ldots, k\}$ (projection/permutation) $\quad (I2)$

$\{[A_1, \ldots, A_k] \subseteq [B_1, \ldots, B_k], [B_1, \ldots, B_k] \subseteq [C_1, \ldots, C_k]\} \vdash$
$[A_1, \ldots, A_k] \subseteq [C_1, \ldots, C_k]$ (transitivity) $\quad (I3)$

$\mathcal{I}$ is a non-redundant sound and complete axiom system for the implication of ids. □

The above axiomatization entails a conceptually simple but, unfortunately, computationally complex procedure to effectively test implication of ids. Anyhow, we may conclude:

Theorem 3.20 *The implication problem for ids is decidable.* □

Since both fds and ids are constraints of indisputable semantical nature, it is appealing to consider the implication problem for fds and ids together. Unfortunately it has been shown that [28]:

Theorem 3.21 *The implication problem for fds and ids is undecidable.* □

In the following and final section of this chapter, we shall better be able to explain why the implication problem for fds and ids is that difficult. Nevertheless we already want to give you a feeling of the untractability of the problem. For all the cases we studied in the previous sections, it was always possible to produce finite counterexample relation instance to illustrate that a certain implication of constraints does not hold. For inclusion dependencies this no longer holds, as is shown in the following example, by which we conclude this section.

Example 3.26 Consider a relation scheme $RS = (\Omega, \Delta, dom, M, SC)$ with:

- $\Omega = \{A, B\}$;
- Δ contains the set of all integers;
- the domain of both A and B is the set of all integers;
- $SC = \{A \rightarrow B, [A] \subseteq [B]\}$.

Let sc be the id $[B] \subseteq [A]$. Each *finite* relation instance of RS satisfies sc. However, $SC \not\models sc$, since the following *infinite* relation instance of RS does not satisfy sc:

A	B
2	1
3	2
4	3
$\vdots$	$\vdots$
$i+1$	i
$\vdots$	$\vdots$

Ids such as $[A] \subseteq [B]$ in the previous example are called *unary ids*. The attribute sequences in unary ids consist of only one attribute. Although the implication problem for fds and ids is undecidable and although even unary ids interact with fds in a strange way, as shown in Example 3.26, the implication problem for fds and unary ids is still decidable [69]! Undecidability arises as soon as *binary ids* are allowed.

□

3.6 Tuple and Equality Generating Dependencies

In the final section of this chapter, we present a formalism that covers all previously introduced types of constraints. Since it seems very difficult to find an axiomatization for jds that involves only jds, researchers have sought for larger classes of constraints that do have a fairly reasonable axiomatization. Finally many authors realized independently that all the dependencies studied so far were special cases of the constraint types we are going to define next. Afterwards we shall briefly discuss some problems with respect to these constraints and introduce some interesting subtypes we did not yet encounter.

Definition 3.16 Let $PRS = (\Omega, \Delta, dom)$ be a primitive relation scheme.

- A *tuple generating dependency* σ over PRS is a constraint which can be written as a first-order sentence:

$$(\forall x_1, \ldots, x_s)((P_1 \wedge \ldots \wedge P_k) \Rightarrow (\exists y_1, \ldots, y_r)(Q_1 \wedge \ldots \wedge Q_l))$$

  in which the P's are expressions of the form $(t \in rs)$ where t is a mapping of Ω to $\{x_1, \ldots, x_s\}$ and the Q's are similar expressions in which the mappings are defined over $\{x_1, \ldots, x_s, y_1, \ldots, y_r\}$. A possible relation instance prs satisfies σ if and only if σ is true in prs, i. e. if and only if prs is a model for σ.

- A *equality generating dependency* σ over *PRS* is a constraint which can be written as a first-order sentence:

$$(\forall x_1, \ldots, x_s)((P_1 \wedge \ldots \wedge P_k) \Rightarrow (Q_1 \wedge \ldots \wedge Q_l))$$

where the P's are as in the case of tuple generating dependencies and the Q's are expressions of the form $(x_i = x_j)$ in which $1 \leq i, j \leq s$. As in the previous case, a possible relation instance prs satisfies σ if and only if σ is true in prs. □

Tuple and equality generating dependencies in this form are due to Beeri en Vardi [19]. Other authors independently defined similar though less general classes of constraints: [43, 57, 86, 112]. Let us now examine how the constraints we already met can be viewed as tuple or equality generating dependencies.

Example 3.27 Let $PRS = (\Omega, \Delta, dom)$ be a primitive relation scheme where $\Omega = \{A, B, C, D\}$ and in which each attribute has the same infinite domain.

- Consider the fd $AB \rightarrow CD$. It can be expressed as the equality generating dependency:
$$(\forall x_1, \ldots, x_6)(((x_1, x_2, x_3, x_4) \in rs \wedge (x_1, x_2, x_5, x_6) \in rs) \Rightarrow ((x_3 = x_5) \wedge (x_4 = x_6)))$$
where e.g. (x_1, x_2, x_3, x_4) denotes the mapping that associates x_1 to A, x_2 to B, etc.
- Consider the jd $ABC \bowtie CD$. It can be expressed as:
$$(\forall x_1, \ldots, x_7)(((x_1, x_2, x_3, x_4) \in rs \wedge (x_5, x_6, x_3, x_7) \in rs) \Rightarrow ((x_1, x_2, x_3, x_7) \in rs))$$
- Finally, consider the id $[A, B] \subseteq [B, C]$. It can be written as:
$$(\forall x_1, \ldots, x_4)(((x_1, x_2, x_3, x_4) \in rs) \Rightarrow (\exists y_1, y_2)((y_1, x_1, x_2, y_2) \in rs))$$
□

Obviously, each fd, jd or id can be written as a tuple or equality generating dependency. Since mvds are a subclass of the jds, it is readily seen:

Theorem 3.22 *Functional dependencies are a special case of equality generating dependencies; multivalued dependencies, join dependencies and inclusion dependencies are special cases of tuple generating dependencies.* □

The formal details of the proof of the above theorem are left to the reader as an exercise.

Our new formalism reveals some of the fundamental differences between fds and jds on the one hand and ids on the other hand which we already expected intuitively. In fds and jds, the variables are *typed*: no variable is associated to more than one attribute. Furthermore, there are no existential variables in a jd. Tuple generating dependencies in which no existential attributes appear are called *full*. Id's are clearly *untyped* and *not full*. Tuple generating dependencies which are not full are also called *embedded*. We summarize:

Definition 3.17 A tuple or equality generating dependency is *typed* if no variable is associated to more than one attribute; otherwise it is *untyped.* A tuple generating dependency is *full* if there are no existential variables; otherwise it is *embedded.*

□

Mvds and fds are clearly typed and full; fds are also typed and ids are both untyped and embedded. What about other possible combinations? It is easy to find a subclass of ids which are untyped and full. We are now going to introduce some types of constraints which are typed and embedded.

Definition 3.18 Let $PRS = (\Omega, \Delta, dom)$ be a primitive relation scheme.

- Let $X_1, \ldots, X_k \subseteq \Omega$. An *embedded join dependency* $X_1 \bowtie \cdots \bowtie X_k$ over PRS is a constraint that is satisfied by a possible relation instance prs if and only if for all $t_1, \ldots, t_k \in sot$ with $t_i[X_i \cap X_j] = t_j[X_i \cap X_j]$ for all $i, j = 1, \ldots, k$ there exists a tuple $t \in sot$ such that $t[X_i] = t_i[X_i]$ for all $i = 1, \ldots, k$.
- An *embedded multivalued dependency* over PRS is an embedded jd over PRS with exactly two components.

□

Examples of embedded jds and embedded mvds will be given soon, in Example 3.28. As you can see, the only difference between the definition of an embedded jd and Definition 3.9 of a (full) jd is the removal of the condition $\bigcup_{i=1}^{k} X_i = \Omega$. This implies that in general the tuple t whose existence is guaranteed by the presence of an embedded jd, is in general not any more entirely determined. The difference between both definitions can be illustrated better if we translate the alternative version Theorem 3.14 to embedded jds:

Theorem 3.23 *Let $RS = (\Omega, \Delta, dom, M, SC)$ be a relation scheme. Let $X_1, \ldots,$ $X_k \subseteq \Omega$ and let $X = \bigcup_{i=1}^{k} X_i$. $SC \models X_1 \bowtie \cdots \bowtie X_k$ if and only if for each relation instance r of RS we have that $\Pi(r, X) = \Pi(r, X_1) \bowtie \cdots \bowtie \Pi(r, X_k)$.* □

So an embedded jd is essentially a jd that must hold in the projection of a relation. We chose to define embedded mvds as a special case of embedded jds, in the same way as full mvds can be seen as a special case of full jds. However it is also possible to define embedded mvds as a generalization of mvds according to the principle we just mentioned.

It is now time to raise two fundamental questions about tuple and equality generating dependencies:

- Is the implication problem decidable?
- Does there exist a sound and complete axiomatization?

Let us first discuss the latter question. Although for fds, mvds and ids, the presence of a sound and complete axiomatization helped us to device an algorithm to decide implication, the existence of an axiom system does not necessarily mean that the implication problem is decidable. Let us illustrate this with the following "axiom system" for an arbitrary type of constraints which consists of only one axiom:

$$D \vdash d \textit{ iff } D \models d$$

We hope no one has doubts concerning the soundness and completeness of the above axiom system: each constraint which is implied by a given set of constraints, and only these, can be derived from that set in one step (so, a finite number of steps) with the above axiom. Of course, our axiom system is of little use, since we do not know whether the condition in it can be verified effectively. In this extreme case, the answer to this last question is also the solution of the implication problem.

Therefore, our quest is for axiom systems that have "nicer conditions" in their rules. We could e.g. impose the following restriction on our axiomatization: *Given an arbitrary primitive relation scheme PRS and an arbitrary finite set of constraints SC of PRS, then for each axiom the set of constraints that can be derived from SC with that axiom must be recursive.* Note that this condition does not guarantee decidability of the implication problem. Unless each primitive relation scheme has only a finite number of constraints of the type under consideration — as is the case for fds, full and embedded mvds, full and embedded jds and ids — the decidability of the implication problem is not guaranteed even if the word "recursive" is replaced by "finite" or an even more severe restriction, since we cannot be sure that there is an upperbound to the length of a valid derivation. Furthermore, we like to find axiom systems that are valid for all possible primitive relation schemes, rather than only a particular one. Hence arguments concerning finiteness become irrelevant.

However, although the presence of a more or less "nice" axiom system does not necessarily lead to an algorithm which can decide implication, it can give us insight into the nature of the constraints under consideration which may lead indirectly to a solution for the implication problem.

In summary, the existence of a sound and complete axiomatization for a type of constraints depends on the conditions we impose on axiom system. We shall not discuss this problem in further detail and refer the interested reader to [20].

Let us now return to the implication problem. In order to get some insight into the problem, we briefly discuss a proof procedure for the implication of tuple and equality generating dependencies. Actually such procedure is obtained by generalizing the chase algorithm. It would be beyond the scope of this book to define this generalized chase procedure formally, although we encourage you to try so. Details can also be found in [22]. Instead, we show how this extended chase works for embedded jds.

Example 3.28 Let $RS = (\Omega, \Delta, dom, M, SC)$ be a relation scheme with

- $\Omega = \{A, B, C, D, E, F, G, H\}$;
- $SC = \{ABCD \bowtie DEFG, ABD \bowtie ACD, DEG \bowtie DFG\}$.

All the constraints in SC are clearly embedded mvds. Now let J be the embedded jd $ABD \bowtie ACD \bowtie DEG \bowtie DFG$. We now show how the chase Algorithm 3.4 can be generalized in order to examine whether $SC \models J$. The construction of the initial tableau $\tau(J)$ is quite similar to Definition 3.12:

rnr.	A	B	C	D	E	F	G	H
1	α_A	α_B	β^1_C	α_D	β^1_E	β^1_F	β^1_G	β^1_H
2	α_A	β^2_B	α_C	α_D	β^2_E	β^2_F	β^2_G	β^2_H
3	β^3_A	β^3_B	β^3_C	α_D	α_E	β^3_F	α_G	β^3_H
4	β^4_A	β^4_B	β^4_C	α_D	β^4_E	α_F	α_G	β^4_H

For convenience, we have numbered the rows as in Example 3.21. If J holds, then we would expect a row of which the projection onto $ABCDEFG$ consists of distinguished variables only. Indeed it can be shown that $SC \models J$ if and only if $chase_{SC}(\tau(J))$ contains such a row. Let us now do the actual chasing. Since $\ell_1[ABD \cap ACD] = \ell_2[ABD \cap ACD]$ we expect that a row ℓ_5 may be added satisfying $\ell_5[ABD] = \ell_1[ABD]$ and $\ell_5[ACD] = \ell_2[ACD]$. Unfortunately, this condition does not determine ℓ_5 entirely; we do not know anything about $\ell_5[EFGH]$. Therefore it seems a good solution to complete ℓ_5 with (new) undistinguished variables. Similarly, since $\ell_3[DEG \cap DFG] = \ell_4[DEG \cap DFG]$ we can add a row ℓ_6 with $\ell_6[DEG] = \ell_3[DEG]$ and $\ell_6[DFG] = \ell_4[DFG]$. After this addition, our tableau becomes:

rnr.	A	B	C	D	E	F	G	H
1	α_A	α_B	β^1_C	α_D	β^1_E	β^1_F	β^1_G	β^1_H
2	α_A	β^2_B	α_C	α_D	β^2_E	β^2_F	β^2_G	β^2_H
3	β^3_A	β^3_B	β^3_C	α_D	α_E	β^3_F	α_G	β^3_H
4	β^4_A	β^4_B	β^4_C	α_D	β^4_E	α_F	α_G	β^4_H
5	α_A	α_B	α_C	α_D	β^5_E	β^5_F	β^5_G	β^5_H
6	β^6_A	β^6_B	β^6_C	α_D	α_E	α_F	α_G	β^6_H

Since $\ell_5[ABCD \cap DEFG] = \ell_6[ABCD \cap DEFG]$ it follows that the row ℓ_7 with $\ell_7[ABCD] = \ell_5[ABCD]$ and $\ell_7[DEFG] = \ell_6[DEFG]$ (and $\ell_7[H] = \beta^7_H$) can also be added to the tableau. Since the projection of this row onto $ABCDEFG$ consists of distinguished variables only, it follows that $SC \models J$.

□

So Theorem 3.15 still holds in a slightly modified form: *Let* $PRS = (\Omega, \Delta, dom)$ *be a primitive relation scheme. Let* $SC \cup \{sc\}$ *be a set of tuple and equality generating dependencies over* PRS. $SC \models sc$ *if and only if* $chase_{SC}(sc)$ *contains a number of rows satisfying some conditions depending only upon* sc. However, the generalized chase is not an algorithm to decide implication. Indeed, during the execution of the chase new undistinguished variables can be added. Hence our argument in Theorem 3.15 to show that the chase terminates does no longer hold: $chase_{SC}(sc)$ can contain an infinite number of rows.

There is however a huge subclass of tuple and equality generating dependencies for which no undistinguished variables need to be added: all the equality generating dependencies (since they only modify rows, not add any) and all full tuple generating dependencies (since the rows that must be added are entirely determined). So for this subclass the termination argument in the proof of Theorem 3.15 still holds. Hence the generalized chase algorithm can decide implication for these dependencies:

Theorem 3.24 *The implication problem for full tuple generating dependencies and equality generating dependencies is decidable.*

□

Although the chase in the form we presented is no longer a decision procedure for embedded tuple generating dependencies, there nevertheless exist classes of embedded tuple generating dependencies for which the implication problem is decidable, e.g. for ids. Note however, as we saw in the previous section, that it suffices to enlarge this class with fds — that are very nice constraints — to make the implication problem undecidable. Note also that ids are untyped constraints. What happens if we restrict ourselves to embedded typed tuple generating dependencies? Even with this restriction, the implication problem remains undecidable. This leaves us with the following question: how far do we have to restrict this class to get decidability? Or, in other words, where is the border between decidability and undecidability?

In order to give a partial answer to this question, we have to introduce yet another type of constraint — the last one in this chapter.

Definition 3.19 Let $PRS = (\Omega, \Delta, dom)$ be a primitive relation scheme. Let $X_1, \ldots, X_k \subseteq \Omega$ and let $X \subseteq \bigcup_{i=1}^{k} X_i$. A *projected embedded join dependency* $X_1 \bowtie \cdots \bowtie X_k$ over PRS is a constraint which is satisfied by a possible relation instance prs if and only if for all $t_1, \ldots, t_k \in prs$ with $t_i[X_i \cap X_j] = t_j[X_i \cap X_j]$ for all $i, j = 1, \ldots, k$ there exists a tuple $t \in prs$ such that $t[X_i \cap X] = t_i[X_i \cap X]$ for all $i = 1, \ldots, k$.

□

We think that the counterpart to Theorem 3.23 is enlightening:

Theorem 3.25 *Let $RS = (\Omega, \Delta, dom, M, SC)$ be a relation scheme. Let $X_1, \ldots, X_k \subseteq \Omega$ and let $X \subseteq \bigcup_{i=1}^{k} X_i$. $SC \models X_1 \bowtie \cdots \bowtie X_k$ if and only if for each relation instance r of RS we have that $\Pi(r, X) = \Pi(\Pi(r; X_1) \bowtie \cdots \bowtie \Pi(r; X_k); X)$.*

□

Theorem 3.25 shows well that projected embedded jds are only a slight generalization of embedded jds. In [58] and [110] it is shown:

Theorem 3.26 *The implication problem for projected embedded join dependencies is undecidable.*

□

Since projected embedded jds are just a slight generalization of embedded jds one might expect the implication problem for embedded jds to be undecidable too. Until now however, nobody has been able to either prove or disprove this. Related to this is the question whether the implication problem for embedded mvds is decidable. Despite much negative evidence ([89, 97]) the answer is not known. The many research efforts in dependency theory and related areas that were motivated by this question, have made the implication problem for embedded mvds to one of the most outstanding open problems in relational database theory, worthy to close this chapter with.

3.7 Exercises

3.1 Show that $\{(K1), (K2)\}$ in Example 3.4 is a sound, complete and non-redundant set of axioms for the inference of key dependencies.

3.2 Write down all the functional dependencies occurring as a relation constraint in one of the relation schemes of the database scheme *HOTELDB* in Example 1.10.

3.3 Try to derive the fds in Example 3.7 from SC using only the definition of an fd.

3.4 Show, using only the definition of an fd, that the only trivial fds over a primitive relation scheme $PRS = (\Omega, \Delta, dom)$ are the fds $X \rightarrow Y$ with $Y \subseteq X$.

3.5 Show that axioms $(F5)$–$(F9)$ can be derived from axioms $(F1)$–$(F3)$ (cfr. Theorem 3.1).

3.6 Show that axioms $(F3)$–$(F9)$ are correct, by using only the definition of an fd.

3.7 Complete the proof of the non-redundancy of the axiom system $\mathcal{F}$ in Theorem 3.2.

3.8 Consider the following rules for the inference of fds:

$$\emptyset \vdash X \rightarrow X \text{ (identical fds)} \qquad (F1')$$
$$\{X \rightarrow YZ\} \vdash X \rightarrow Y \text{ (generalized fragmentation)} \qquad (F2')$$
$$\{X \rightarrow Y, Y \rightarrow Z\} \vdash X \rightarrow YZ \text{ (augmented transitivity)} \qquad (F3')$$

Show that $\{(F1'), (F2'), (F3')\}$ is also a non-redundant, sound and complete set of axioms for the implication of fds.

3.9 Is it possible to find a sound and complete set of axioms for the inference of fds that consists of only two rules? (Hint: try to combine rules $(F1')$ and $(F2')$ in the previous exercise into one axiom!)

3.10 Try to derive the fds in Example 3.7 from SC using the rules of axiom system $\mathcal{F}$ in Theorem 3.2.

3.11 Let $RS = (\Omega, \Delta, dom, M, SC)$ be a relation scheme with $\Omega = \{A, B, C, D, E, F, G\}$ and $SC = \{A \rightarrow BC, BD \rightarrow E, EC \rightarrow A, FG \rightarrow E\}$. Compute the fd-closures of all sets of up to three attributes.

3.12 Prove that Algorithm 3.2 is correct.

3.13 Implement Algorithm 3.2 on your computer system.

3.14 Write an algorithm that decides the implication problem for fds based on Algorithm 3.2 and show that its time complexity is also $O(np)$.

3.15 We say that a set of fds SC is a *reduced cover* for a set of fds SC if:

1. $SC \Leftrightarrow SC'$;
2. SC is non-redundant;
3. for each fd $X \rightarrow Y$ in SC' and for each $B \in Y$, $SC - \{X \rightarrow Y\} \cup \{X \rightarrow (Y - B)\}$ is not equivalent to SC;
4. for each fd $X \rightarrow Y$ in SC' and for each $B \in X$, $SC - \{X \rightarrow Y\} \cup \{(X - B) \rightarrow Y\}$ is not equivalent to SC.

Clearly, a canonical cover is reduced. Given a canonical cover for a set of fds, show now that the set of fds obtained from this canonical cover by applying the union rule as many times as possible is also a reduced cover.

3.16 Find another canonical cover for the set of fds in Example 3.10 by considering the fds in another order.

3.17 Try to derive the fds and mvds in Example 3.13 from SC using the definition of an mvd.

3.18 Do the following rules for the implication of fds and mvds by a set of fds and mvds hold? If so, proof it and if not, give a counterexample!

- $\{X \rightarrow\rightarrow Y, Y \rightarrow\rightarrow Z\} \models X \rightarrow\rightarrow Z$
- $\{X \rightarrow\rightarrow Y, Y \rightarrow Z\} \models X \rightarrow Z$

3.19 Try to derive the fds and mvds in Example 3.13 from SC using the rules of axiom system $\mathcal{M}$ in Theorem 3.10.

3.20 Complete the details in the proof of Lemma 3.1.

3.21 Prove the correctness of rule $M4$ in Lemma 3.1 using only the definition of multivalued dependency. Derive rules $M5$ and $M6$ from the axiom system $\mathcal{M}$ of Theorem 3.10, i. e. without using rule $M4$.

3.22 Show, by giving a counterexample, that in Example 3.14, $A \rightarrow\rightarrow C$ cannot be derived from SC.

3.23 Show Theorem 3.11.

3.24 Complete the proof of Theorem 3.13 by showing that the axiom system $\mathcal{M}$ is non-redundant.

3.25 Write down the details of the proof of Theorem 3.12.

3.26 Write an algorithm that decides the implication problem for fds and mvds based on Algorithm 3.3, implement it on your computer system and calculate its time complexity.

3.27 Compute the dependency basis of X in Example 3.14 using Algorithm 3.3.

3.28 In the proof of Theorem 3.15, we mentioned a few facts which we associated with the terms "readily seen", "easy" and "obvious". Nevertheless we would like you to be able to prove them formally!

3.29 Compute the entire tableau $chase_{SC}(\tau(J))$ in Example 3.21. Are there other ways to derive the row of all distinguished variables?

3.30 Show that $chase_{SC}(\tau(J))$ is independent of the order in which the dependencies were applied during the chase algorithm.

3.31 Consider a relation scheme $PRS = (\Omega, \Delta, dom, M, SC)$ with $\Omega = \{A, B, C, D, E, F\}$. Let $SC = \{AB \bowtie BC \bowtie CD \bowtie DE \bowtie EF \bowtie DF, ABCDE \bowtie EF\}$. Use the chase algorithm to decide whether $SC \models AB \bowtie BC \bowtie CD \bowtie DE \bowtie EF$.

3.32 Use Corollary 3.4 to establish a necessary and sufficient condition for an mvd $X \rightarrow\!\!\!\rightarrow Y$ to be implied by a jd $X_1 \bowtie \cdots \bowtie X_k$.

3.33 Compute the time complexity of Algorithm 3.4. Show that the chase algorithm is polynomial under the assumption that there exists a fixed (constant) upperbound for the number of components of the jds that are allowed.

3.34 A jd is called *reduced* if no component of that jd is contained in another one. The *reduction of a join dependency* is obtained by removing each component that is contained in another one. The reduction of a jd is obviously unique except perhaps for the order of the components. Use Corollary 3.4 to show that a jd and its reduction are always equivalent.

3.35 Use Theorem 3.15 to find a characterization for trivial jds (i.e. jds that are always valid).

3.36 Let us assume that $J: X_1 \cdots \bowtie \cdots X_k$ is a reduced jd (see Exercise 3.34). Let $\mathcal{E} \subset \{X_1, \ldots, X_k\}$ with $|\mathcal{E}| > 1$. $\mathcal{E}$ is called a *hinge* of J if for each connected component[8] $\mathcal{F}$ of $\{X_1, \ldots, X_k\} - \mathcal{E}$ there exists $X_i \in \mathcal{E}$ such that $(\cup\mathcal{F}) \cap (\cup\mathcal{E})$ is contained within X_i. A hinge is called minimal if it does not properly contain another hinge. We now mention the following result of [61]: *A jd is n-cyclic if and only if it contains no minimal hinge with more than n edges.* Show now that the jd J in Example 3.17 is 4-cyclic.

3.37 Use the Graham algorithm to show that the jd J' in Example 3.23 is acyclic.

3.38 Obviously, Algorithm 3.5 is not an optimal implementation of the Graham algorithm. E.g. the number of occurrences of an attribute is counted again during each cycle of the algorithm. Avoid this excessive counting by modifying Algorithm 3.5.

3.39 Let $PRS = (\Omega, \Delta, dom)$ be a primitive relation scheme. Let $X \neq \emptyset$ and Y be subsets of Ω. The *inclusion* $X \geq Y$ over PRS is a constraint that is satisfied by a possible relation instance prs if $\bigcup_{A \in Y} \Pi(prs; A) \subseteq \bigcup_{B \in X} \Pi(prs; B)$. Show, that, though these constraints are defined completely different, their implication problem is the same as for fds $X \rightarrow Y$ with $X \neq \emptyset$. *Hint:* show that they satisfy the same axiomatization. Also, explain why we need to impose the condition $X \neq \emptyset$.

[8]In the normal hypergraph-theoretical meaning of the word.

3.40 Let RS_1 and RS_2 be two relation schemes of a certain primitive database scheme. Now consider a possible database instance in which rs_1 and rs_2 correspond to RS_1 and RS_2 respectively. This possible database instance satisfies the *database inclusion dependency (did)* $RS_1[A_1, \ldots, A_k] \subseteq RS_2[B_1, \ldots, B_k]$ (where the A's and B's are attributes of the corresponding schemes) if and only if:

$$\forall t \in rs_1 \, \exists t' \in rs_2 \, \forall i = 1, \ldots, k : t(A_i) = t'(B_i)$$

So dids are database constraints. Write down all the database constraints in the hotel database of Example 1.10 which can be described — fully or partially — as dids. Also, modify the axiomatization in Theorem 3.19 into an axiomatization for dids. Use the result of Theorem 3.19 to show that this axiomatization is non-redundant, sound and complete.

3.41 Show the soundness of the following mixed rules for the inference of fds and ids: [80]

$$\begin{array}{ll} \{[A_1, \ldots A_l, A_{l+1}, \ldots, A_k] \subseteq [B_1, \ldots, B_l, B_{l+1}, \ldots, B_k], & \\ B_1 \ldots B_l \rightarrow B_{l+1} \ldots B_k\} \vdash A_1 \ldots A_l \rightarrow B_1 \ldots B_l & (FI1) \\ \{[A_1, \ldots A_l, A_{l+1}, \ldots, A_k] \subseteq [B_1, \ldots, B_l, B_{l+1}, \ldots, B_k], & \\ [A_1, \ldots A_l, A_{k+1}, \ldots, A_m] \subseteq [B_1, \ldots, B_l, B_{k+1}, \ldots, B_m], & \\ B_1 \ldots B_l \rightarrow B_{l+1} \ldots B_k\} \vdash [A_1, \ldots, A_m] \subseteq [B_1 \ldots B_m] & (FI2) \end{array}$$

3.42 Let $RS = (\Omega, \Delta, dom, M, SC)$ be a relation scheme. Let $A_1, \ldots, A_{k+1}, B_1, \ldots, B_{k+1} \in \Omega$ and assume that SC contains both $[A_1, \ldots, A_k] \subseteq [B_1, \ldots, B_k]$ and $B_1 \ldots B_k \rightarrow B_{k+1}$. Find conditions under which $[A_1, \ldots, A_{k+1}] \subseteq [B_1, \ldots, B_{k+1}]$ is implied by SC. [80]

3.43 From the viewpoint of integrity checking, it would be nice if we could "translate" a relation constraint in some relational query language, e. g. the algebra. Let $RS = (PRS, M, SC)$ be a relation scheme and let sc be a constraint over PRS. Let rs be a instance identifier of RS. We call an *algebraic translation* of sc in RS any algebraic instance expression having as only operand rs the value of which is rs itself whenever rs satisfies sc and the empty instance of RS otherwise. Find algebraic translations for the following constraints:

- the functional dependency $X \rightarrow Y$;
- the join dependency $X_1 \bowtie \cdots \bowtie X_k$;
- the inclusion dependency $[A_1, \ldots, A_k] \subseteq [B_1, \ldots, B_k]$.

3.44 Write down the proof of Theorem 3.22.

3.45 Give an example of an id which can be described as an untyped full tuple generating dependency.

3.46 Write down embedded typed tuple generating dependencies that are equivalent to embedded jds, embedded mvds and projected embedded jds respectively.

3.47 Define embedded mvds as a generalization of full mvds.

3.48 Try to generalize the chase of Algorithm 3.4 to tuple and equality generating dependencies.

3.49 In Example 3.28, SC and J are actually equivalent. Use the generalized chase to show that $J \models SC$.

3.50 Show that a projected embedded jd is a tuple generating dependency.

Chapter 4

Vertical Decompositions

In Example 3.11 and Theorem 3.7 we saw that the presence of fds can give rise to lossless decompositions of a given relation scheme. We summarize the main advantages of decomposing a relation scheme:

- smaller relations are easier to understand;
- independent information should not be stored in one relation;
- it is often possible to eliminate redundancy;
- in distributed databases different components can be located in different sites.

Of course several questions now arise. Which fds have to be used? How far do we have to decompose? Which properties of the original relation should be preserved by a decomposition? The answers to this questions resulted in an number of *normal forms* for relations that we shall discuss in this chapter.

4.1 First Normal Form

We shall first deal with the first normal form. A relation is said to be in *first normal form* if all the domain values that can occur in a relation instance are atomic. A value is called atomic if we do not consider the structure or parts of the value. We deliberately did not make a "Definition" of this concept, because of its rather fuzzy nature. Indeed, it can depend on the particular application whether or not certain data are considered as atomic. We illustrate this with an example.

Example 4.1 Consider again the relation scheme *ADDRESSES* and the instance *addresses* introduced in Example 3.11. There are now two possible attitudes towards this relation. The first is that we completely disregard the structure of a phone number, in other words that we consider a phone number as a whole in which no separate parts are distinguished or accessed. If we take this attitude, the relation scheme *FRIENDS* is in first normal form. The second attitude is that a phone number consists of several distinguishable parts, such as a country code, a city code and the actual number. If we would specify constraints such as *the country uniquely determines the country code* and *the city uniquely determines the* *city code* (as we did in Example 3.1 in less explicit terms) then we clearly choose for the second attitude and hence *FRIENDS* is *not* in first normal form. If we want to convert our relation into first normal form, we have to split up the attribute *PHONE-NUMBER* into three attributes, say *COUNTRY-CODE*, *CITY-CODE* and *LOCAL-NUMBER*. By this operation, *ADDRESSES* is converted into a new relation scheme that is in first normal form provided we agree not to look into the internal structure of the actual local number. The constraints specified above can now be expressed as the fds *COUNTRY-WHERE-LIVING* $\rightarrow$ *COUNTRY-CODE* and *CITY-WHERE-LIVING* $\rightarrow$ *CITY-CODE*.

□

As can be seen from Example 4.1, converting a relation scheme into first normal form can have as a consequence that some constraints become expressible as fds. Hence converting a relation into first normal form if necessary can give rise to further decompositions and to the removal of redundancies, i. e. to a higher degree of normalization, as we shall see in the following sections.

It would be a wrong conclusion however that non-first normal form relations should be avoided at any cost. On the contrary, allowing domains with structured values makes it possible to build relations that can represent better the structure of the data. Non-first normal form relations will be discussed in Chapter 7. In the remainder of this chapter though, we assume that all the relation schemes under consideration are in first normal form.

4.2 Second and Third Normal Form

The major part of this section will be devoted to *third normal form*, since *second normal form* was only historically an intermediate step towards third normal form and is not used any more in database design. For sake of completeness, we shall briefly discuss second normal form as well. In order to define these normal forms, we first need some additional terminology.

Definition 4.1 Let $RS = (\Omega, \Delta, dom, M, SC)$ be a relation scheme. We define:

- A set of attributes $X \subseteq \Omega$ is called a *superkey* for RS if $SC \models X \rightarrow \Omega$.
- A set of attributes of Ω is called a *key* for RS if it is a superkey for RS and no superkey for RS is properly contained in it.
- An attribute $A \in \Omega$ is called a *prime attribute* of RS if it belongs to some key for RS. A *non-prime attribute* of RS does not belong to any key for RS.

□

Example 4.2 Consider again the relation scheme

$$VISITORS = (\Omega_V, \Delta_V, dom_V, M_V, SC_V)$$

of Example 1.10 where

- Ω_V = { *VIS-NUMBER, VIS-NAME, VIS-STREET, VIS-CITY, VIS-COUNTRY*};
- SC_V = {*VIS-NUMBER*→ *VIS-NAME, VIS-STREET, VIS-CITY, VIS-COUNTRY*; *VIS-CITY*→ *VIS-COUNTRY*}.

(See also Example 3.5.) Obviously, *VIS-NUMBER* is a key for *VISITORS*. Hence any set of attributes containing this key is a superkey of *VISITORS*. By definition, *VIS-NUMBER* is a prime attribute. Since *VIS-NUMBER* is clearly the only key for *VISITORS*, all the other attributes are non-prime.

□

As we saw earlier, the presence of an fd can give rise to redundant information, which can be eliminated by performing a decomposition. This observation has led to the definition of several normal forms for relational databases. We are now ready to define the third (and second) normal form.

Definition 4.2 Let $RS = (\Omega, \Delta, dom, M, SC)$ be a relation scheme. We define:

- RS is in *third normal form* if whenever $Y \to A$ is in SC^* then either $A \in Y$ or A is prime or Y is a superkey. A database scheme is in third normal form if all its relation schemes are in third normal form.
- RS is in *second normal form* if whenever $Y \to A$ is in SC^* where Y is properly contained in some key for RS then either $A \in Y$ or A is prime. A database scheme is in second normal form if all its relation schemes are in second normal form.

□

Let us first rephrase Definition 4.2 in a more conventional way. Third normal form implies that the constraints $X \to Y$, where X is a key and Y is not a superkey, and $Y \to A$, where A is a non-prime attribute not in XY, cannot occur simultaneously. This phrase is usually summarized by saying that a *transitive dependency* $X \to Y \to A$ may not occur. So we may conclude that *a relation is in third normal form if there are no transitive dependencies*. Now, second normal form says that there are no such transitive dependencies in which Y is properly contained in X. These special transitive dependencies are called *partial dependencies*. So *a relation is in second normal form if there are no partial dependencies*. Hence any relation in third normal form is also in second normal form. The opposite inclusion however does not hold as can be easily verified by constructing a counterexample.

Example 4.3 Consider again the relation scheme of Example 4.2. In this relation we have (among others) the transitive dependency:

$$VIS\text{-}NUMBER \rightarrow VIS\text{-}CITY \rightarrow VIS\text{-}COUNTRY.$$

Hence *VISITORS* is not in third normal form.

□

What could be the motivation behind third normal form, or, in other words, what is wrong in having a relation that is not in third normal form? If a relation scheme is not in third normal form, we know that there exists a transitive dependency $X \rightarrow Y \rightarrow A$. Reconsider e. g. Example 4.3 and the transitive dependency given there. If an instance of *VISITORS* would e. g. contain 100 visitors living in the same city, then the information to which country this city belongs is also repeated 100 times. This *redundancy* can cause *update anomalies.* In the unlikely but nevertheless not impossible event of a border correction, it might be necessary to change the country in 100 tuples. Forgetting to change even one tuple would cause an inconsistency!

Another problem with this transitive dependency is that it is impossible to store the city in which a visitor lives, if it is not known to which country this city belongs. This problem would not occur if these three attributes would not all occur in the same relation. So transitive dependencies can also cause *insertion* and *deletion anomalies.*

Now, what can we do if we are given a database scheme which is not in third normal form (i. e. in which some relation schemes are not in third normal form)? Theorem 3.7 suggests a way to get rid of transitive dependencies by decomposing the relation schemes in which these transitive dependencies occur. The process of transforming a relation or database scheme into a database scheme in a (e. g. third) normal form is called *normalization.*

For sake of simplicity we shall assume that we start with one relation scheme (otherwise, just apply the operations described and discussed below to each of the relation schemes in the database). The most important property the database scheme generated during the normalization process must satisfy, is its being a *(lossless join) decomposition* of the original relation scheme. We first formalize this notion:

Definition 4.3 Let $RS = (\Omega, \Delta, dom, M, SC)$ be a relation scheme. A database scheme $DS = (PDS, DM, SDC)$ with $PDS = \{RS_i = (\Omega_i, \Delta_i, dom_i, M_i, SC_i) \mid i \in I\}$ is called a *(lossless join) decomposition* if:

- $\forall i \in I: \Omega_i \subseteq \Omega$;
- $\bigcup_{i \in I} \Omega_i = \Omega$;
- DM expresses dat DS is a representation of the relation RS with meaning M (we shall not be concerned with DM in the sequel);

- $SDC = \emptyset$;
- for each instance r of RS we have that $\bowtie_{i \in I} \Pi(r; \Omega_i) = r$.

□

In Definition 4.3, nothing is specified about the sets of constraints SC_i. As a first attempt, one might wish SC_i to consist of the constraint of $\Pi(RS; \Omega_i)$, as defined in Chapter 2. In general however, this constraint is not recursive. Now, in the remainder of this section we shall assume that only fds are involved. Unfortunately, it has been shown in [54] that in this case it is in general impossible to express the projection constraint as a set of fds. Therefore we define a projection of a set of fds as follows:

Definition 4.4 Let $RS = (\Omega, \Delta, dom, M, SC)$ be a relation scheme where SC is a set of fds. Let $\Omega_i \subseteq \Omega$. A *projection of the set of fds* SC onto Ω_i is a set of fds SC_i that is logically equivalent to $\{X \rightarrow Y \mid X \rightarrow Y \in SC^* \ \& \ XY \subseteq \Omega_i\}$. □

In practical situations, each SC_i in Definition 4.3 will be a projection of the original set of fds SC onto Ω_i. We illustrate Definition 4.4 with an example:

Example 4.4 Consider again the relation scheme $RS = (\Omega, \Delta, dom, M, SC)$ from Example 3.7 in Chapter 3, with

- $\Omega = \{A, B, C, D\}$;
- $SC = \{A \rightarrow B, B \rightarrow C, AC \rightarrow D\}$.

One can easily check that a projection of SC onto ABD is $\{A \rightarrow B, A \rightarrow D\}$. □

Since the size of SC^* can be exponential in the size of SC, it unfortunately will take exponential time in the worst case to compute the projection of a set of fds. We shall come back to this point later on and will not worry about it for the time being. We are now ready to present an algorithm for normalization in third normal form.

Algorithm 4.1 *Decomposition into third normal form*

Input: A relation scheme $RS = (\Omega, \Delta, dom, M, SC)$ in which SC is a set of fds.

Output: A decomposition $DS = (PDS, DM, \emptyset)$ of RS which is in third normal form.

Method:

1. Initialize DS as $(\{RS\}, DM, \emptyset)$ where DM is as in Definition 4.3;
2. Look for a relation scheme $RS_i(\Omega_i, \Delta_i, dom_i, M_i, SC_i)$ in PDS and a transitive dependency $X \rightarrow Y \rightarrow A$ in RS_i. If such a relation scheme and such fds do not exist, then *return*(DS) and stop;

3. Replace RS_i by $\Pi(RS_i; YA)$ and $\Pi(RS_i; \Omega - A)$ in which the sets of constraints are replaced by a projection of SC_i onto YA and $\Omega - A$ respectively. Return to step 2.

□

Theorem 4.1 *Algorithm 4.1 is correct.*

Proof Left to the reader.

□

In general, the above algorithm will take exponential time, because of the remark made earlier about the size of SC^*. There is also another fundamental problem in connection with decomposing into third normal form [73]:

Theorem 4.2 *Let $RS = (\Omega, \Delta, dom, M, SC)$ be a relation scheme in which SC is a set of fds. Let $A \in \Omega$. It is NP-complete to decide whether A is a prime or a non-prime attribute.*

□

As promised we will come back to the problem of finding an efficient algorithm for normalization in third normal form later on. We now conclude this section with an example illustrating Algorithm 4.1.

Example 4.5 Consider again Example 4.4. Clearly, A is the only key and hence C a non-prime attribute. As a consequence, $A \rightarrow B \rightarrow C$ is a transitive dependency. Hence we decompose RS into $RS_1 = (BC, \Delta_1, dom_1, M_1, SC_1)$ with $SC_1 = \{B \rightarrow C\}$ and $RS_2 = (ABD, \Delta_2, dom_2, M_2, SC_2)$ with $SC_2 = \{A \rightarrow B, A \rightarrow D\}$. Since both schemes are in third normal form, the algorithm stops.

□

4.3 Boyce-Codd Normal Form

We recall that in defining third normal form, our purpose was to eliminate redundancy and update anomalies that could be caused by the presence of fds. This removing of redundancy was realized by further decomposing the database according to some fds in the sense of Theorem 3.7. We now want to answer the following question: which fds, in general, can be used to decompose a relation in a meaningful way? First of all, we ask the reader to convince himself that it suffices to consider fds of the form $Y \rightarrow A$ where A is a single attribute. Of these fds $Y \rightarrow A$, we of course do not consider those for which $A \in Y$ (since they are trivial). Furthermore, it also makes no sense to use an fd for which Y is a superkey. Indeed, since in that case, all the attributes of the relation are functionally determined by Y, decomposition would not remove any redundancy! These considerations give rise to the following definition:

Definition 4.5 Let $RS = (\Omega, \Delta, dom, M, SC)$ be a relation scheme. RS is in *Boyce-Codd normal form* if whenever $Y \rightarrow A$ is in SC^*, then either $A \in Y$ or Y is a superkey for RS. A database scheme is in Boyce-Codd normal form if all its relation schemes are in Boyce-Codd normal form.

□

So, Boyce-Codd normal form (BCNF) is the nec plus ultra we may expect. From Definition 4.2 and Definition 4.5 it immediately follows:

Theorem 4.3 *Each database scheme or relation scheme in BCNF is also in third normal form.*

□

Example 4.6 Reconsider the relation scheme *VISITORS* we last discussed in Example 4.2. We saw in Example 4.3 that *VISITORS* is *not* in third normal form. As a consequence, it is not in Boyce-Codd normal form either.

□

We leave it as an exercise to the reader to show that the opposite implication does not hold.

It can be seen in a straightforward manner that Algorithm 4.1 can be easily adapted to yield decompositions in BCNF:

Algorithm 4.2 *Decomposition into Boyce-Codd normal form*

Input: A relation scheme $RS = (\Omega, \Delta, dom, M, SC)$ in which SC is a set of fds.

Output: A decomposition $DS = (PDS, DM, \emptyset)$ of RS which is in Boyce-Codd normal form.

Method:

1. Initialize DS as $(\{RS\}, DM, \emptyset)$ where DM is as in Definition 4.3;
2. Look for a relation scheme $RS_i(\Omega_i, \Delta_i, dom_i, M_i, SC_i)$ in PDS and a non-trivial fd $Y \rightarrow A$ in SC_i^* in which Y is not a superkey for RS_i. If such relation scheme and such fd do not exist, then *return*(DS);
3. Replace RS_i by $\Pi(RS_i; YA)$ and $\Pi(RS_i; \Omega - A)$ in which the sets of constraints are replaced by the projections of SC onto YA and $\Omega - A$ respectively. Go back to step 2.

□

Theorem 4.4 *Algorithm 4.2 is correct.*

□

Example 4.7 Consider a relation scheme $RS = (\Omega, \Delta, dom, M, SC)$ where

- $\Omega = \{A, B, C, D\}$;
- $SC = \{A \rightarrow B, B \rightarrow C, CD \rightarrow A, AC \rightarrow D\}$.

This relation scheme is not in BCNF since in $B \rightarrow C$, B is not a superkey. Hence we decompose RS into $RS_1 = (BC, \Delta_1, dom_1, M_1, SC_1)$ with $SC_1 = \{B \rightarrow C\}$ and $RS_2 = (ABD, \Delta_2, dom_2, M_2, SC_2)$ with $SC_2 = \{A \rightarrow B, A \rightarrow D, BD \rightarrow A\}$. Since both schemes are in BCNF, the algorithm terminates.

□

As was the case for the normalization algorithm in third normal form, Algorithm 4.2 usually takes exponential time to compute a BCNF decomposition of a relation scheme.

At this point, one might wonder why we discussed third normal form at all, since BCNF obviously is a more desirable goal for normalization. Unfortunately, we have [73, 16]:

Theorem 4.5 *Let* $RS = (\Omega, \Delta, dom, M, SC)$ *be a relation scheme in which* SC *is a set of fds. It is NP-complete to decide whether or not* RS *is in BCNF.*

□

A third normal form decomposition can be found in polynomial time, as we shall see in the next section. There is however a more fundamental objection that can be made against BCNF, which will be discussed in the following section.

4.4 Constraint Preserving Normalization

In striving towards a normal form, we of course want the normalized result to convey the same information as the original one. That is why we want our decompositions to be lossless. Indeed, lossless decompositions allow us to reconstruct the instance of the original scheme from the instance of the normalized scheme. A database however does not only consist of raw data, but also of constraints and we might as well like not to loose information about the constraints during normalization, because weaker constraints automatically imply less rigorous integrity checking. Therefore we define:

Definition 4.6 Let $RS = (\Omega, \Delta, dom, M, SC)$ be a relation scheme. A database scheme $DS = (PDS, DM, SDC)$ with $PDS = \{RS_i(\Omega_i, \Delta_i, dom_i, M_i, SC_i) \mid i \in I\}$ is called a *constraint preserving representation* of RS if:

- $\forall i \in I: \Omega_i \subseteq \Omega$;
- $\bigcup_{i \in I} \Omega_i = \Omega$;
- $SDC = \emptyset$;
- $SC^* = (\bigcup_{i \in I} SC_i)^*$

If, in addition, DS is a (lossless join) decomposition of RS, DS is called a *constraint preserving decomposition* of RS.

□

Let us now recall to some earlier examples of decompositions obtained by normalization and check if they are constraint preserving.

Example 4.8 Reconsider Example 4.3. It is readily seen that the third normal form decomposition we obtained is constraint preserving. There are however cases in which Algorithm 4.1 does *not* yield a constraint preserving decomposition.

Now, reconsider Example 4.7. The BCNF decomposition we found is *not* constraint preserving, since it is impossible to obtain $CD \to A$ from SC_1 and SC_2.

□

Unfortunately there are relation schemes that do not have a constraint preserving decomposition into BCNF (see Exercise 4.8). So, if we want to achieve BCNF, which is a very desirable goal as explained in the previous section, we might have to sacrifice a few dependencies. There is however an alternative if you do not want to make that sacrifice. It is possible to obtain a constraint preserving decomposition of an arbitrary relation scheme in third normal form! This observation also answers a question raised earlier why we discussed third normal form at all; third normal form can provide a reasonable compromise if we are put before a choice between BCNF and preservation of dependencies.

As noted earlier, Algorithm 4.1 does not always produce constraint preserving decompositions. Below, we present an algorithm that always generates constraint preserving decompositions in third normal form. This algorithm is often called a *synthesis algorithm* because of its different approach. Nevertheless, it also generates a decomposition!

Algorithm 4.3 *Constraint preserving decomposition into third normal form*

Input: A relation scheme $RS = (\Omega, \Delta, dom, M, SC)$ in which SC is a set of fds.

Output: A constraint preserving decomposition $DS = (PDS, DM, \emptyset)$ of RS which is in third normal form.

Method:

1. Compute a canonical cover $SC' = \{Y_i \to A_i \mid 1 \leq i \leq m\}$ for SC (Definition 3.7);
2. Look for an arbitrary key X for RS;
3. Let RS_0 be the projection of RS onto X in which the set of constraints is replaced by a projection of SC' onto X;
4. Construct $DS = (PDS, DM, \emptyset)$ with:
   - $PDS = \{RS_0\} \cup \{RS_i \mid 1 \leq i \leq m\}$ where for all $i = 1, \ldots, m$, RS_i is the projection of RS onto Y_iA_i, in which the set of constraints is replaced by a projection of SC' onto Y_iA_i;
   - DM is as in Definition 4.3;
5. If there exists $0 \leq i \leq m$ and $0 \leq j \leq m$ with $i \neq j$ such that the scheme of RS_i is contained in the scheme of RS_j, then delete RS_i from PDS. Repeat this step until no more deletions are possible.
6. *return*(DS).

□

Before we investigate the correctness of this algorithm, let us first try it out on an example.

Example 4.9 Consider again the relation scheme RS in Example 4.7. A canonical cover for SC is $SC' = \{A \rightarrow B, B \rightarrow C, CD \rightarrow A, A \rightarrow D\}$. A is a key for RS. Hence Algorithm 4.3 generates a decomposition consisting of

$$RS_0(A, \Delta_0, dom_0, M_0, \emptyset)$$
$$RS_1(AB, \Delta_1, dom_1, M_1, \{A\rightarrow B\})$$
$$RS_2(BC, \Delta_2, dom_2, M_2, \{B\rightarrow C\})$$
$$RS_3(ACD, \Delta_3, dom_3, M_3, \{CD\rightarrow A, A\rightarrow C, A\rightarrow D\})$$
$$RS_4(AD, \Delta_4, dom_4, M_4, \{A\rightarrow D\})$$

Clearly, RS_0 and RS_4 can be eliminated. So our final database scheme consists of RS_1, RS_2 and RS_3. It is easily checked that this represents a constraint preserving decomposition of RS in third normal form. □

At this time, you probably wonder why we included RS_0 in the decomposition generated by Algorithm 4.3. The reason for this is that the minimal cover SC' (as well as SC itself) need not involve all the attributes of Ω. Clearly, each attribute of RS must appear in some scheme of a lossless decomposition of RS. An attribute not appearing in any fd of the given set of constraints (SC or SC', it does not matter) however is contained in every key of RS. Hence including the projection of RS onto an arbitrary key ensures that each attribute occurs in the proposed decomposition. We are now ready to show that Algorithm 4.3 is correct.

Theorem 4.6 *Each relation scheme has a constraint preserving decomposition into third normal form. Such a decomposition can be obtained with Algorithm 4.3.*

Proof Let $RS = (\Omega, \Delta, dom, M, SC)$ be the given relation scheme in which SC is a set of fds and let $SC' = \{Y_i \rightarrow A_i \mid 1 \leq i \leq m\}$ be a canonical cover for SC. Let X be a key for RS. We shall show here that the database scheme generated by steps 1–4 of Algorithm 4.3 satisfies the required properties. It can be easily seen that these properties are not violated in the last step of the algorithm (see Exercise 4.11).

Let $DS = (PDS, DM, \emptyset)$ with $PDS = \{RS_0, RS_1, \ldots, RS_m)$ be the aforementioned database scheme. So, in $RS_i = (\Omega_i, \Delta_i, dom_i, M_i, SC_i)$, SC_i is the projection of SC onto Ω_i where $\Omega_0 = X$ and for $i = 1, \ldots, m$, $\Omega_i = Y_i A_i$. First, it is obvious by construction that DS is a constraint preserving representation of RS since for all $i = 1, \ldots, m:\ Y_i \rightarrow A_i \in SC_i$.

We now show that each of the RS_i, $0 \leq i \leq m$ is in third normal form. First, consider RS_0. Suppose there exists an fd $V \rightarrow W$ in SC^* with $VW \subseteq X$ and $W \not\subseteq V$. This would imply that $X - (W - V)$ is a superkey of RS, contradicting the assumptions. Hence SC_0 only contains trivial fds, whence RS_0 is in third normal form. Let us now consider the RS_i, $i \neq 0$. First note that Y_i is a key for RS_i. (Indeed, Y_i is obviously a superkey for RS_i. If it were not a key, a proper subset Z of Y_i would be a key, whence $Z \rightarrow A \in SC^*$, contradicting SC' being left reduced.) Suppose there is an fd $Y \rightarrow A$ in SC^* with $YA \subseteq \Omega_i$, and $A \notin Y$. We have to distinguish two cases:

- *Case 1:* $A = A_i$*:* Then $Y \subseteq Y_i$. Since SC' is left reduced, $Y \subset Y_i$ cannot occur. Hence $Y = Y_i$, so Y is a superkey.
- *Case 2:* $A \neq A_i$*:* Then $A \in Y_i$. Hence, A is prime.

So each of the schemes in DS is in third normal form.

It just remains to show that DS is a lossless decomposition of RS. Therefore, let $\Omega - X = A_{i_1} \ldots A_{i_l}$ where the indices $1, \ldots, l$ are determined by the order in which the attributes are added to X in the computation of $\overline{X}$ w.r.t. SC' by Algorithm 3.1. First, we show by reverse induction on j that for all $j = 1, \ldots, l+1$, RS has a lossless decomposition $DS_j = (PDS_j, DM_j, \emptyset)$ with $PDS_j = \{RS_{i_t} \mid j \leq t \leq l\} \cup \{RS^j\}$ where RS^j is the projection of RS onto $\Omega - \{A_{i_t} \mid j \leq t \leq l\}$ (in which the set of constraints is replaced by a projection of SC'). For $j = l+1$, this condition is trivially satisfied. Suppose we showed the above assertion for $j = l+1, l, \ldots$ down to $k+1$. Hence RS has a lossless join decomposition $DS_{k+1} = (PDS_{k+1}, DM_{k+1}, \emptyset)$ with $PDS_{k+1} = \{RS_{i_t} \mid k+1 \leq t \leq l\} \cup \{RS^{k+1}\}$ where RS^{k+1} is the projection of RS onto $\Omega - \{A_{i_t} \mid k+1 \leq t \leq l\}$. Since in the computation of $\overline{X}$ w.r.t. SC', $A_{i_{k+1}}, \ldots, A_{i_l}$ were added after A_{i_k} was added, it follows that necessarily $Y_{i_k} \subseteq \Omega - \{A_{i_t} \mid k+1 \leq t \leq l\}$. We now have to distinguish two cases:

- *Case 1:* $Y_{i_k}A_{i_k} = \Omega - \{A_{i_t} \mid k+1 \leq t \leq l\}$. In this case, $RS^{k+1} = RS_{i_k}$ and all the relation schemes of DS_{k+1} are contained in DS_k. Since all the schemes in DS_k are projections of RS and since DS_{k+1} is a lossless join decomposition of RS, it follows that DS_k is a lossless join decomposition of RS.
- *Case 2:* $Y_{i_k}A_{i_k} \subset \Omega - \{A_{i_t} \mid k+1 \leq t \leq l\}$. Then, by Theorem 3.7 in Chapter 3, we have that RS^{k+1} can be decomposed into a database scheme consisting of RS_k and RS^k, whence DS_k is a lossless decomposition of RS.

So, our assertion holds. Since $PDS_1 \subseteq PDS$, since PDS consists only of projections of RS and since DS_1 is a lossless join decomposition of RS, it follows that DS is a lossless join decomposition of RS.

□

As an immediate corollary, we get (if we extend the definition of constraint preserving decomposition in the obvious way to databases):

Corollary 4.1 *Each database scheme has a constraint preserving decomposition into third normal form. Such a decomposition can be obtained by applying Algorithm 4.3 on each of its relation schemes.*

□

The proof of Theorem 4.6 suggests some comments. First, we saw that the RS_0 has an empty set of constraints. Second, it follows from the last part of the proof that in general not all the relation schemes of DS are needed in order to have a lossless join decomposition. Nevertheless, the relation schemes in DS not needed for a lossless join decomposition, might be indispensable from the point of view of constraint preservation.

Although the last step of Algorithm 4.3 removes some redundancy, it is at the other hand not guaranteed that no more relation schemes are redundant, as is shown by the following counterexample:

Example 4.10 Consider a relation scheme $RS = (\Omega, \Delta, dom, M, SC)$ where

- $\Omega = \{A, B, C, D, E\}$;
- $SC = \{AD \rightarrow B, AB \rightarrow C, C \rightarrow E, BE \rightarrow C\}$.

Clearly SC is a canonical cover of itself. By using steps 1–4 of Algorithm 4.3, it follows that RS can be decomposed in a constraint preserving third normal form decomposition, consisting of the projections of RS onto ADB, ABC, CD and BDC, in which the sets of constraints are replaced by the corresponding projections of SC. The last step of the algorithm eliminates the third scheme, leaving the projections of RS onto ADB, ABC, BDC. Note that the first and the last scheme are sufficient for a lossless join decomposition. (Indeed, the presence of $BD \rightarrow C$ in SC guarantees by Theorem 3.7 that RS can be decomposed into its projections on BDC and ABD.) Note that, by transitivity, $AB \rightarrow D \in SC^*$. Hence $AB \rightarrow D$ is in the projection of SC onto ADB. $AB \rightarrow D$ and $BD \rightarrow C$ which is of course in the projection of SC onto BDC imply $AB \rightarrow C$. Hence $AB \rightarrow C$ is also redundant for constraint preservation. Hence the projections of RS onto ADB, BDC yield a constraint preserving decomposition of RS in third normal form with fewer schemes than the one generated by Algorithm 4.3. □

We want to conclude this section with a remark about the time complexity of Algorithm 4.3. The only hard things to compute in this algorithm are the projections of SC onto the sets of attributes of the various subschemes. We know already that these projections are weaker than the actual projection constraint defined in Chapter 2. We could weaken it further by putting $SC_i = \{Y_i \rightarrow A_i\}$ for all $i = 1, \ldots, m$ (and, as noticed earlier, $SC_0 = \emptyset$). By doing this, Algorithm 4.3 not only becomes polynomial, but generates a constraint preserving decomposition in which no scheme can be removed. However we are not sure that this advantage outweights the disadvantage of losing integrity checking power in each of the subschemes separately.

4.5 Fourth and Fifth Normal Form

Until now, we (at least in practice) only considered fds in this chapter. We might want to define a normal form in the case where SC consists of both mvds and fds:

Definition 4.7 A relation scheme $RS = (\Omega, \Delta, dom, M, SC)$ is in *fourth normal form* if for each non-trivial mvd $X \rightarrow\!\!\!\rightarrow Y$ with $SC \models X \rightarrow\!\!\!\rightarrow Y$, X is a superkey for RS. A database scheme is in fourth normal form if each of its relations schemes is in fourth normal form.

□

Now let $X \rightarrow A$ be a non-trivial fd implied by SC. Then the mvd $X \rightarrow\!\!\!\rightarrow A$ is also implied by SC, and hence X must be a superkey for RS to be in fourth normal form. So we immediately derive:

Theorem 4.7 *A database scheme or a relation scheme in fourth normal form is also in BCNF.*

□

In the case where only fds are involved, the opposite inclusion also holds. Decomposing into fourth normal form goes in about the same way as decomposing in BCNF. We leave it to the reader to construct an example for decomposing in fourth normal form. Whenever there is an mvd $X \rightarrow\!\!\!\rightarrow Y$ implied by SC that violates the condition for fourth normal form, we decompose the relation scheme into its projections of XY and $X(\Omega - Y)$ (compare with Theorem 3.9). Hence decomposing into fourth normal form means we have to deal with all the problems of decomposing into BCNF: a time-expensive algorithm and in general no preservation of constraints.

The last normal form we choose to discuss here deals with the case in which the constraints are jds and fds (note that mvds can be considered as special jds, by Corollary 3.3). We define [40]:

Definition 4.8 A relation scheme $RS = (\Omega, \Delta, dom, M, SC)$ is in *fifth normal form* or *project-join normal form* if each jd implied by SC is already implied by $\{X \rightarrow \Omega \mid SC \models X \rightarrow \Omega\}$, i. e. by the key dependencies that are a consequence of SC. A database scheme is in fifth normal form if each of its relation schemes is in fifth normal form.

□

The jds that are allowed by fifth normal form are jds that would give no rise to elimination of redundancy if they were used to decompose the relation. Furthermore, the conditions for fifth normal form are chosen in such a way that:

Theorem 4.8 *A database scheme or relation scheme in fifth normal form is also in fourth normal form.*

Proof Left as an exercise to the reader.

□

4.6 Vertical Decomposition and Consistency Checking

In Chapter 3, we discussed constraints mainly from the viewpoint of *integrity checking*. We saw constraints in the first place as a tool to ensure that contents of a database or a relation still corresponds to a representation of a part of the real world, according to the meaning of that database or relation. However we also saw that constraints, such as fds, can give rise to decomposition as well, and we discussed some strategies for this in the previous sections of the present chapter. Whereas fds are constraints that give also information on the contents of a database, jds in most cases only tell you something about the structure of your database. Even more, whenever a certain decomposition of a relation is the most suitable way to represent that relation, you can express this fact by adding the corresponding jd to the constraints of that relation.

In this section, we therefore assume that we have to deal with a relation scheme $RS = (\Omega, \Delta, dom, M, SC)$ where SC contains a jd $X_1 \bowtie \cdots \bowtie X_k$ that expresses the "structure" of the relation, as explained in the previous paragraph.

Since jds rarely tell you anything about the data represented in the relation, it makes little sense to use jds for integrity checking purposes. Since jds precisely express the most favorable way to represent your relation, the best thing one can do is decomposing the relation according to that jd. By doing so, we are freed at the same time from the burden of integrity checking, which can be quite painful. Indeed, since the size of the join of a number of relations can be exponential in the size of these relations (the exponent being the number of joins that has to be performed), integrity checking for fds in general takes exponential time.

Unfortunately, we have to pay a price for being freed of integrity checking, which is as high as that of integrity checking itself. Indeed, the database resulting from the decomposition of the given relation consists of various projections of that relation. Of course, we have to make sure that this condition remains satisfied. Updates of the database have to be simulatable by updates of the original relation. In other words, after some update of our database, there still has to exist an instance of the original relation scheme the projections of which are the updated relation instances in our database. This problem is called *consistency checking*. We formally define:

Definition 4.9 Let $DS = (PDS, DM, SDC)$ be a database with $PDS = \{RS_1, \ldots, RS_k\}$ and let $RS = (\Omega, \Delta, dom, M, SC)$ be $RS_1 \bowtie \cdots \bowtie RS_k$. Hence RS_i is the projection of RS onto some $X_i \subseteq \Omega$ for all $i = 1, \ldots, k$. Let $(rs_1, \ldots, rs_k)$ be an instance of DS. $(rs_1, \ldots, rs_k)$ is *consistent* iff there exists some instance rs of RS such that for all $i = 1, \ldots, k$, $\Pi(rs; X_i) = rs_i$.

□

It can be easily seen that Definition 4.9 can be rephrased as follows:

Theorem 4.9 *Let $DS = (PDS, DM, SDC)$ be a database with $PDS = \{RS_1, \ldots, RS_k\}$. Let X_i be the set of attributes of RS_i for $i = 1, \ldots, k$. Let $(rs_1, \ldots, rs_k)$ be an instance of DS. $(rs_1, \ldots, rs_k)$ is consistent iff for all $i = 1, \ldots, k$, $\Pi(rs_1 \bowtie \cdots \bowtie rs_k; X_i) = rs_i$.*

Proof Left as an exercise to the reader.

□

Since Theorem 4.9 involves taking joins, we may suspect that consistency checking, as integrity checking, in general takes exponential time. This is indeed the case. Therefore, we might want to set an upperbound on the number of components of the jds which to consider. This idea strongly reminds us of *m-cyclic jds* which were introduced in Section 3.4. A natural question to ask now is whether consistency checking can be done in polynomial time, provided one is restricted to m-cyclic jds, for a fixed value of m. In order to answer this question, we need to extend our notion of consistency:

Definition 4.10 Let $DS = (PDS, DM, SDC)$ be a database with $PDS = \{RS_1, \ldots, RS_k\}$. Let X_i be the set of attributes of RS_i for $i = 1, \ldots, k$. Let $(rs_1, \ldots, rs_k)$ be an instance of DS. $(rs_1, \ldots, rs_k)$ is *m-wise consistent* iff for each subsequence $j_1, \ldots, j_m$ of length m of $1, \ldots, k$ and for all $i = j_1, \ldots, j_m$, $\Pi(rs_{j_1} \bowtie \cdots \bowtie rs_{j_m}; X_i) = rs_i$.

□

In other words, a database instance consisting of k relations is m-wise consistent if each database obtained by choosing m relation instances out of these k is consistent. To make the distinction more clearly, we shall often use the phrase *global consistency* for consistency. It turns out that the following result holds (proof omitted, see [61]):

Theorem 4.10 *Let $DS = (PDS, DM, SDC)$ be a database with $PDS = \{RS_1, \ldots, RS_k\}$. Let X_i be the set of attributes of RS_i for $i = 1, \ldots, k$. Each m-wise consistent instance of DS is globally consistent if and only if the jd $X_1 \bowtie \cdots \bowtie X_k$ is m-cyclic.*

□

Since it is possible to perform a number of joins bounded by a constant in polynomial time we can derive in the same way as we derived Theorem 3.17 [61]:

Theorem 4.11 *Let m be a fixed constant. Let $DS = (PDS, DM, SDC)$ be a database with $PDS = \{RS_1, \ldots, RS_k\}$. Let X_i be the set of attributes of RS_i for $i = 1, \ldots, k$ and suppose that $X_1 \bowtie \cdots \bowtie X_k$ is an m-cyclic jd. Then each instance of DS can be checked for consistency in polynomial time.*

□

We shall not deal with the general case in the remainder of this section, but limit our attention to the case $m = 2$, i. e. to 2-cyclicity or *acyclicity* (see Definition 3.14). As an immediate corollary to Theorems 4.9 and 4.11, we can state:

Corollary 4.2 *Let $DS = (PDS, DM, SDC)$ be a database with $PDS = \{RS_1, \ldots, RS_k\}$. Let X_i be the set of attributes of RS_i for $i = 1, \ldots, k$. Each pairwise consistent instance of DS is globally consistent if and only if the jd $X_1 \bowtie \cdots \bowtie X_k$ is acyclic. In this case, each instance of DS can be checked for consistency in polynomial time.*

□

There is a more elegant way to check pairwise consistency than taking all joins of two relations and projecting them. We have:

Theorem 4.12 *Let $DS = (PDS, DM, SDC)$ be a database with $PDS = \{RS_1, \ldots, RS_k\}$. Let X_i be the set of attributes of RS_i for $i = 1, \ldots, k$. Let $(rs_1, \ldots, rs_k)$ be an instance of DS. $(rs_1, \ldots, rs_k)$ is pairwise consistent if and only if for all $i, j = 1, \ldots, k$, $i \neq j$, $\Pi(rs_i; X_i \cap X_j) = \Pi(rs_j; X_i \cap X_j)$.*

Proof Left as an exercise to the reader.

□

Example 4.11 Consider a database (instance) consisting of the following three relation instances:

A	B	C
a	b	c
a	d	c
e	d	f

B	C	D
b	c	g
b	c	h
d	f	g
d	c	h

D	E
g	k
h	k

Obviously, $ABC \bowtie BCD \bowtie DE$ is acyclic. In order to verify pairwise consistency we have to check that the projections of the first two relations onto BC are equal and that the projections of the last two relations onto D are equal. Clearly, this is the case. We do not have to check anything for the first and last relation, since $ABC \cap DE = \emptyset$. Hence the above database instance is pairwise consistent and thus globally consistent.

□

In many practical situations, the set of constraints of a relation will consist of only fds. As explained in the beginning of this section, we can associate a jd to a decomposition of that relation. On the one hand, we would like our decomposition to be constraint preserving and in BCNF, but we now that both conditions can not always be simultaneously satisfied. On the other hand, as explained above, we would like the jd associated to our decomposition to be acyclic. We call a decomposition satisfying all these conditions a *desirable decomposition*. Yuan ans Özsoyoğlu [115] gave sufficient and necessary conditions for the existence of a desirable decomposition, hereby generalizing results of [72, 18]. Moreover, they showed that whenever a desirable decomposition exists, it is possible to construct one in polynomial time.

We want to close this section (and this chapter) with a comment. In this chapter as well as in the previous one we only dealt with situations in which essentially just one relation scheme was involved. If we considered databases with several relation schemes, it was as a result of the decomposition of single relations. One might wonder whether this approach can always be followed, i. e. is it sufficient to consider only databases with instances that are always consistent? If one answers this question in the positive, one accepts (one of the various interpretations of) the *universal relation assumption*. We do not want to elaborate on this issue since there has already been written far too much about it. We just want to point out that the universal relation assumption in the form we presented it, is too restrictive for many applications. Consider e. g. a library database consisting of two relations, the first over the attributes *ISBN-NR* and *BOOK-DATA*, the latter over *ISBN-NR* and *LIB-NR*. A universal relation for this database should be over the attributes *ISBN-NR*, *LIB-NR* and *BOOK-DATA*. In many practical situations it can take several weeks before a newly acquired book gets registered and receives a library catalog number. If one sticks to the universal relation assumption as formulated above, one would not be able to enter a new book in the database before the registration procedure is completed, a highly undesirable situation. A way to solve this problem and relax the universal relation assumption is to introduce a special symbol that is used to indicate that a certain value does not yet exist or is unknown. Such a value is called a *null value*. Another closely related relaxation of the universal relation assumption is the *weak instance model*. Both topics will be discussed later on, in Chapter 6.

4.7 Exercises

4.1 Find an example yourself of a relation scheme in second normal form that is not in third normal form.

4.2 What is the minimal number of attributes needed to construct a relation scheme in second normal form which is not in third normal form? Prove your answer!

4.3 Let RS be a relation scheme and let $DS = (PDS, DM, \emptyset)$ be a decomposition of RS. Suppose $RS_1 \in PDS$ and let $DS_1 = (PDS_1, \emptyset)$ is a decomposition of RS_1. Show that $DS' = ((PDS - RS_1) \cup PDS_1, \emptyset)$ is also a decomposition of RS.

4.4 Prove Theorem 4.1.

4.5 Show that a relation $RS = (\Omega, \Delta, dom, M, SC)$ is in BCNF if and only if there does not exist a key X, $Y \subset \Omega$ with $X \not\rightarrow Y$ and $A \notin XY$ such that $X \rightarrow Y \rightarrow A$.

4.6 Find an example yourself of a relation scheme in third normal form that is not in BCNF.

4.7 What is the minimal number of attributes needed to construct a relation scheme in third normal form which is not in BCNF? Prove your answer!

4.8 Consider a relation scheme $RS = (\Omega, \Delta, dom, M, SC)$ with $\Omega = \{A, B, C\}$ and $SC = \{A \rightarrow B, BC \rightarrow A\}$. Show that there does not exist a constraint preserving decomposition of RS in BCNF.

4.9 Give an example which shows that Algorithm 4.1 does not always produce constraint preserving decompositions in third normal form.

4.10 Let $RS = (\Omega, \Delta, dom, M, SC)$ be a relation scheme where SC is a set of fds. Suppose that the attribute $A \in \Omega$ does not appear in any fd of SC. Let X be an arbitrary key for RS. Show that $A \in X$.

4.11 Let $DS = (PDS, DM, \emptyset)$ be a database scheme with $PDS = \{RS_1, \ldots, RS_m\}$ and for all $i = 1, \ldots, m$, $RS_i = (\Omega_i, \Delta_i, dom_i, M_i, SC_i)$. Suppose furthermore that DS is a constraint preserving decomposition in third normal form of a relation scheme $RS = (\Omega, \Delta, dom, M, SC)$ where SC is a set of fds. (We assume that SC_i is the projection of SC onto Ω_i). Show that the database scheme DS' obtained by recursively eliminating from PDS each relation scheme whose set of attributes is contained into the set of attributes of another relation scheme until no further action is possible, is also a constraint preserving decomposition in third normal form of RS.

4.12 Show that a relation scheme $RS = (\Omega, \Delta, dom, M, SC)$ where SC is a set of fds and which is in BCNF, is also in fourth normal form.

4.13 Give an example of a relation scheme which is *not* in fourth normal form. Then decompose that scheme into fourth normal form! What can you say about preservation of constraints in your example?

4.14 Let $RS = (\Omega, \Delta, dom, M, SC)$ be a relation scheme in fifth normal form. Let $X_1 \bowtie \cdots \bowtie X_k$ be a jd implied by SC. Show that for each $i = 1, \ldots, k$ there exists j, $1 \leq j \leq k$, such that $X_i \subseteq X_j$ and X_j is a superkey for RS. Explain why such jds are admissible in a fifth normal form relation!

4.15 Show that a relation scheme in fifth normal form is also in fourth normal form.

4.16 Show that a relation scheme $RS = (\Omega, \Delta, dom, M, SC)$ where SC is a set of fds and mvds and which is in fourth normal form, is also in fifth normal form.

4.17 Give an example of a relation scheme which is *not* in fifth normal form. Then decompose that scheme into fifth normal form! What can you say about preservation of constraints in your example?

4.18 Prove Theorem 4.9.

4.19 Prove Theorem 4.12.

4.20 Show that the database instance in Example 4.11 is globally consistent by using Theorem 4.9.

4.21 Consider a database scheme consisting of three relation schemes over the attribute sets AB, BC and AC respectively. Obviously $AB \bowtie BC \bowtie AC$ is not acyclic. Give an example of an instance of this database which is pairwise consistent, but not globally consistent.

Chapter 5

Horizontal Decompositions

The vertical decomposition, explained in Chapter 4, is a useful tool for reducing redundancy in the database and for improving the speed of query evaluation and updating. However, in the real world the constraints on which the decomposition relies may not be easy to find, and exceptions may appear after a database system is in use for some period of time.

In this chapter we provide a tool for handling such exceptions, by using another kind of decomposition [37, 36, 38]. We emphasize on functional dependencies (fds) in a single relation scheme.

In Section 5.1 we define the *horizontal decomposition* based on *"goals"*. These "goals" represent fds for which there may be exceptions in the real world. By decomposing the scheme horizontally we will create two (sub)schemes: one for the exceptions and one where the fd holds. We formalize the notion of an "exception" by means of a new constraint: the *afunctional dependency* (ad). In Section 5.2 we show the interaction between fds and ads, a problem similar to that of functional and multivalued dependencies. In the next section we show that the horizontal decomposition is not *dependency preserving* in general, and we give the constraints which are preserved. In the last section we define some normal forms for horizontal decompositions and say how the horizontal decomposition interacts with the vertical decomposition.

5.1 Horizontal Decompositions

Recall Example 1.10. In the scheme *STAYS* the attribute *VIS-NUMBER* may seem to be a key, i. e. every visitor arrives on only one day, leaves on only one day, stays in one room, has one number of accompanying persons and has to pay only one bill.

The disadvantage of this assumption is that a visitor who wishes to reserve two rooms (because he has more accompanying persons than fit into one room) needs to have two visitor-numbers. Hence his name and address appear twice in *VISITORS*, and there is a problem obtaining the correct bill for that visitor. One can also circumvent this problem by mentioning only one room for that visitor. But then there is no way to keep track of rooms that are reserved in reality, but not reserved in the database.

To avoid this problem we propose to split up the relation (scheme) into two subrelations: one for the visitors with only one room, and one for the others. Clearly, in the subrelation for the visitors with only one room, *VIS-NUMBER* is a key.

The horizontal decomposition (applied to an instance of *STAYS*) will keep the tuples with the same *VIS-NUMBER* in the same subinstance, i. e. a visitor does not occur in both subinstances.

Definition 5.1 Let X be a set of attributes of a scheme RS and let rs be an instance of RS. A set of tuples, s, $s \subseteq rs$, is called *X-complete* iff the tuples belonging to s all have other X-projections than those belonging to $rs - s$. Formally: $\forall t_1 \in s, t_2 \in rs - s : t_1[X] \neq t_2[X]$. s is said to be *X-unique* iff all tuples of s have the same X-value.

□

One can easily see that the empty set of tuples is X-complete for every set X of attributes of RS. The set of tuples of an instance of *STAYS*, consisting of just all the tuples with a given *VIS-NUMBER*, is both *VIS-NUMBER*-complete and *VIS-NUMBER*-unique. In the sequel we shall use the term *X-set* instead of "X-complete X-unique set of tuples".

In Chapter 2 we have seen that the condition of a selection in the relational algebra can be any computable boolean function on attributes. In most cases we have met so far, this condition was a simple operator like $\leq$. We shall define the horizontal decomposition using a more complicated selection.

Definition 5.2 Let $RS = (\Omega, \Delta, dom, M, SC)$ be a scheme. Let $X, Y \subseteq \Omega$. The *selection for $X \rightarrow Y$ of RS*, $\sigma(RS, X \rightarrow Y)$, is a scheme $RS_1 = (\Omega, \Delta, dom, M_1, SC_1)$. The calculation of SC_1 will be described in Section 5.3 (SC_1 contains $X \rightarrow Y$). M_1 explains that all instances of RS_1 must be the selection for $X \rightarrow Y$ of the instances of RS. For every instance rs of RS, the *selection for $X \rightarrow Y$ of rs*, $\sigma(rs, X \rightarrow Y)$, is the largest X-complete subset (of tuples) of rs in which $X \rightarrow Y$ holds.[1]

□

Clearly $\sigma(rs, X \rightarrow Y)$ is defined unambiguously, since there is only one set of tuples satisfying this definition.

When decomposing a relation horizontally for eliminating exceptions to a functional dependency, we want to keep as many tuples in the "good" subrelation

[1] The attentive reader will note that this selection is not a selection in the sense of the relational algebra, given in Chapter 2. However, it can be simulated using relational algebra expressions.

as possible, without splitting up X-sets. Therefore we select the largest X-complete set of tuples in which $X \to Y$ holds. Whether the fd $X \to Y$ holds for some X-value does not depend on the tuples having other X-values. So one can obtain the largest X-complete set of tuples satisfying $X \to Y$ by taking all tuples such that $X \to Y$ holds in "their" X-set.

Note that although the largest X-complete (sub)set of tuples satisfying $X \to Y$ (exists and) is unique, the largest (sub)set of tuples satisfying $X \to Y$ is not unique. A visitor with two rooms can be included in the largest subset with either of these rooms. This ambiguity does not occur with our horizontal decomposition, since we keep the tuples concerning one visitor together.

The selection for *VIS-NUMBER→ROOM-STAY* of *STAYS* contains the visitors staying in only one room.

The horizontal decomposition of a relation scheme will consist of the selection for $X \to Y$ of that scheme and of the "remaining part" of the scheme. These two subschemes have the same set of attributes as the original relation (they have the same primitive relation scheme) but different meaning and constraints.

Definition 5.3 • A *goal* is an ordered pair of sets of attributes, denoted $X \overset{?}{\to} Y$ to indicate that this is an fd with possible exceptions.

- The *horizontal decomposition of a scheme RS, according to the goal $X \overset{?}{\to} Y$* is the ordered pair (RS_1, RS_2), where: $RS_1 = \sigma(RS, X \to Y)$ and $RS_2 = RS - \sigma(RS, X \to Y)$.[2]

□

Example 5.1 Recall Example 1.11. The table shown in Figure 5.1 represents an instance *stays*, together with the decomposition according to *VIS-NUMBER*$\overset{?}{\to}$ *ROOM-STAY*. Visitors 101 and 102 occupy only one room, whereas visitor 105 needs 2 rooms. From this example one can see that there are a few anomalies when trying to update this instance: if visitor 101 wants a second room, then the first tuple of $stays_1$ has to move to $stays_2$ where it will be accompanied by a new tuple with another roomnumber for that visitor. Likewise, if visitor 105 wishes to cancel room 402, the remaining tuple has to move to $stays_1$ since visitor 105 is no longer an exception to *VIS-NUMBER→ROOM-STAY*. The reader is invited to construct an efficient algorithm to perform these updates.

□

By decomposing RS horizontally we obtain a subscheme RS_1 in which an additional fd $X \to Y$ holds. In the other subscheme $RS2$ we also have a new constraint: for every X-value (in every instance of RS_2) there must be at least two different Y-values. In Example 5.1 this means that all visitors in the second

[2]To keep the notation easier, we shall not use multiple subscripts when applying several decomposition steps after another. So we write RS_{11} instead of RS_{1_1}, etc.

stays

VIS-NUMBER	ARRIV-DATE	LEAV-DATE	ROOM-STAY	NUMBER-OF-ACCOMP-PERSONS	BILL
101	1/7/87	15/7/87	205	1	10000
102	1/8/87	7/8/87	310	2	3000
105	1/7/87	15/7/87	401	4	12000
105	1/7/87	15/7/87	402	4	12000

$stays_1$

VIS-NUMBER	ARRIV-DATE	LEAV-DATE	ROOM-STAY	NUMBER-OF-ACCOMP-PERSONS	BILL
101	1/7/87	15/7/87	205	1	10000
102	1/8/87	7/8/87	310	2	3000

$stays_2$

VIS-NUMBER	ARRIV-DATE	LEAV-DATE	ROOM-STAY	NUMBER-OF-ACCOMP-PERSONS	BILL
105	1/7/87	15/7/87	401	4	12000
105	1/7/87	15/7/87	402	4	12000

Figure 5.1: Decomposition of *stays*.

subrelation occupy more than one room. This constraint is called an *afunctional dependency.*

Definition 5.4 The *afunctional dependency (ad)* $X \not\twoheadrightarrow Y$ holds in the relation scheme RS if in every nonempty X-complete set of tuples in every instance of RS the fd $X \rightarrow Y$ does not hold.

□

The ad *VIS-NUMBER*$\not\twoheadrightarrow$*ROOM-STAY* means that every visitor must occupy more than one room. This can be seen in $stays_2$ in Example 5.1. Obviously, Definition 5.4 can be rewritten as: *The ad* $X \not\twoheadrightarrow Y$ *holds in the scheme* RS *if for every instance* rs *of* RS*, for every tuple* $t \in rs$*, there is a tuple* $t' \in rs$ *such that* $t[X] = t'[X]$ *and* $t[Y] \neq t'[Y]$.

Note that $X \not\twoheadrightarrow Y$ holds in the empty instance, for all X and Y.

From now on we shall assume that the set of constraints SC of a relation scheme RS only consists of a set $\mathcal{F}$ of fds and a set $\mathcal{A}$ of ads.

The subscheme for the exceptions can be redefined as follows, using the definition of ads:

Definition 5.5 The *selection for* $X \not\twoheadrightarrow Y$ *of* RS, $\sigma(RS, X \not\twoheadrightarrow Y)$, is a scheme $RS_2 = (\Omega, \Delta, dom, M_2, SC_2)$. The calculation of SC_2 will be described in Section 5.3. SC_2 contains $X \not\twoheadrightarrow Y$. M_2 explains that all instances of RS_2 must be the selection for $X \not\twoheadrightarrow Y$ of the instances of RS. For every instance rs of RS, the *selection for* $X \not\twoheadrightarrow Y$ *of* RS, $\sigma(rs, X \not\twoheadrightarrow Y)$, is the largest X-complete subset (of tuples) of rs in which $X \not\twoheadrightarrow Y$ holds.[3]

□

The reader will note that the horizontal decomposition of RS according to $X \overset{?}{\twoheadrightarrow} Y$ is the ordered pair (RS_1, RS_2), where $RS_1 = \sigma(RS, X \rightarrow Y)$ and $RS_2 = \sigma(RS, X \not\twoheadrightarrow Y)$.

The presence of several constraints of different kinds in a relation scheme involves the danger that the constraints may be in contradiction with each other. In such a case there are no possible instances that satisfy all constraints. In general, i. e. when all kinds of constraints are allowed, this problem is undecidable.

When only fds and ads are considered the constraints cannot be in contradiction with each other, since at least the empty set of tuples does not violate any fd or ad. However there is a weak kind of contradiction that turns out to be a useful tool in the next sections.

Definition 5.6 A set $\mathcal{F} \cup \mathcal{A}$ of fds and ads is said to be *in conflict* if the empty set of tuples is the only instance in which all constraints of $\mathcal{F} \cup \mathcal{A}$ hold.

□

We shall always suppose that $\mathcal{F} \cup \mathcal{A}$ is not in conflict. An easy example of a set of fds and ads in conflict is $\{A \rightarrow B, A \not\twoheadrightarrow B\}$.

In the next section we shall show how to decide whether a set of fds and ads is in conflict. In the theory of that section we shall need a special instance, known in literature as the *Armstrong relation for fds* [42].

Definition 5.7 Let $\mathcal{F}$ be a set of fds over a set Ω of attributes. An *Armstrong relation for* $\mathcal{F}$ is an instance in which only the fds of $\mathcal{F}$ hold, together with their consequences.

□

Example 5.2 The table shown below shows an Armstrong relation for $\{AB \rightarrow C\}$ (in a scheme with no other attributes).

A	B	C
0	0	0
0	1	1
2	2	0
0	2	0
1	0	1
2	0	0

□

[3] This again is no selection in the sense of the relational algebra.

In Theorem 3.2 the following instance is used to prove the completeness of the inference rules for fds:

$r_X =$

$\overline{X}$	$\Omega \setminus \overline{X}$
$0_X \ldots 0_X$	$0_X \ldots 0_X$
$0_X \ldots 0_X$	$1_X \ldots 1_X$

($\overline{X} = \{A : \mathcal{F} \models X \rightarrow A\}$, i. e. the closure of X.) We use the subscripts to obtain different domains for different X-es.

The reader is invited to prove that $\bigcup_{X \subseteq \Omega} r_X$ is an Armstrong relation for $\mathcal{F}$. However, this instance is useless if we also consider ads.

The instances we need in the next sections have a somewhat stronger property than the Armstrong relations:

Definition 5.8 Let $\mathcal{F}$ be a set of fds over a set Ω of attributes. A *strong Armstrong relation for* $\mathcal{F}$ is an instance in which all the fds of $\mathcal{F}$ hold, and also their consequences, but in which for every other fd $X \rightarrow Y$ the "corresponding" ad $X \not\twoheadrightarrow Y$ holds.

□

The Armstrong relation shown in Example 5.2 is not a strong Armstrong relation since e. g. $A \not\twoheadrightarrow B$ does not hold. Neither is $\bigcup_{X \subseteq \Omega} r_X$ a strong Armstrong relation. However

A	B
0	0
1	0

is a strong Armstrong relation for $\{A \not\twoheadrightarrow B\}$ (in a scheme with only these two attributes).

In the sequel we shall only use strong Armstrong relations.

Theorem 5.1 *For every set $\mathcal{F}$ of fds there exists a strong Armstrong relation.*

Proof We consider a construction similar to that of Fagin [42]. For every set of attributes $X \subseteq \Omega$ consider the instance r_X as above. In the proof of Theorem 3.2 it is shown that $\mathcal{F}$ holds in r_X and if $\mathcal{F} \not\models X \rightarrow Y$ then $X \rightarrow Y$ does not hold in r_X. Hence $X \not\twoheadrightarrow Y$ holds, since there is only one X-complete set of tuples in r_X.

Let r_1 and r_2 be sets of tuples over Ω. The direct product of r_1 and r_2, $r_1 \otimes r_2$, is constructed as follows: if $(a_1, \ldots, a_n) \in r_1$ and $(b_1, \ldots b_n) \in r_2$ then $r_1 \otimes r_2$ contains $((a_1, b_1), \ldots, (a_n, b_n))$. One can easily see that an fd holds in $r_1 \otimes r_2$ if it holds in both r_1 and r_2, and that an ad holds in $r_1 \otimes r_2$ if it holds in r_1 or r_2 (or in both).

Consider

$$Arm(\mathcal{F}) = \bigotimes_{X \subseteq \Omega} r_X$$

In $Arm(\mathcal{F})$, $\mathcal{F}$ holds since it holds in all r_X. For every fd $X \rightarrow Y$ that is not a consequence of $\mathcal{F}$, $X \not\twoheadrightarrow Y$ holds in r_X, hence also in $Arm(\mathcal{F})$.

□

5.2 The Membership and Inference Problem for Fds and Ads

For fds only, we already know the solution for the membership and the inference problem from Chapter 3. We shall first prove that these algorithms are not affected by the presence of ads.

Lemma 5.1 *If $\mathcal{F} \cup \mathcal{A}$ is not in conflict then $\mathcal{F} \cup \mathcal{A} \models X \rightarrow Y$ iff $\mathcal{F} \models X \rightarrow Y$.*

Proof The if-part is trivial, since $\mathcal{F} \subseteq \mathcal{F} \cup \mathcal{A}$.

For the only-if-part, suppose $\mathcal{F} \cup \mathcal{A} \models X \rightarrow Y$. In $Arm(\mathcal{F})$, $\mathcal{F}$ holds and if an ad $T \not\twoheadrightarrow U$ of $\mathcal{A}$ does not hold then $\mathcal{F} \models T \rightarrow U$ by Theorem 5.1, and $\mathcal{F} \cup \mathcal{A}$ would have been in conflict, a contradiction. Hence $\mathcal{F} \cup \mathcal{A}$ holds in $Arm(\mathcal{F})$. Hence $X \rightarrow Y$ holds in $Arm(\mathcal{F})$ and by Theorem 5.1 this implies that $\mathcal{F} \models X \rightarrow Y$. □

Lemma 5.2 *$\mathcal{F} \cup \mathcal{A}$ is in conflict iff for some ad $X \not\twoheadrightarrow Y$ of $\mathcal{A}$, $\mathcal{F} \models X \rightarrow Y$ holds.*

Proof The if-part is trivial.

For the only-if-part, suppose that $\mathcal{F} \cup \mathcal{A}$ is in conflict and hence the empty instance is the only instance in which $\mathcal{F} \cup \mathcal{A}$ holds. Hence in $Arm(\mathcal{F})$, in which $\mathcal{F}$ holds, some ad $X \not\twoheadrightarrow Y$ of $\mathcal{A}$ does not hold. By Theorem 5.1 this implies that $X \rightarrow Y$ holds in $Arm(\mathcal{F})$ and that $\mathcal{F} \models X \rightarrow Y$. □

This lemma suggests a very important property of ads: ads do not "work" together. For instance, if $A \rightarrow B$ and $B \rightarrow C$ hold then $A \rightarrow C$ holds by transitivity. For ads no such rule can exist: if for every A-value there are at least two B-values, and for every B-value at least two C-values, then it is still possible that not for every A-value there are at least two C-values. In fact the following table shows that it is still possible that for some A-value there is only one C-value. Even a stronger property holds: the following instance shows that $A \not\twoheadrightarrow B$, $B \not\twoheadrightarrow C$ and $A \rightarrow C$ are not in conflict.

A	B	C
0	0	0
0	1	0
1	0	1
1	1	1

From Lemma 5.2 one can easily deduce the following algorithm to detect conflict:

Algorithm 5.1 *Conflict Detection*

Input: $\mathcal{F}, \mathcal{A}$, a set of fds and a set of ads.

Output: *true* or *false*.

Method:

for each $T \not\twoheadrightarrow U$ **in** $\mathcal{A}$ **do**
  if $\mathcal{F} \vdash T \rightarrow U$
    then return(*true*) {and exit}
od
return(*false*) {only reached if for-loop is done}

□

We propose the following set of inference rules for (mixed) fds and ads:

$$\{XV \not\twoheadrightarrow YW, W \subseteq V\} \vdash X \not\twoheadrightarrow Y \quad (A1)$$
$$\{X \rightarrow Y, X \not\twoheadrightarrow Z \vdash Y \not\twoheadrightarrow Z \quad (FA1)$$
$$\{Y \rightarrow Z, X \not\twoheadrightarrow Z \vdash X \not\twoheadrightarrow Y \quad (FA2)$$

Lemma 5.3 *The rules FA1, FA2 and A1 are sound.*

Proof We only prove rule $FA1$. The proof for the other rules follows a similar argument and is therefore left to the reader.

Suppose that $X \rightarrow Y$ holds, and for some Y-value $Y \not\twoheadrightarrow Z$ does not hold (hence $Y \rightarrow Z$ holds for that Y-value). Consider an (arbitrary) X-value, that corresponds to that Y-value (meaning that there is a tuple in that X-value having that Y-projection). Since $X \rightarrow Y$ holds, all tuples in that X-complete set of tuples have that same Y-value. And since we assumed that $Y \rightarrow Z$ holds for that Y-value these tuples all have the same Z-value. This means that $X \rightarrow Z$ holds for that X-value, hence $X \not\twoheadrightarrow Z$ cannot hold.

□

As suggested above, there are no rules for deducing an ad from two (or more) other ads. Rule $A1$ is the "opposite" of the augmentation rule for fds, and $FA1$ and $FA2$ "reverse" the transitivity rule for fds. The following Example illustrate rule $FA1$ (in a more informal way):

If every visitor has only one bill, but every visitor has at least two rooms, then for every bill there must be at least two rooms. (Otherwise there would be some visitor having a bill for which there is only one room, so this visitor could have only one room by transitivity.)

The following theorem shows the link between the membership problem for mixed fds and ads and the conflict concept.

Theorem 5.2 *Let* $\mathcal{F} \cup \mathcal{A}$ *be not in conflict,* $X \not\twoheadrightarrow Y$ *an ad. Then* $\mathcal{F} \cup \mathcal{A} \models X \not\twoheadrightarrow Y$ *iff* $\mathcal{F} \cup \mathcal{A} \cup \{X \rightarrow Y\}$ *is in conflict.*

Proof The only-if-part is trivial.

For the if-part, suppose that $\mathcal{F} \cup \mathcal{A} \cup \{X \rightarrow Y\}$ is in conflict. Then, by Lemma 5.2 $\mathcal{F} \cup \{X \rightarrow Y\} \models T \rightarrow U$ for some $T \not\twoheadrightarrow U \in \mathcal{A}$. We prove that this implies $\mathcal{F} \cup \{T \not\twoheadrightarrow U\} \models X \not\twoheadrightarrow Y$.

Let P be a set of attributes, and let $\overline{P}$ indicate (as usual) $\{A \mid \mathcal{F} \models P \rightarrow A\}$. There are two possibilities (of which we shall prove that only the second can occur):

1. $X \not\subset \overline{T}$. Consider the following instance r:

$\overline{T}$	$\Omega \setminus \overline{T}$
$0 \ldots 0$	$0 \ldots 0$
$0 \ldots 0$	$1 \ldots 1$

In r, $\mathcal{F}$ holds, because of the definition of $\overline{T}$; $X \rightarrow Y$ holds since $X \not\subset \overline{T}$; and $T \not\twoheadrightarrow U$ holds since $U \not\subset \overline{T}$ (otherwise $\mathcal{F} \cup \mathcal{A}$ would have been in conflict). Hence $\mathcal{F} \cup \{X \rightarrow Y\} \not\models T \rightarrow U$, since r is a counterexample, in which $\mathcal{F} \cup \{X \rightarrow Y\} \cup \{T \not\twoheadrightarrow U\}$ holds. So this case ($X \not\subset \overline{T}$) is impossible if $\mathcal{F} \cup \{X \rightarrow Y\} \models T \rightarrow U$. This means that the following case must hold:

2. $X \subseteq \overline{T}$. There are (again) two cases (of which we shall prove that only the second is possible):

   (a) $U \not\subset \overline{YT}$. Consider the following instance r:

$\overline{YT}$	$\Omega \setminus \overline{YT}$
$0 \ldots 0$	$0 \ldots 0$
$0 \ldots 0$	$1 \ldots 1$

   In r, $\mathcal{F}$ holds, because of the definition of $\overline{YT}$, $X \rightarrow Y$ holds since $Y \subseteq \overline{YT}$, and $T \not\twoheadrightarrow U$ holds, since $U \not\subset \overline{YT}$. Hence $\mathcal{F} \cup \{X \rightarrow Y\} \not\models T \rightarrow U$, since $\mathcal{F} \cup \{X \rightarrow Y\} \cup \{T \not\twoheadrightarrow U\}$ holds in r. So this case is also impossible if $\mathcal{F} \cup \{X \rightarrow Y\} \models T \rightarrow U$. This means that the following (final) case must be true:

   (b) $U \subset \overline{YT}$ (and $X \subset \overline{T}$). We show that not only $\mathcal{F} \cup \{T \not\twoheadrightarrow U\} \models X \not\twoheadrightarrow Y$ but even $\mathcal{F} \cup \{T \not\twoheadrightarrow U\} \vdash X \not\twoheadrightarrow Y$, i.e. we shall show how to infer $X \not\twoheadrightarrow Y$ from $\mathcal{F} \cup \{T \not\twoheadrightarrow U\}$ using the inference rules for fds (see chapter 3) and for fds and ads.

   $T \not\twoheadrightarrow U$ and $TY \rightarrow U$ induce $T \not\twoheadrightarrow TY$ by $FA2$, $T \not\twoheadrightarrow TY$ induces $T \not\twoheadrightarrow Y$ by $A1$ and $T \rightarrow X$ and $T \not\twoheadrightarrow Y$ induce $X \not\twoheadrightarrow Y$ by $FA1$.

The proof is completed by remarking that $\mathcal{F} \cup \{T \not\twoheadrightarrow U\} \subseteq \mathcal{F} \cup \mathcal{A}$.

□

By using the inference rules in the above proof, this also proves the following corollary:

Corollary 5.1 *The inference rules for fds (reflexivity, augmentation and transitivity) and the rules $A1$, $FA1$ and $FA2$ are complete for mixed fds and ads.*

□

Using Theorem 5.2 and Lemma 5.2 one can easily prove the correctness of the following membership algorithm for ads (in the presence of fds).

Algorithm 5.2 *Membership Detection*

Input: $\mathcal{F}, \mathcal{A}$, a set of fds and a set of ads, not in conflict; $X \not\twoheadrightarrow Y$ an ad.

Output: *true* or *false.*

Method:

for each $T \not\twoheadrightarrow U$ **in** $\mathcal{A}$ **do**
  if $\mathcal{F} \cup \{X \rightarrow Y\} \models T \rightarrow U$
    then return(*true*) {and exit}
od
return(*false*) {only reached if for-loop is done}

□

This algorithm confirms our previous note, that ads do not "work" together: the membership problem for ads always depends on only one ad.

5.3 The Inheritance of Dependencies

In general, more than one goal may be associated with a relation scheme RS, and after decomposing RS using one goal, the resulting subschemes may be decomposed further on, using the other goals. However, a goal $X \overset{?}{\twoheadrightarrow} Y$ cannot be used for the horizontal decomposition of RS if $X \rightarrow Y$ or $X \not\twoheadrightarrow Y$ holds in RS since this would yield a set of dependencies that is in conflict in one of the subschemes. The same restriction applies to the subschemes that are the result of earlier decomposition steps.

Determining whether for a goal $X \overset{?}{\twoheadrightarrow} Y$ either $X \rightarrow Y$ or $X \not\twoheadrightarrow Y$ holds in RS is described in the previous section. After one decomposition step, this decision depends on the sets of dependencies that hold in the subschemes that result from that decomposition step. In the present section we show how these sets of dependencies can be calculated. Since they are derived from the "parent" scheme, we call them *inherited* dependencies.

In the sequel we treat the horizontal decomposition of a scheme $RS = (\Omega, \Delta, dom, M, \mathcal{F} \cup \mathcal{A})$, according to $X \overset{?}{\twoheadrightarrow} Y$, into the schemes $RS_1 = (\Omega, \Delta, dom, M_1, \mathcal{F}_1 \cup \mathcal{A}_1)$ and $RS_2 = (\Omega, \Delta, dom, M_2, \mathcal{F}_2 \cup \mathcal{A}_2)$. We assume that $\mathcal{F} \cup \mathcal{A}$ is not in conflict, $\mathcal{F} \cup \mathcal{A} \not\models X \rightarrow Y$ and $\mathcal{F} \cup \mathcal{A} \not\models X \not\twoheadrightarrow Y$.

In this section we show how to calculate the sets $\mathcal{F}_1$, $\mathcal{F}_2$, $\mathcal{A}_1$ and $\mathcal{A}_2$. Since there are many sets of fds and ads that are equivalent (that have the same closure), we shall only show how to find a generating set for the dependencies.

For the fds the "inheritance problem" is easy to formulate and to prove.

Theorem 5.3 *Using the notation introduced in the beginning of this section,* $\mathcal{F}_1 = \mathcal{F} \cup \{X \rightarrow Y\}$ *and* $\mathcal{F}_2 = \mathcal{F}$.

□

This theorem only says that fds are always inherited. This is fairly obvious: if a visitor has only one bill in the whole relation, then he obviously cannot have more that one bill in any subrelation.

For ads the inheritance problem is more complicated. Some ads can be violated by decomposing a relation horizontally. This is illustrated by the following example:

Example 5.3 *Let* $\Omega = \{A, B, C\}$, *with integer domains. Let* $\mathcal{F} = \emptyset$ *and* $\mathcal{A} = \{A \not\twoheadrightarrow B\}$. *Consider the following instance* rs:

A	B	C
0	0	0
0	1	0
0	1	1

Let rs *be decomposed according to* $B \overset{?}{\twoheadrightarrow} C$. *This yields*

rs_1

A	B	C
0	0	0

rs_2

A	B	C
0	1	0
0	1	1

The ad $A \not\twoheadrightarrow B$ *is violated in both* rs_1 *and* rs_2. *This is caused by the fact that the A-complete sets in* rs_1 *and* rs_2 *are not A-complete in* rs.

□

The example suggests that for an ad $T \not\twoheadrightarrow U$ to be inherited by RS_1 or RS_2, the T-values of rs_1 (resp. rs_2) must be T-complete in rs, i. e. the T-values that occur in rs_1 must not occur in rs_2 and vice versa. Hence, by dividing the tuples in two X-complete sets (that is what the horizontal decomposition does) the T-unique sets of tuples must not be split up. A sufficient condition is to require that all T-unique sets of tuples are also X-unique (i. e. every T-value corresponds to only one X-value. We shall prove that this condition is also necessary.

The above observation is formalized in the following lemma:

Lemma 5.4 *Using the notation introduced in the beginning of this section, an ad* $T \not\twoheadrightarrow U$ *holds in both* RS_1 *and* RS_2 *if* $\mathcal{F} \cup \mathcal{A} \models T \not\twoheadrightarrow U$ *and* $\mathcal{F} \models T \rightarrow X$. *(Note that the "only if" is not true).*

□

Now that we have a sufficient condition for ads to be inherited, we shall develop a necessary condition. First we prove a partial result, which shows that although it is possible to lose some ads, it is not possible to create new ones:

Lemma 5.5 *If* $T \not\twoheadrightarrow U$ *holds in* RS_1 *(resp.* RS_2*) then* $\mathcal{F} \cup \mathcal{A} \cup \{X \rightarrow Y\} \models T \not\twoheadrightarrow U$ *(resp.* $\mathcal{F} \cup \mathcal{A} \cup \{X \not\twoheadrightarrow Y\} \models T \not\twoheadrightarrow U$*).*

Proof We only prove the case for RS_1; the other case is similar.

Consider an ad $T \not\twoheadrightarrow U$ such that $\mathcal{F} \cup \mathcal{A} \cup \{X \rightarrow Y\} \not\models T \not\twoheadrightarrow U$. Then $\mathcal{F} \cup \mathcal{A} \cup \{X \rightarrow Y\} \cup \{T \rightarrow U\}$ is not in conflict, by Theorem 5.2.

We shall prove that there exists an rs in which $\mathcal{F} \cup \mathcal{A}$ holds, and for which $T \not\twoheadrightarrow U$ does not hold in rs_1.

Let $rs = Arm(\mathcal{F} \cup \{X \rightarrow Y\} \cup \{T \rightarrow U\}) \cup Arm(\mathcal{F})$ and suppose that both Armstrong relations have disjoint domains[4]. In rs, $\mathcal{F} \cup \mathcal{A}$ holds since it holds in both Armstrong relations (by Theorem 5.1). After decomposing rs according to $X \overset{?}{\twoheadrightarrow} Y$ $rs_1 = Arm(\mathcal{F} \cup \{X \rightarrow Y\} \cup \{T \rightarrow U\})$ and $rs_2 = Arm(\mathcal{F})$. In rs_1 $T \not\twoheadrightarrow U$ does not hold.

□

Lemma 5.5 states (in other terms) that $(\mathcal{F}_1 \cup \mathcal{A}_1)^* \subseteq (\mathcal{F} \cup \mathcal{A} \cup \{X \rightarrow Y\})^*$ and $(\mathcal{F}_2 \cup \mathcal{A}_2)^* \subseteq (\mathcal{F} \cup \mathcal{A} \cup \{X \not\twoheadrightarrow Y\})^*$.

The result of Lemma 5.5 does not take into account the ads of $\mathcal{A}$ that may not be inherited. Therefore we first define a smaller set of ads, using the notation introduced in the beginning of this section:

$$\hat{\mathcal{A}} = \{T \not\twoheadrightarrow U \in \mathcal{A} \mid \mathcal{F} \models T \rightarrow X\}$$

Note from Lemma 5.4 that the ads of $\hat{\mathcal{A}}$ are inherited by both RS_1 and RS_2.

If an ad $T \not\twoheadrightarrow U$ does not hold in an instance then for some T-value $T \rightarrow U$ must hold in that instance. Such a T-value (i. e. T-unique and T-complete set of tuples) will be called a *violation* of $T \not\twoheadrightarrow U$.

In the proof of the inheritance of ads a special instance is needed, of which the construction is described below. This construction starts with a set of tuples in which some ads of $\mathcal{A}$ do not hold, and by adding some more tuples the violations of the ads of $\mathcal{A}$ are eliminated.

Lemma 5.6 *Let $\mathcal{A}' \subseteq \mathcal{A}$ and let $\mathcal{F} \cup \mathcal{A}$ be not in conflict. Let sot be a set of tuples in which $\mathcal{F} \cup \mathcal{A}'$ holds, but in which some ad $P \not\twoheadrightarrow Q \in \mathcal{A} \setminus \mathcal{A}'$ does not hold. Then one can construct a set sot′ of tuples, containing sot as a subset, in which $\mathcal{F} \cup \mathcal{A}'$ still holds, and in which the number of violations of $P \not\twoheadrightarrow Q$ is less than in sot.*

Proof Suppose that the domains of $Arm(\mathcal{F})$ and sot are disjoint[5]. Suppose also that in $Arm(\mathcal{F})$ the domains of the attributes all are disjoint. (This can be easily achieved by replacing $Arm(\mathcal{F})$ by an equivalent instance with other domains.)

Let $\overline{P} = \{A \in \Omega \mid \mathcal{F} \models P \rightarrow A\}$. Let t be a tuple in an arbitrary violation of $P \not\twoheadrightarrow Q$ (in sot). Let s be an arbitrary tuple of $Arm(\mathcal{F})$. The domain of $Arm(\mathcal{F})$ is changed such that $s[\overline{P}] := t[\overline{P}]$. Let r' be the union of this adapted Armstrong relation and sot.

In r', $\mathcal{F}$ still holds, since $\mathcal{F}$ holds in sot and $Arm(\mathcal{F})$, and since if $V \not\subseteq \overline{P}$ then $V \rightarrow W \in \mathcal{F}$ still holds because no tuple of sot has the same V-projection

[4]Strictly speaking we must assume that the domains of both Armstrong relations are the same, but that the instances use no common elements of the domains.

[5]Strictly speaking only the used part of the domains must differ; the domains themselves must be the same in order to be able to take the union.

as any tuple of $Arm(\mathcal{F})$, and if $V \subseteq \overline{P}$ then $V \to W \in \mathcal{F}$ still holds because also $W \subseteq \overline{P}$ and if the V-projection of a tuple of *sot* and of a tuple of $Arm(\mathcal{F})$ are equal then this projection is $t[V]$, and hence for the tuple of *sot* and the tuple of $Arm(\mathcal{F})$ the W-projection is $t[W]$ by the construction of r'.

In r', $\mathcal{A}'$ holds since $\mathcal{A}'$ holds in *sot* and $\mathcal{A} \supseteq \mathcal{A}'$ holds in $Arm(\mathcal{F})$ and since an ad cannot be violated by taking a union.

In $Arm(\mathcal{F})$, $P \not\twoheadrightarrow Q \in \mathcal{A}$ holds, hence $Arm(\mathcal{F})$ does not contain any violation of $P \not\twoheadrightarrow Q$. In r' the violation of $P \not\twoheadrightarrow Q$ in *sot* that contains t is no longer a violation of $P \not\twoheadrightarrow Q$. Hence in r' the number of violations of $P \not\twoheadrightarrow Q$ is (strictly) less than in *sot*.

□

The construction, used in the proof of the above lemma is illustrated by the following, (simplified) example.

Example 5.4 Consider a scheme RS with attributes $\{A, B, C, D\}$, fds $\mathcal{F} = \{A \to B, B \to A, C \to D, D \to A\}$ and ads $\mathcal{A} = \{A \not\twoheadrightarrow C, A \not\twoheadrightarrow D\}$. Let $\mathcal{A}' = \{A \not\twoheadrightarrow C\}$. Consider the following set of tuples *sot*:

A	B	C	D
a	a	a	a
a	a	b	a
b	b	c	b
b	b	d	b
c	c	e	c
c	c	f	d

In *sot* $\mathcal{F} \cup \mathcal{A}'$ holds, but $A \not\twoheadrightarrow D$ does not hold. There are two violations of $A \not\twoheadrightarrow D$: {tuples 1 and 2} and {tuples 3 and 4}.

The following instance is equivalent to $Arm(\mathcal{F})$:

A	B	C	D
0	0	0	0
1	1	1	1
0	0	2	2
0	0	3	0
1	1	4	4
1	1	5	1
0	0	6	2
1	1	7	4

With the notation of Lemma 5.6, $\overline{P} = AB$. Let t be the tuple over RS consisting only of as and let s be the tuple over RS consisisting only of 0s. After the renaming of $Arm(\mathcal{F})$, the union of *sot* and $Arm(\mathcal{F})$ is the instance:

$r' =$

A	B	C	D
a	a	a	a
a	a	b	a
b	b	c	b
b	b	d	b
c	c	e	c
c	c	f	d
a	a	0	0
1	1	1	1
a	a	2	2
a	a	3	0
1	1	4	4
1	1	4	4
1	1	5	1
a	a	6	2
1	1	7	4

In r', $\mathcal{F} \cup \mathcal{A}'$ still holds, and the number of violations of $A \not\twoheadrightarrow D$ in r' is less than in *sot*: only {tuples 3 and 4} is still a violation of $A \not\twoheadrightarrow D$.

□

The effect of repeatedly performing the above construction is described by the following corollary:

Corollary 5.2 *Let $\mathcal{A}' \subseteq \mathcal{A}$ and let $\mathcal{F} \cup \mathcal{A}$ be not in conflict. Let sot be a set of tuples in which $\mathcal{F} \cup \mathcal{A}'$ holds. Then there exists a set of tuples sot', containing sot as a subset, in which $\mathcal{F} \cup \mathcal{A}$ holds.*

Proof *sot'* is obtained by repeating the above construction for every violation of every ad of $\mathcal{A} \setminus \mathcal{A}'$ which does not hold in *sot*.

□

The solution of the inheritance problem is not hard to prove now:

Theorem 5.4 *Using the notation introduced in the beginning of this section, $\mathcal{F}_1 = \mathcal{F} \cup \{X \rightarrow Y\}$, $\mathcal{A}_1 = \hat{\mathcal{A}}$, $\mathcal{F}_2 = \mathcal{F}$ and $\mathcal{A}_2 = \hat{\mathcal{A}} \cup \{X \not\twoheadrightarrow Y\}$.*

Proof We already know that $(\mathcal{F} \cup \{X \rightarrow Y\} \cup \hat{\mathcal{A}}) \subseteq (\mathcal{F}_1 \cup \mathcal{A}_1) \subseteq (\mathcal{F} \cup \{X \rightarrow Y\} \cup \mathcal{A})$ and $(\mathcal{F} \cup \{X \not\twoheadrightarrow Y\} \cup \hat{\mathcal{A}}) \subseteq (\mathcal{F}_2 \cup \mathcal{A}_2) \subseteq (\mathcal{F} \cup \{X \not\twoheadrightarrow Y\} \cup \mathcal{A})$[6].

Consider an ad $T \not\twoheadrightarrow U$ such that $\mathcal{F} \cup \{X \rightarrow Y\} \cup \mathcal{A} \models T \not\twoheadrightarrow U$ but $\mathcal{F} \cup \{X \rightarrow Y\} \cup \hat{\mathcal{A}} \not\models T \not\twoheadrightarrow U$. We prove that $T \not\twoheadrightarrow U$ does not hold in RS_1.

Since $\mathcal{F} \cup \{X \rightarrow Y\} \cup \hat{\mathcal{A}} \not\models T \not\twoheadrightarrow U$ we know that $\mathcal{F} \cup \{X \rightarrow Y\} \cup \hat{\mathcal{A}} \cup \{T \rightarrow U\}$ is not in conflict, by Theorem 5.2. Hence there exists a set of tuples *sot* in which $\mathcal{F} \cup \{X \rightarrow Y\} \cup \hat{\mathcal{A}} \cup \{T \rightarrow U\}$ holds. Suppose the domains of *sot* and $Arm(\mathcal{F})$ are disjoint.

Let $r' = sot \cup Arm(\mathcal{F})$. When r' is decomposed according to $X \overset{?}{\twoheadrightarrow} Y$, $r_1' = sot$ and $r_2' = Arm(\mathcal{F})$. In *sot* $\mathcal{F} \cup \hat{\mathcal{A}}$ holds, but a number of ads of $\mathcal{A} \setminus \hat{\mathcal{A}}$ may not hold.

[6]The inclusion stated in this theorem only holds for the closure of these sets, not for every arbitrary generating set.

By the construction of Lemma 5.6 and Corollary 5.2 one can build an instance rs which contains sot and in which $\mathcal{F} \cup \mathcal{A}$ is satisfied. In this construction a number of copies of $Arm(\mathcal{F})$ are added to sot. Since $X \not\twoheadrightarrow Y$ holds in $Arm(\mathcal{F})$, and since $\mathcal{F} \cup \mathcal{A} \not\models T \rightarrow X$ (hence $X \not\subset \overline{T}$), these copies are added to rs_2. Hence rs_1 remains unchanged, implying that $T \rightarrow U$ holds in rs_1. Hence $T \not\twoheadrightarrow U$ does not hold in rs_1, which means that $\mathcal{F}_1 \cup \mathcal{A}_1 \not\models T \not\twoheadrightarrow U$.

The proof of the other case is similar and left to the reader. □

5.4 Normal Forms for Horizontal Decompositions

When decomposing a relation scheme both horizontally (according to goals) and vertically (according to fds) one should decide which decomposition has to be performed first. Our approach is to perform the horizontal decomposition steps first. This is based on Theorem 5.4, which states that the horizontal decomposition, according to a goal, preserves fds. Also, performing the vertical decomposition first would cause problems: only the "real fds" (without exceptions) can be used for this decomposition, and after it there may be no more subrelation with all attributes of a goal (since the subrelations that result from vertical decompositions have fewer attributes), so the horizontal decomposition may not be possible after all, and last but not least, if the horizontal decomposition is still possible, it will generate new fds, which can be used for vertical decomposition again.

So we perform the horizontal decomposition first. This means that we do not have to consider the normal forms for the vertical decomposition when designing normal forms for the horizontal decomposition.

There is one gap in the theory of the previous sections: we have proved the inheritance for fds and ads, but we said nothing about the inheritance of goals. The reason is that, since goals are not constraints, they are not necessarily inherited; it is an arbitrary choice whether we want a certain goal to be inherited by the subrelations or not. The goals are actually part of the meaning of the relation, but the meaning of the subrelations has not yet been defined. In the sequel the set of goals of RS will be denoted by $\mathcal{G}$.

In this section we show two possible ways of defining the inheritance of goals, and the normal forms they lead to.

Definition 5.9 Let $RS = (\Omega, \Delta, dom, M, \mathcal{F} \cup \mathcal{A})$ have a set $\mathcal{G}$ of goals.[7] Decomposing $(RS, \mathcal{G})$ according to $X \stackrel{?}{\twoheadrightarrow} Y \in \mathcal{G}$, for which $\mathcal{F} \cup \mathcal{A} \not\models X \rightarrow Y$ and $\mathcal{F} \cup \mathcal{A} \not\models X \not\twoheadrightarrow Y$, into $(RS_1 = (\Omega, \Delta, dom, M_1, \mathcal{F}_1 \cup \mathcal{A}_1), \mathcal{G}_1)$ and $(RS_2 = (\Omega, \Delta, dom, M_2, \mathcal{F}_2 \cup \mathcal{A}_2), \mathcal{G}_2)$ is called a *horizontal decomposition step* (or *decomposition step* for short.

[7]The goals are in fact a part of the meaning M of the relation, but we prefer to write them explicitly.

The decomposition steps and the (sub)schemes together are called a *decomposition tree.* The "final" subschemes of a decomposition tree together are called a *decomposition.*

□

First we give a "trivial" way to decompose relation schemes (with goals) and we show that it is too simple to be useful.

Definition 5.10 Let $RS = (\Omega, \Delta, dom, M, \mathcal{F} \cup \mathcal{A})$ have a set $\mathcal{G}$ of goals. $(RS, \mathcal{G})$ is called an *atomic (relation) scheme* if for all $X \stackrel{?}{\rightarrow} Y \in \mathcal{G}$, $\mathcal{F} \cup \mathcal{A} \models X \rightarrow Y$ or $\mathcal{F} \cup \mathcal{A} \models X \nrightarrow Y$.

□

Definition 5.11 • A decomposition step in which the whole set of goals $\mathcal{G}$ is (defined to be) inherited by both subschemes (i. e. $\mathcal{G}_1 = \mathcal{G}_2 = \mathcal{G}$) is called a *trivial decomposition step.*

- A decomposition $((RS_1, \mathcal{G}_1), \ldots, (RS_n, \mathcal{G}_n))$ of $(RS, \mathcal{G})$ is said to be a *trivial decomposition* of RS if it is obtained by means of trivial decomposition steps. (This implies that $\mathcal{G}_1 = \ldots = \mathcal{G}_n = \mathcal{G}$.)
- A decomposition $((RS_1, \mathcal{G}_1), \ldots, (RS_n, \mathcal{G}_n))$ of $(RS, \mathcal{G})$ is said to be in *Horizontal Normal Form (HNF)* iff all the $(RS_i, \mathcal{G}_i), i = 1, \ldots, n$, are atomic schemes.

□

Figure 5.2 shows a trivial decomposition step for an arbitrary scheme $(RS, \mathcal{G})$. (the calculation of $\mathcal{A}_1$ and $\mathcal{A}_2$ is described in Section 5.3):

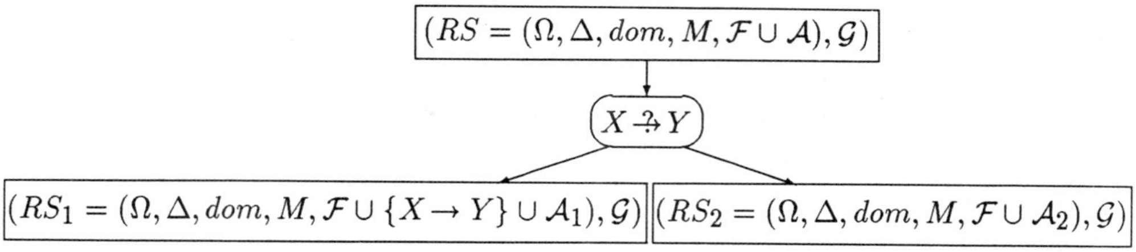

Figure 5.2: A trivial decomposition step.

We now show an example that illustrates how a "bad" choice of goals can make it impossible to obtain a trivial decomposition which is in *HNF* because all decompositions generate "non-atomic" schemes.

Example 5.5 Let a scheme RS have neither fds nor ads, but two goals: $X \stackrel{?}{\rightarrow} Y$ and $Y \stackrel{?}{\rightarrow} X$. Since RS has no constraints, both goals can be used for horizontal decomposition.

Decomposing $(RS, \mathcal{G})$ according to $X \stackrel{?}{\rightarrow} Y$ produces two subschemes: RS_1 with the fd $X \rightarrow Y$ and RS_2 with the ad $X \nrightarrow Y$. Both RS_1 and RS_2 (still having the same set $\mathcal{G}$ of goals) can be decomposed further on using $Y \stackrel{?}{\rightarrow} X$. For RS_1 this produces two atomic subschemes: RS_{11} with $X \rightarrow Y$ and $Y \rightarrow X$,

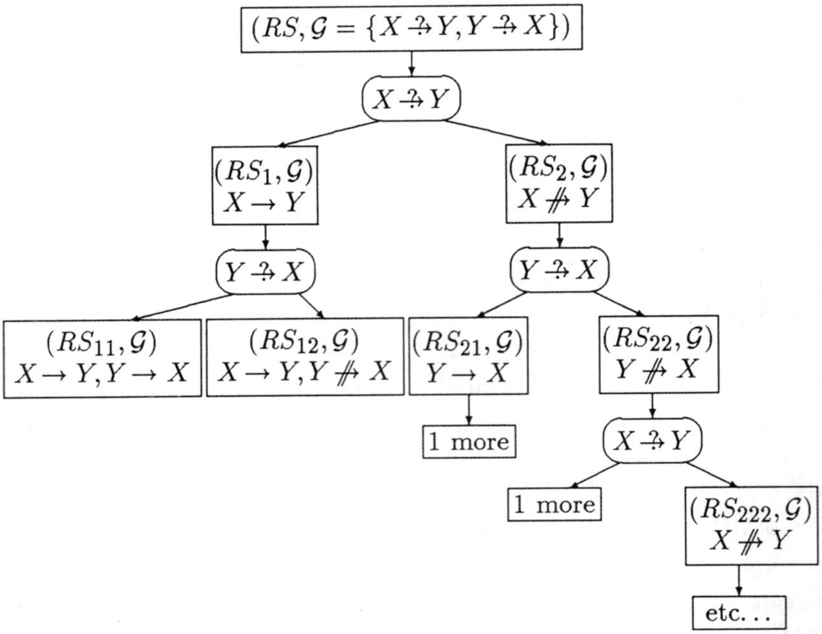

Figure 5.3: Infinite trivial decomposition tree.

and RS_{12} with $X \rightarrow Y$ and $Y \not\twoheadrightarrow X$. For RS_2 the situation is different: if we decompose RS_2 according to $Y \overset{?}{\twoheadrightarrow} X$ the ad $X \not\twoheadrightarrow Y$ is lost. So the resulting subschemes RS_{21} with $Y \rightarrow X$ and RS_{22} with $Y \not\twoheadrightarrow X$ are not atomic: they can be decomposed (again) using $X \overset{?}{\twoheadrightarrow} Y$. One can easily see that this decomposition process can go on for ever: the "rightmost" subrelation $RS_{2\ldots2}$ is never atomic Figure 5.3 shows a decomposition tree from which the effect of losing ads but keeping goals is clear.

□

There are two ways of solving the problem with trivial decomposition steps: since the infinite decomposition is caused by the fact that ads may be lost, but goals are preserved, one can either decide to restrict the decompositions to avoid the loss of ads, or one can define the goals not always to be inherited. Both solutions can be used, and lead to useful decomposition steps and normal forms, described below.

Definition 5.12 • A goal $X \overset{?}{\twoheadrightarrow} Y$ is said to be *clean* iff

1. neither $X \rightarrow Y$ nor $X \not\twoheadrightarrow Y$ holds in RS and
2. all ads of $\mathcal{A}$ are inherited by the decomposition of $(RS, \mathcal{G})$ according to $X \overset{?}{\twoheadrightarrow} Y \in \mathcal{G}$.

- Decomposing $(RS, \mathcal{G})$ according to a clean goal, into $((RS_1, \mathcal{G}), (RS_2, \mathcal{G}))$, is called a *clean decomposition step.* A decomposition $((RS_1, \mathcal{G}), \ldots, (RS_n, \mathcal{G}))$

is said to be a *clean decomposition* of $(RS, \mathcal{G})$ if it is obtained by clean decomposition steps.

- A scheme $(RS, \mathcal{G})$ is called a *clean scheme* iff $\mathcal{G}$ does not contain any clean goal.
- A decomposition $((RS_1, \mathcal{G}_1), \ldots, (RS_n, \mathcal{G}_n))$ is in *Clean Normal Form (CNF)* iff all the $(RS_i, \mathcal{G}_i)$, $i = 1, \ldots, n$, are clean (sub)schemes.
- The decomposition steps and the subschemes together are called a *clean decomposition tree*.

□

Figure 5.4 shows a clean decomposition step for a scheme RS:

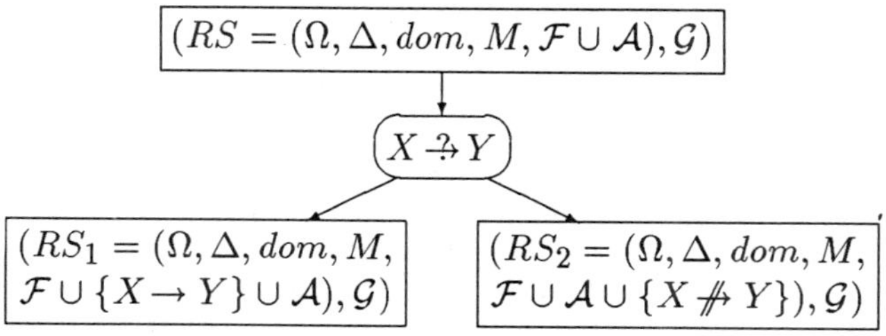

Figure 5.4: A clean decomposition step.

Note that both $\mathcal{F}$ and $\mathcal{A}$ are inherited by the subschemes. This means that clean decomposition steps are *dependency preserving*.

Since no fd or ad can be lost by clean decomposition steps, it is obvious that the clean decomposition into *CNF* cannot produce an infinite number of subschemes. In fact the maximum number of subschemes is $2^{\sharp\mathcal{G}}$. The (sub)schemes of a clean decomposition into *CNF* are not necessarily atomic schemes: there may still be goals which can be used in trivial decomposition steps, but which are not clean.

We now present an example to illustrate the clean decomposition into *CNF*.

Example 5.6 Recall Example 5.1. The scheme *STAYS* satisfies the following fds:

- Every visitor arrives on one day, leaves on one day and has one bill, i. e. *VIS-NUMBER*$\rightarrow$*ARRIV-DATE, LEAV-DATE, BILL.*
- For every room, arrival date and departure date, there is only one visitor, i. e. *ARRIV-DATE, LEAV-DATE, ROOM-STAY*$\rightarrow$ *VIS-NUMBER.*
- Every visitor has only one number of accompanying persons per room, i. e. *VIS-NUMBER, ROOM-STAY*$\rightarrow$*NUMBER-OF-ACCOMP-PERSONS.*

The following fds may or may not hold; since we expect few exceptions we put them in the set of goals $\mathcal{G}$:

- Most visitors have only one room, i. e. *VIS-NUMBER*$\overset{?}{\rightarrow}$ *ROOM-STAY.*

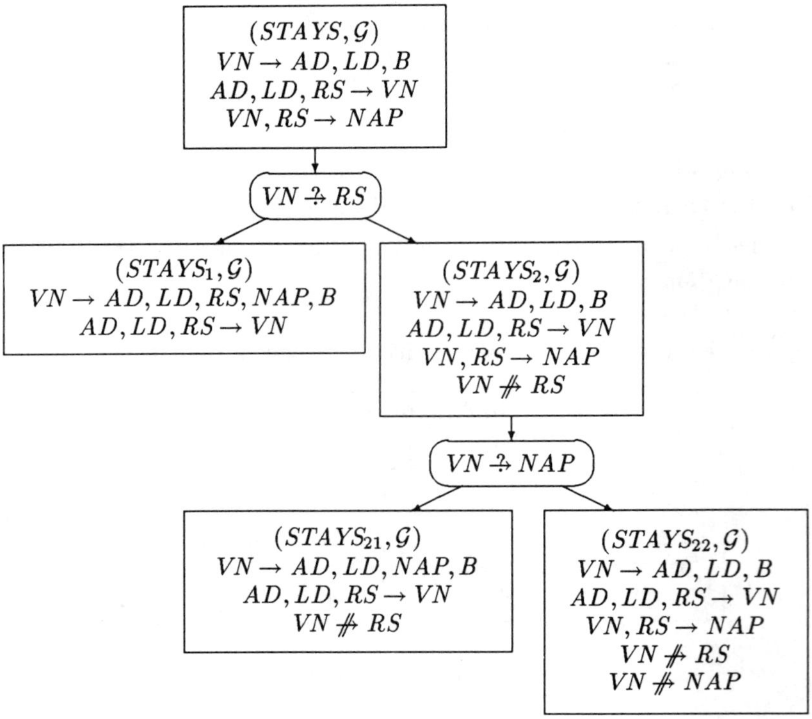

Figure 5.5: Clean decomposition tree for *STAYS*.

- Most visitors have only one number of accompanying persons, i. e. *VIS-NUMBER* $\overset{?}{\rightarrow}$ *NUMBER-OF-ACCOMP-PERSONS*. This could be a real fd if the total number of accompanying persons was written for all the rooms that a visitor has reserved, but if only the actual number of accompanying persons that stay in the room are listed this may not be an fd.

Figure 5.5 shows the decomposition of *STAYS* into *CNF*. To keep the size of the picture reasonable, the attributes have been given shorter names: *VN*, *AD*, *LD*, *RS*, *NAP*, *B*. In the subschemes different fds with the same left-hand side have been written as one fd (which is equivalent) and "redundant" fds have been omitted.

The condition that only clean decomposition steps are allowed is always satisfied, since there are no ads initially, and since both goals have the same left-hand side (*VIS-NUMBER*) (and hence only produce ads with the same left-hand side). (This means that the trivial decomposition of *STAYS* into *HNF* would produce the same result.) This will be the case in most databases, since the main problem is that a nice candidate for "key" of the scheme is not really a key. After the decomposition, *VIS-NUMBER* is a key in $STAYS_1$, which is the (main) part of the relation, containing the visitors with only one room and one number of accompanying persons.

Note also that the number of subrelations is not 2^2 ($2^{\sharp\mathcal{G}}$): after decomposing *STAYS* according to *VIS-NUMBER*$\overset{?}{\not\rightarrow}$*ROOM-STAY* the second goal is useless in $STAYS_1$, since *VIS-NUMBER*$\rightarrow$*NUMBER-OF-ACCOMP-PERSONS* already holds.

If the order in which the goals are used in the decomposition is reversed, an equivalent decomposition is generated (only the names of the subschemes differ; the reader is invited to construct the decomposition tree). In general however, the decomposition strongly depends on the order in which the goals are used. (The subschemes may be different, and even their number may differ.)

The two goals could have been combined into one goal: *VIS-NUMBER*$\overset{?}{\not\rightarrow}$ *ROOM-STAY*, *NUMBER-OF-ACCOMP-PERSONS*, but the decomposition would differ: there would be no subrelation for the visitors with only one number of accompanying persons, but with more than one room.

□

The second alternative for solving the problem with trivial decomposition steps is to define the inheritance of goals differently.

Definition 5.13 Let the scheme $(RS = (\Omega, \Delta, dom, M, \mathcal{F} \cup \mathcal{A}), \mathcal{G})$ be decomposed according to $X \overset{?}{\not\rightarrow} Y \in \mathcal{G}$. A goal $T \overset{?}{\not\rightarrow} U \in \mathcal{G}$ is *inherited* by RS_1 (resp. RS_2) (i. e. is in $\mathcal{G}_1$, resp. $\mathcal{G}_2$) if $\mathcal{F}_1 \not\models T \rightarrow U$ (resp. $\mathcal{F}_2 \not\models T \rightarrow U$) and $\mathcal{F}_1 \cup \mathcal{A}_1 \not\models T \not\twoheadrightarrow U$ (resp. $\mathcal{F}_2 \cup \mathcal{A}_2 \not\models T \not\twoheadrightarrow U$).

□

In particular, the goal $X \overset{?}{\not\rightarrow} Y$ is not inherited by RS_1, nor by RS_2.

When considering this definition of the inheritance of goals, we speak about *inherited decomposition steps*, *inherited decompositions* and *inherited decomposition trees.* When decomposing subschemes only inherited goals can be used.

Figure 5.6 shows an inherited decomposition step for a scheme $(RS, \mathcal{G})$:

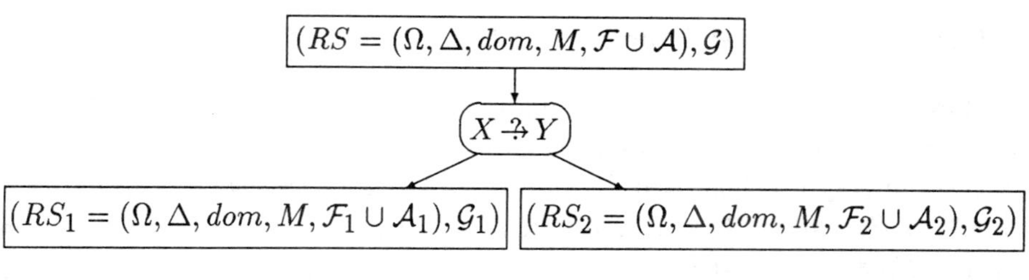

Figure 5.6: An inherited decomposition step.

The inherited decomposition of *STAYS* into *HNF* produces the same result as for *CNF* (if we disregard the obtained sets of goals in the "final" subschemes). In general however this is not the case.

Example 5.7 Recall the scheme $(RS, \mathcal{G})$ of Example 5.5. Figure 5.7 shows a clean decomposition of R into *CNF*, whereas Figure 5.8 shows an inherited decomposition of R into *HNF*. □

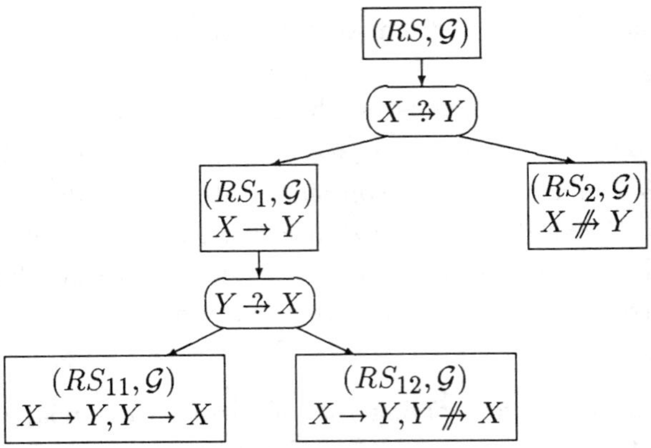

Figure 5.7: Clean decomposition for $(RS, \{X \overset{?}{\rightarrow} Y, Y \overset{?}{\rightarrow} X\})$.

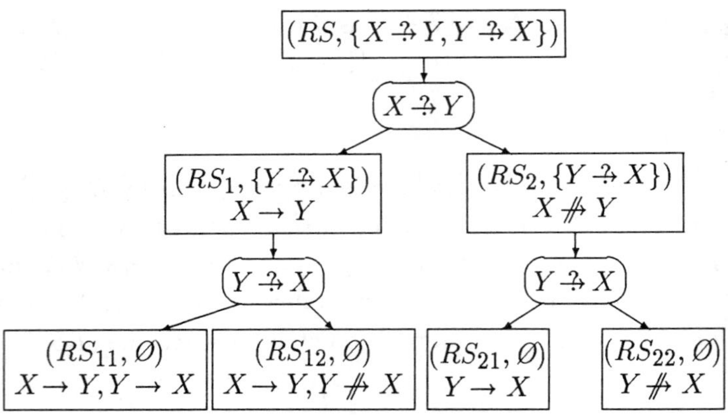

Figure 5.8: Inherited decomposition tree for $(RS, \{X \overset{?}{\rightarrow} Y, Y \overset{?}{\rightarrow} X\})$.

A third possibility for avoiding infinite decompositions is to combine the clean and inherited decomposition steps. One can easily define a *clean inherited decomposition step* (an inherited decomposition step according to a clean goal) and a *Clean Horizontal Normal Form (CHNF)*. The reader is invited to prove that this *CHNF* is equivalent to the *CNF*, or in other words, that goals which are not inherited by the schemes that result from a clean inherited decomposition step can never become clean in the remaining part of the decomposition process.

The relationship between *HNF*, *CNF*, trivial, clean and inherited decompositions is as follows:

- A trivial decomposition into *HNF* is also in *CNF* (if we disregard differences in the sets of goals of the final subrelations). However it may not be possible to generate it using clean decomposition steps.
- An inherited decomposition in *HNF* is also in *CNF* (disregarding goals again). It may not be possible to generate it using clean decomposition steps.
- The schemes obtained by clean decomposition steps can also be obtained using inherited decomposition steps, (disregarding goals again), but the resulting decomposition (in *CNF*) may not (yet) be in *HNF*.

Due to space limitations we cannot discuss the influence of the different normal forms on the possible update algorithms.

5.5 Exercises

5.1 The selection operator $\sigma(RS, X \rightarrow Y)$ does not satisfy the definition given in Chapter 2. Why not?

5.2 Using the notation of Definition 5.2, prove that there is a unique largest X-complete subset of rs in which $X \rightarrow Y$ holds.

5.3 Simulate the selection operator $\sigma(RS, X \rightarrow Y)$ using the relational algebra, the domain calculus and SQL. Do the same for $\sigma(RS, X \not\twoheadrightarrow Y)$.

5.4 Give an (efficient) algorithm for generating $\sigma(rs, X \rightarrow Y)$, and calculate its time-complexity.

5.5 Construct an efficient algorithm to update a relation rs that is decomposed horizontally into $\sigma(rs, X \rightarrow Y)$ and $rs - \sigma(r, X \rightarrow Y)$.

5.6 Consider $\Omega = \{A, B, C\}$ and an instance $rs = \{t \mid 2 \leq t(A), t(B), t(C) \leq 0,$ $t(A)$ is a multiple of $t(B)$ and $t(A) + 1$ is a multiple of $t(C)\}$.
Find rs. Decompose rs into $rs_1 = \sigma(rs, A \rightarrow B)$ and $rs_2 = \sigma(rs, A \not\twoheadrightarrow B)$. Decompose $rs_i, i = 1, 2$ into $rs_{i1} = \sigma(rs_i, C \rightarrow A)$ and $rs_{i2} = \sigma(rs_i, C \not\twoheadrightarrow A)$.

5.7 Prove that the horizontal decomposition of a scheme RS, according to the goal $X \overset{h}{\rightarrow} Y$ is the ordered pair (RS_1, RS_2), where $RS_1 = \sigma(RS, X \rightarrow Y)$ and $RS_2 = \sigma(RS, X \not\twoheadrightarrow Y)$.

5.8 Can a set of fds and ads be contradictory, i.e. such that no set of tuples satisfies all dependencies?

5.9 Find a single constraint that is in contradiction (not just in conflict) with $A \rightarrow B$.

5.10 In Section 5.2 we claimed that $\{X \rightarrow Y, X \not\twoheadrightarrow Y\}$ is an easy example of a set of fds and ads that is in conflict. Find a smaller example.

5.11 Prove or disprove:

- $A \not\twoheadrightarrow B$, $B \rightarrow C$ implies $A \not\twoheadrightarrow C$.
- $A \rightarrow B$, $AB \not\twoheadrightarrow C$ implies $A \not\twoheadrightarrow C$.
- $A \rightarrow B$, $AB \not\twoheadrightarrow C$, $D \rightarrow C$ implies $D \not\twoheadrightarrow B$.
- $A \rightarrow B$, $AB \not\twoheadrightarrow C$, $D \rightarrow C$ implies $D \rightarrow B$.
- $A \not\twoheadrightarrow C$, $B \not\twoheadrightarrow C$ implies $AB \not\twoheadrightarrow C$.
- $AB \not\twoheadrightarrow D$, $BC \not\twoheadrightarrow D$ implies $B \not\twoheadrightarrow D$.

5.12 Let $r_X =$

$\overline{X}$	$\Omega - \overline{X}$
$0_X \ldots 0_X$	$0_X \ldots 0_X$
$0_X \ldots 0_X$	$1_X \ldots 1_X$

Prove that $\bigcup_{X \subseteq \Omega} r_X$ is an Armstrong relation for fds, but not a strong Armstrong relation.

5.13 Let r_1 and r_2 be instances with the same attributes. Let $s_1 = r_1 \cup r_2$, $s_2 = r_1 \cap r_2$, $s_3 = r_1 - r_2$, $s_4 = r_1 \Delta r_2$, $s_5 = r_1 \otimes r_2$, $s_6 = r_1 \boxtimes r_2$, $s_7 = r_1 \overline{\times} r_2$, where

- $r_1 \Delta r_2 = (r_1 - r_2) \cup (r_2 - r_1)$;
- $r_1 \boxtimes r_2 = \{((a_1, b_1), a_2, \ldots, a_n), \ldots, (a_1, \ldots, a_{i-1}, (a_i, b_i), a_{i+1}, \ldots, a_n), \ldots, (a_1, \ldots, a_{n-1}, (a_n, b_n)) \mid (a_1, \ldots, a_n) \in r_1$ and $(b_1, \ldots, b_n) \in r_2$ or $(a_1, \ldots, a_n) \in r_2$ and $(b_1, \ldots, b_n) \in r_1\}$;
- $r_1 \overline{\times} r_2 = \Theta(r_1 \otimes r_2)$, Θ substitutes (a_i, b_i) by a_i if $a_i = b_i$.

Prove or disprove the following 14 facts for an fd f, and for $i = 1, \ldots, 7$:

- if f holds in both r_1 and r_2 then f holds in s_i.
- if f holds in r_1 or r_2 then f holds in s_i.

Prove or disprove the same facts for an ad a.

5.14 Prove Lemma 5.3 (i. e. the inference rules are sound).

5.15 Give a formal proof of Lemma 5.4.

5.16 In Lemma 5.4 a sufficient condition is given for the inheritance of ads. Show that this condition is not necessary, i. e. give an example in which an ad $T \not\twoheadrightarrow U$ holds in both RS_1 and RS_2 although $\mathcal{F} \cup \mathcal{A} \not\models T \not\twoheadrightarrow U$ or $\mathcal{F} \not\models T \rightarrow X$.

5.17 Prove Theorem 5.3.

5.18 Prove that an fd $X \rightarrow Y$ is equivalent to "every X-unique set of tuples (in every instance) is also Y-unique" and also to "every Y-complete set of tuples (in every instance) is also X-complete.

5.19 Prove the remaining case of Theorem 5.4, i. e. the inheritance of ads in RS_2.

5.20 Give a small example of a scheme that leads to decompositions in *CNF* that are not in *HNF*.

5.21 Prove that decompositions that are in *HNF* also are in *CNF*.

5.22 Show that *CNF* and *CHNF* are equivalent.

5.23 Construct an efficient (i. e. polynomial) algorithm for inserting and deleting tuples in a horizontally decomposed relation.

5.24 Consider a scheme *ADDRESSBOOK* with two attributes: *family* and *address*. A family may have several addresses (although most have only one address). An address may be shared by several families, although usually only by one.

Let $\mathcal{G} = \{family \overset{?}{\rightarrow} address, address \overset{?}{\rightarrow} family\}$. Decompose (*ADDRESSBOOK*, $\mathcal{G}$) into *HNF* and *CNF* (using trivial-, clean- and inherited decomposition steps), and describe the meaning of the obtained (sub-) schemes.

Chapter 6

Incomplete Information

In the previous chapters we have usually assumed that tuples are complete, i. e. that a tuple of a relation instance has, for each attribute of the relation scheme, a value of the domain of that attribute. In a "real" database however it is sometimes necessary to insert a new tuple into an instance, although the value of that tuple for some attributes is (still) unknown. In Example 1.10 we said that if a stay is not yet finished, the *LEAV-DATE*-value of a tuple is *unknown*. The definition of a relation instance (Definition 1.4) however does not allow the use of *unknown* unless this is a "normal" element of the domain of the attribute *LEAV-DATE*.

The main concept for handling incomplete information is called the *null value*. Many authors have been using different meanings for null values. Basically, most of them fall into one of the following categories:

1. *existing but unknown* values. These kinds of nulls are used when we know that a value exists, but we don't know what the value is. Everyone has an age for instance, but we may not know some people's age.
2. *non-existing* values. We may have attributes for which a tuple cannot have a value, depending on the values it has for other attributes. For unmarried people for instance the name of their spouse is non-existing.
3. *no-information* nulls. In some cases we do not even know whether there exists a value or not. If we want to record all employee's home phonenumber, some employees may not want to reveal the information whether they have a phone or not.

It can be very difficult to find out what kind of null-values are being used, just from looking at a table. The value *unknown* could mean that we do not know whether or when a visitor has left the hotel, in which case it is a no-information null, but if it means that the visitor has not yet left the hotel then the value for *LEAV-DATE* is actually a non-existing null. The description of Chapter 1 ("If a stay is not finished yet, then the *LEAV-DATE*-value is *unknown*") does not rule out the no-information interpretation, because it does not say what the *LEAV-DATE*-value will be if the visitor has left but we do not know when.

The exact meaning of the kind of null-values being used is important, because the answers to queries and updates depend on that meaning. In most cases a query, when given in "plain" English, must be rephrased in order to produce the expected answer. The question "List all the employees, younger than 40" should result in a reply like "Insufficient data", whereas "List all the employees who for sure are younger than 40" is probably what the user really meant with the first query. Under the "non-existing" interpretation the question "List the names of all spouses" can be answered, whereas under the "no-information" interpretation it cannot.

Even when not using natural language, but operators like the relational algebra, one must redefine these in such a way that they provide the expected result, depending on the meaning of null-values. In fact, the questions given above illustrate the problem of redefining the selection, depending on the meaning of nulls. In the sequel we shall (partially) redefine the relational database theory for the three kinds of nulls. The "existing but unknown" nulls have been discussed by many authors, including Codd [32] and Imieliński and Lipski [66]. "Non-existing" nulls are used mostly in the *weak instance model* defined by Honeyman [65], which is a relaxation of the *universal instance model.* Zaniolo [117] introduced the "no-information" nulls and showed that these null-values, although they contain the least information (none at all) lead to the most straightforward generalization of the relational database model.

The problem of updating databases must also be reconsidered in the presence of null-values. This problem is studied by Abiteboul and Grahne [3] (also among many others). The incompleteness of an update can be of three different natures:

- The database contains null values which may be affected by the update [47, 71].
- The update itself is not completely specified. This is the case for e. g. view updates [13].
- The database scheme may be altered, for instance by adding a new attribute, for which no values have been given (yet), hence leading to no-information nulls [117].

6.1 Representation Systems for Existing-but-Unknown Nulls

In the "existing but unknown" interpretation of null-values, one can argue that since the unknown values exist, we should be able to represent whatever information we have about the unknown values. In particular, we should be able to represent the equality or inequality of two null-values, but possibly even more specific information. In the literature three representation systems have been studied thoroughly, which we shall examine in this section.

The first representation system is based on tables with the so called Codd null values @. We call them *Codd tables.* They use only one null value to represent all missing values. Figure 6.1 shows an example of a Codd table.

VIS-NUMBER	*ARRIV-DATE*	*LEAV-DATE*	*ROOM-STAY*	*NUMBER-OF-ACCOMP-PERSONS*	*BILL*
101	Jul 01	Jul 15	205	1	10000
102	Aug 01	@	310	2	3000
105	Jul 01	@	401	4	12000
105	Jul 01	@	402	4	12000

Figure 6.1: Codd table for *stays*.

This table represents the information that the *LEAV-DATE* of visitors 102 and 105 is unknown. However, it is not possible to express that visitor 105 will vacate rooms 401 and 402 at the same time. The second representation system, called *V-tables* allows many different "marked" null values. The table for *stays* then becomes Figure 6.2.

VIS-NUMBER	*ARRIV-DATE*	*LEAV-DATE*	*ROOM-STAY*	*NUMBER-OF-ACCOMP-PERSONS*	*BILL*
101	Jul 01	Jul 15	205	1	10000
102	Aug 01	x	310	2	3000
105	Jul 01	y	401	4	12000
105	Jul 01	y	402	4	12000

Figure 6.2: V-table for *stays*.

The table contains different symbols, x and y in our example, to indicate different null-values. Using y twice means that visitor 105 will vacate rooms 401 and 402 at the same (but still unknown) time.

A very desirable property of V-tables is that all relational operators on V-tables are performed in exactly the same way as in the case of relations without null-values, treating variables as if they were regular elements of the attribute domains. This is often referred to as *naive evaluation*, and the tables are also called *naive tables.*

Both Codd tables and V-tables have severe limitations. We shall show that Codd tables cannot support projection and join at the same time, whereas V-tables cannot support projection and (arbitrary) selection at the same time. A third representation system, which overcomes these restrictions, is the *conditional table*, or *C-table* for short. It is a V-table, with an additional column, *con*, containing a condition. Figure 6.3 shows an example of a C-table.

This table represents the fact that visitor 105 will get room 401 if visitor 102

VIS-NUMBER	*ARRIV-DATE*	*LEAV-DATE*	*ROOM-STAY*	*NOAC*	*BILL*	con
101	Jul 01	Jul 15	205	1	10000	
102	Aug 01	x	401	2	3000	
105	Jul 01	y	401	4	12000	$x <$ Aug 01
105	Jul 01	y	402	4	12000	$x \geq$ Aug 01

Figure 6.3: C-table for *stays*.

leaves before August 1 and room 402 otherwise. (In either case visitor 105 gets only one room.)

C-tables have nicer properties than the other two representation systems, but they are difficult to implement. Therefore they are mainly of theoretical interest. Some authors use not only conditions for each tuple, but also some "global" conditions.

The *selection* operator, defined in Chapter 2, allows for arbitrary computable functions on tuples. In the sequel we call this *general selection.* We shall only use the equality test for attributes (written $A = B$ for instance), combined with the logical connectives $\vee$, $\wedge$ and $\neg$. If the expression of a selection does not contain $\neg$ we call it a *positive* selection.

To simplify the terminology, we use one-letter abbreviations to indicate the kind of operators that occur in a relational algebraic expression. We use P for projection, S for selection, S^+ for positive selection, J for join, U for union, D for difference and R for renaming. A *relational β-expression* is a well-formed expression using the operators of β only. For instance, $\sigma(r_1; A = a) \bowtie \Pi(r_2; B, C)$ is a relational PS^+J-expression.

For the representation of incomplete information we need to extend relations with null-values. We call them *tables.* Whenever we use the term instance or relation we refer to relations without null values. A table in fact represents a (possibly infinite) set of instances. We use the symbol $\Im$ to denote the set of all sets of instances over the same set of attributes. We use boldface characters to denote tables.

Definition 6.1 A *representation system* is a triple $\langle \mathcal{I}, Rep, \beta \rangle$, where $\mathcal{I}$ is a set of *tables*, *Rep* is a mapping, $Rep : \mathcal{I} \rightarrow \Im$ and β is a set of relational operators. The three components of a representation system must satisfy an additional condition, which we will not describe formally. Intuitively, it means that *Rep* must be chosen in such a way that for every relational β-expression f and every table $\mathbf{T}$ it is possible to define a table $f(\mathbf{T})$ such that $Rep(f(\mathbf{T}))$ and $f(Rep(\mathbf{T}))$ are in a sense equivalent with respect to β.

□

This equivalence of two tables is defined as follows:

Definition 6.2 Let f be a relational expression and $\mathcal{X} \in \Im$. The *f-information* in $\mathcal{X}$, denoted $\mathcal{X}^f$ is $\bigcap f(\mathcal{X})$. $\mathcal{X}$ and $\mathcal{Y}$ are *β-equivalent*, denoted $\mathcal{X} \equiv_\beta \mathcal{Y}$, if $\mathcal{X}^f = \mathcal{Y}^f$ for any β-expression f. A table $\mathbf{T}$ is said to *β-represent* $\mathcal{X}$ if $Rep(\mathbf{T}) \equiv_\beta \mathcal{X}$.

□

We now return to the three representation systems, described earlier.

Theorem 6.1 *Any $\mathcal{X} \in \Im$ can be P-represented by a Codd table* [66].
Proof Let $\mathcal{X}$ have a set of attributes X, let $Y \subset X$. Let $Q(Y)$ be obtained from $\mathcal{X}^{\Pi_Y}$ by extending every tuple $t \in \mathcal{X}^{\Pi_Y}$ with @s to an @-tuple (a tuple with @s) $\bar{t}$ on X. Let $\mathbf{T} = \bigcup_{Y \subset X} Q(Y)$. We have to prove that $Rep(\mathbf{T}) \equiv_P \mathcal{X}$, where $Rep(\mathbf{T}) = \{r$ (instance over X) : for every $t \in \mathbf{T}$ there is $t' \in r$ such that for all $A \in X : t[A] = @$ or $t[A] = t'[A]\}$.

Consider an arbitrary $Y \subset X$. If $t \in \mathcal{X}^{\Pi_Y}$, then clearly $\mathbf{T}$ contains a @-tuple t' that agrees with t on Y, and consequently every $r \in Rep(\mathbf{T})$ contains a tuple u that agrees with t on Y; hence $t \in Rep(\mathbf{T})^{\Pi_Y}$. Conversely, assume that $t \notin \mathcal{X}^{\Pi_Y}$, for a tuple t over Y. Then no @-tuple in $\mathbf{T}$ agrees with t on Y, and hence there exists a relation $r \in Rep(\mathbf{T})$ not containing any tuple agreeing with t on Y. Hence $t \notin Rep(\mathbf{T})^{\Pi_Y}$.

□

From the above theorem we can easily deduce:

Corollary 6.1 *Any two P-equivalent Codd tables are Rep-equivalent (where Rep is defined as above).*

□

The S-equivalence for Codd tables is somewhat easier to prove.

Theorem 6.2 *For any $\mathcal{X}, \mathcal{Y} \in \Im$ (with the same set of attributes X), $\mathcal{X} \equiv_S \mathcal{Y}$ iff $\mathcal{X} \equiv_\emptyset \mathcal{Y}$.*
Proof Let $f(r) = \sigma(r; E)$ be an arbitrary relational S-expression (where r has X as set of attributes). $\mathcal{X} \equiv_\emptyset \mathcal{Y}$ is (trivially) equivalent with $\bigcap \mathcal{X} = \bigcap \mathcal{Y}$, and $\sigma(r; E)$ can be expressed as $r \cap \sigma(\mathbf{1_X}; E)$, where $\mathbf{1}_X = \times_{A \in X} dom(A)$. Hence

$$\begin{aligned} \mathcal{X}^f = \bigcap_{r\in\mathcal{X}} \sigma(r;E) &= \bigcap_{r\in\mathcal{X}} (r \cap \sigma(\mathbf{1}_X;E)) = \sigma(\mathbf{1}_X;E) \cap \bigcap_{r\in\mathcal{X}} (r) = \\ &= \sigma(\mathbf{1}_X;E) \cap \bigcap_{r\in\mathcal{Y}} (r) = \bigcap_{r\in\mathcal{Y}} (r \cap \sigma(\mathbf{1}_X;E)) = \bigcap_{r\in\mathcal{Y}} \sigma(r;E) = \mathcal{Y}^f, \end{aligned}$$

which implies $\mathcal{X} \equiv_S \mathcal{Y}$.

□

Clearly, by Theorem 6.2, $\mathcal{X} \equiv_P \mathcal{Y}$ implies $\mathcal{X} \equiv_S \mathcal{Y}$. However, the PS-equivalence is not the same as the P-equivalence, as shown by the following example:

Example 6.1 Let $\mathcal{X} = \{\{abc'\}, \{ab'c\}\}$, $\mathcal{Y} = \{\{abc\}, \{ab'c'\}\}$ be sets of two instances, each with only one tuple. We have $\mathcal{X} \equiv_P \mathcal{Y}$ since both $\mathcal{X}$ and $\mathcal{Y}$ can be P-represented by $T = \{a@@\}$. Hence also $\mathcal{X} \equiv_S \mathcal{Y}$. But $\mathcal{X} \not\equiv_{PS} \mathcal{Y}$

since for the PS-expression $f(r) = \Pi(\sigma(r; (B = b) \wedge (C = c)); A)$ we have $\mathcal{X}^f = \{a\} \neq \emptyset = \mathcal{Y}^f$.

In other words, $\mathcal{X}$ and $\mathcal{Y}$ cannot be distinguished by P-expressions or S-expressions, but they are distinguishable by PS-expressions.

□

We now turn to the main property of Codd tables:

Theorem 6.3 *It is possible to correctly evaluate PS-expressions over Codd tables* [66].

Proof We omit the proof, but we show how to construct f such that $Rep(f(\mathbf{T})) \equiv_{PS} f(Rep(\mathbf{T}))$. We define $f(\mathbf{T})$ inductively by using the following rules:

- $\Pi(\mathbf{T}; Y) = \{t[Y] : t \in \mathbf{T}\}$,
- $\sigma(\mathbf{T}; E) = \{t \in \mathbf{T} : E_*(t) = true\}$,

where

- $E_*(t) = true$ if $E(u)$ for every u which is t with @s replaced by arbitrary values of the domain,
- $E_*(t) = false$ otherwise.

□

Theorem 6.3 is the only positive result about Codd tables. A number of representations are not possible:

Theorem 6.4 *It is not possible to correctly evaluate PSU-expressions over Codd tables. It is also not possible to correctly evaluate PJ-expressions over Codd tables.*

□

We do not prove the above theorem. A proof can be found in [66]. For the PJ-expressions for instance, one can show that if $\mathbf{T} = \{a@c, a'@c'\}$ with $a \neq a'$ and $c \neq c'$, one cannot find a Codd table $\mathbf{U}$ which PJ-represents $\Pi(r; AC) \bowtie \Pi(r; B)$.

Let us now consider the case of V-tables. The problem with the Codd tables, that we were not able to represent the information that two occurrences of @ should represent the same (unknown) value indicates that it may be possible to correctly evaluate joins with V-tables. The positive result is:

Theorem 6.5 *It is possible to correctly evaluate PS^+UJ-expressions over V-tables.*

□

The complicated proof is omitted. The evaluation of PS^+UJ-expressions over V-tables treats the null-values *exactly the same way* as normal elements of the attribute domains. The proof that this simple method of evaluating PS^+UJ-expressions gives correct results is not trivial at all [66], and is based on the properties of C-tables.

A negative result about V-tables is:

Theorem 6.6 *It is not possible to correctly evaluate PS-expressions over V-tables.*

Proof We only give the general idea: consider the V-table $\mathbf{T}$:

A	B	C
a	y	c
a'	y	c

and consider the PS-expression (in fact only an S-expression) $f(r) = \sigma(r; (A = a) \wedge (B = b) \vee (A = a') \wedge (B \neq b))$. There is no V-table $\mathbf{U}$ PS-representing $f(Rep(\mathbf{T}))$.

□

The most powerful representation system are the *C-tables*. Rather than proving the main result we will give a non-trivial example to show how they can be used.

Theorem 6.7 *It is possible to correctly evaluate PSUJ-expressions over C-tables.*

□

Example 6.2 Let us evaluate $f(r) = \sigma(\Pi(\Pi(r; AB) \bowtie \Pi(r; BC); AC); C = c)$ over the following C-table $\mathbf{T}$:

A	B	C	con
a	b	z	$z \neq c$
a	y	c	$y \neq b$
x	b	c	$x \neq a$

The projection is executed by simply removing the attributes that are projected out. The join is executed as follows: the tuples are joined by taking the first tuple and completing it with attribute values of the second; the conditions are taken together, and an additional condition expresses the join. The join of $\{a, b, z \neq c\}$ and $\{y, c, y \neq b\}$ becomes $\{a, b, c, (z \neq c) \wedge (y \neq b) \wedge (b = y)\}$. We have $\mathbf{U} = \Pi(\mathbf{T}; AB) \bowtie \Pi(\mathbf{T}; BC) =$

A	B	C	con
a	b	z	$(z \neq c) \wedge (z \neq c) \wedge (b = b)$
a	b	c	$(z \neq c) \wedge (y \neq b) \wedge (b = y)$
a	b	c	$(z \neq c) \wedge (x \neq a) \wedge (b = b)$
a	y	z	$(y \neq b) \wedge (z \neq c) \wedge (y = b)$
a	y	c	$(y \neq b) \wedge (y \neq b) \wedge (y = y)$
a	y	c	$(y \neq b) \wedge (x \neq a) \wedge (y = b)$
x	b	z	$(x \neq a) \wedge (z \neq c) \wedge (b = b)$
x	b	c	$(x \neq a) \wedge (y \neq b) \wedge (b = y)$
x	b	c	$(x \neq a) \wedge (x \neq a) \wedge (b = b)$

After removing impossible tuples (such as those with a condition $y = b$ and also $y \neq b$) and redundant conditions we obtain

A	B	C	*con*
a	b	z	$(z \neq c)$
a	b	c	$(z \neq c) \wedge (x \neq a)$
a	y	c	$(y \neq b)$
x	b	z	$(x \neq a) \wedge (z \neq c)$
x	b	c	$(x \neq a)$

After the projection $\mathbf{W} = \Pi(\mathbf{U}; AC)$ we obtain

A	C	*con*
a	z	$(z \neq c)$
a	c	$(z \neq c) \wedge (x \neq a)$
a	c	$(y \neq b)$
x	z	$(x \neq a) \wedge (z \neq c)$
x	c	$(x \neq a)$

For the selection we add the condition of the selection. $\sigma(\mathbf{W}; C = c)$ then becomes

A	C	*con*
a	z	$(z \neq c) \wedge (z = c)$
a	c	$(y \neq b)(z \neq c) \wedge (x \neq a) \wedge (z = c)$
a	c	$(y \neq b) \wedge (z = c)$
x	z	$(x \neq a) \wedge (z \neq c) \wedge (z = c)$
x	c	$(x \neq a) \wedge (z = c)$

This is finally simplified to

A	C	*con*
a	c	$(y \neq b)$
x	c	$(x \neq a)$

□

6.2 Updating Relations with Existing-but-Unknown Nulls

A database instance with null-values is in fact a notation for a set of possible database instances. As such, updates can be viewed as mappings from sets of instances to sets of instances. We present some large classes of updates based on classical operations on sets. Some of them (e. g. deletion and insertion) are generalizations of updates on relations without null-values. Other updates are more closely related to the concept of incompleteness of information. In particular, we introduce new updates like *integration*, *subjection*, *negative subjection* and *augmentation* [3].

Definition 6.3 An *elementary condition* over r is an expression of the form $A = a$ or $A \neq a$, where A is an attribute of r and $a \in dom(A)$. A *condition* is a conjunction of elementary conditions. A tuple *satisfies* a condition F if the condition evaluates to true when each attribute A appearing in F is substituted by $t[A]$.

An *insertion* on r is an expression $ins(F)$, where F is a condition specifying a complete tuple t (i. e. R lists values for all attributes of r). The *result* of performing an insertion on an instance r is defined by: $ins(F)(r) = r \cup t$.

A *deletion* on r is an expression $del(F)$, where F is a condition (over attributes of r). The *result* of performing a deletion on an instance r is defined by $del(F)(r) = r - \{t : t \text{ satisfies } F\}$.

A *modification* on r is an expression $mod(F; F')$, where F and F' are conditions, the latter not containing inequalities. The *result* of a modification on an instance r is such that the condition F selects the tuples to be updated, and F' lists new values for some of the attributes.

□

$mod((\mathit{VIS\text{-}NUMBER} = 102) \wedge (\mathit{ROOM\text{-}STAY} = 401); \mathit{ROOM\text{-}STAY} = 400)$ for instance, moves visitor 102 from room 401 to room 400.

For the updates on tables (i. e. instances with null values), we use some set operations, which we have not met before. Let $\mathcal{X}$ and $\mathcal{Y}$ be sets of instances.

- *Pairwise union*: $\mathcal{X}(\cup)\mathcal{Y} = \{r \cup r' : r \in \mathcal{X} \textit{ and } r' \in \mathcal{Y}\}$.
- *Pairwise intersection*: $\mathcal{X}(\cap)\mathcal{Y} = \{r \cap r' : r \in \mathcal{X} \textit{ and } r' \in \mathcal{Y}\}$.
- *Pairwise difference*: $\mathcal{X}(-)\mathcal{Y} = \{r - r' : r \in \mathcal{X} \textit{ and } r' \in \mathcal{Y}\}$.

The classical operations can be generalized in a straightforward way to tables. Since a table represents a set of possible instances, inserting a tuple is generalized to inserting the tuple in all of these possible instances for instance. The situation becomes more complicated when the update itself is incompletely specified. Inserting a tuple with null values then is translated into combining every possible value of the tuple with every possible instance.

The updates on tables are:

Definition 6.4 Let $\mathcal{X}$ and $\mathcal{Y}\ldots$ be sets of instances.

- The *general insertion* of $\mathcal{Y}$ into $\mathcal{X}$ is the pairwise union $\mathcal{X}(\cup)\mathcal{Y}$.
- The *general deletion* of $\mathcal{Y}$ from $\mathcal{X}$ is the pairwise difference $\mathcal{X}(-)\mathcal{Y}$.
- The *integration* of $\mathcal{X}$ and $\mathcal{Y}$ is the pairwise intersection $\mathcal{X}(\cap)\mathcal{Y}$.
- The *subjection* of $\mathcal{X}$ and $\mathcal{Y}$ is the intersection $\mathcal{X} \cap \mathcal{Y}$.
- The *negative subjection* of $\mathcal{X}$ and $\mathcal{Y}$ is the difference $\mathcal{X} - \mathcal{Y}$.
- The *augmentation* of $\mathcal{X}$ with $\mathcal{Y}$ is the union $\mathcal{X} \cup \mathcal{Y}$.
- The *modification* is similar to that for instances.

□

The meaning of the *(general) insertion* and *deletion* is clear. The *integration* means that the knowledge contained in the databases $\mathcal{X}$ and $\mathcal{Y}$ is integrated into one database by taking the tuples common to a possible state in $\mathcal{X}$ and a possible state in $\mathcal{Y}$ as one possible state of the new database.

The *subjection* means that we keep only those instances of $\mathcal{X}$ that are also in $\mathcal{Y}$. The name subjection means that the set of possible states are subjected to be among the states in $\mathcal{Y}$.

The *negative subjection* means that we know that the possible states of $\mathcal{X}$ are subjected not to be among the states in $\mathcal{Y}_1$.

The *augmentation* means that we know that the instances of $\mathcal{X}$ and of $\mathcal{Y}$ are possible, so all possible instances are those in $\mathcal{X}$ or in $\mathcal{Y}$.

The reader may have noted the resemblance between the subjection update and dependency enforcement. Indeed, a subjection restricts the possible instances to be among the instances of $\mathcal{Y}$. An important difference however is that a subjection update is satisfied only immediately after it is applied, whereas constraints are generally considered to be time independent. To impose a set of dependencies $\mathcal{G}$ on $\mathcal{X}$, one takes the subjection of $sat(\mathcal{G})$ on $\mathcal{X}$, where $sat(\mathcal{G})$ is the set of complete instances satisfying $\mathcal{G}$. This set of instances is guaranteed to exist for *equality generating dependencies with constants* [20].

So far we have considered the databases to be updated as sets of possible instances. For practical use it is necessary to represent these sets by tables. It is not obvious how to translate the updates on sets of instances into updates on tables, and here again not all updates can be translated for all three representation systems. We only give some results, and then illustrate the update problems with a non-trivial example.

Theorem 6.8

- *It is possible to use the relational algebra and all update operations with C-tables.*
- *It is possible to use projection, positive selection, union, join, renaming, insertion, integration and subjection by positive dependencies without constants with V-tables.*
- *It is not possible to use positive selection, projection and deletion (even with complete conditions) with V-tables.*
- *It is not possible to use positive selection, projection and modification (even with complete conditions) with V-tables.*
- *It is not possible to use positive selection, projection and augmentation with V-tables.*
- *It is not possible to use positive selection, projection and subjection with V-tables.*
- *It is possible to use projection, selection, insertion, integration and deletion with complete conditions with Codd tables.*
- *It is not possible to use selection and modification (even with complete conditions) with Codd tables.*
- *It is not possible to use selection and subjection with Codd tables.*
- *It is not possible to use selection and augmentation with Codd tables.*

□

Example 6.3 Recall Example 1.10. The only *unknown* value mentioned in Chapter 1 is the *LEAV-DATE* for visitors who have not yet left. However, in a more realistic approach, many more values will sometimes be unknown, as we have seen in Figure 6.3. Figure 6.4 shows another example, which represents the table *stays* on July 17, .

VIS-NB	*ARRIV-DATE*	*LEAV-DATE*	*ROOM-STAY*	*NOAC*	*BILL*	con $(y_2 = 0) \wedge (z_3 = 0) \wedge$ $(x_2 \geq 3000) \wedge$ $(x_1 \geq \text{Jul } 20) \wedge$ $(y_1 \geq \text{Aug } 10) \wedge$ $(z_1 \geq \text{Jul } 17)$
101	Jul 01	Jul 15	205	1	10000	
102	Jul 15	x_1	401	2	x_2	
106	z_1	z_2	401	2	z_3	$(z_2 \geq z_1) \wedge$ $(x_1 < z_1)$
106	z_1	z_2	402	2	z_3	$(z_2 \geq z_1) \wedge$ $(x_1 \geq z_1)$
105	Aug 01	y_1	401	4	y_2	$(x_1 < \text{Aug } 01) \wedge$ $(z_2 < \text{Aug } 01)$
105	*Aug*01	y_1	302	4	y_2	$(x_1 \geq \text{Aug } 01) \vee$ $(z_2 \geq \text{Aug } 01)$

Figure 6.4: *C*-table for *stays* on July 17.

This table can be interpreted as follows:

- The tuple concerning visitor 101 is completely known.
- Visitor 102 has arrived on July 15, has reserved until July 20 (but he may possibly leave later) and has a non-final bill of 3000.
- Visitor 106 was due to arrive, but has currently not shown up. If he arrives, his *LEAV-DATE* will be later than his *ARRIV-DATE* of course. His bill is currently 0 but is not yet final. He will get room 401 if visitor 102 leaves before 106 arrives, otherwise he will get room 402.
- Visitor 105 will arrive on August 1, and has reserved until August 10. His non-final bill is still 0. He will get room 401 if both visitors 102 and 106 have left before August 1, otherwise he will get room 302.

The reader who has got some experience with hotels will note that this kind of information is indeed the kind that hotels usually have available. People request a room if it is free, otherwise they have a second preference. If that is not free either they may have a third choice, etc. The information about the bill is usually only a guess (except when you leave). And finally, some people show up late, or not at all.

Now let us follow the evolution of this table, as time goes by. Suppose visitor 102 leaves on July 20, as expected, and visitor 106 arrives on July 21 and indicates he will stay until August 5. The table then may look like Figure 6.5. Note that

VIS-NB	*ARRIV-DATE*	*LEAV-DATE*	*ROOM-STAY*	*NOAC*	*BILL*	con $(y_2 = 0) \wedge (z_3 \geq 100) \wedge$ $(y_1 \geq \text{Aug } 10) \wedge$ $(z_2 \geq \text{Aug } 05)$
101	Jul 01	Jul 15	205	1	10000	
102	Jul 15	Jul 20	401	2	7000	
106	Jul 21	z_2	401	2	z_3	
105	Aug 01	y_1	401	4	y_2	$(z_2 < \text{Aug } 01)$
105	Aug 01	y_1	302	4	y_2	$(z_2 \geq \text{Aug } 01)$

Figure 6.5: C-table for *stays* on July 21.

we have not deleted the second tuple containing visitor 105. Otherwise we would lose the information that he prefers room 401, should visitor 106 decide to leave earlier. It is only when information becomes complete that tuples can be deleted. Indeed one of two contradictory conditions can be denied later on, even without making the information complete.

Suppose now that visitor 106 leaves the hotel early, on July 25. The table could then become figure 6.3. Visitor 105 now definitely gets room 401.

VIS-NB	*ARRIV-DATE*	*LEAV-DATE*	*ROOM-STAY*	*NOAC*	*BILL*	con $(y_2 = 0) \wedge$ $(y_1 \geq \text{Aug } 10) \wedge$
101	Jul 01	Jul 15	205	1	10000	
102	Jul 15	Jul 20	401	2	7000	
106	Jul 21	Jul 25	401	2	9000	
105	Aug 01	y_1	401	4	y_2	

Figure 6.6: C-table for *stays* on July 25.

□

6.3 Constraints in Incomplete Databases

In the previous section we have shown that some constraints can be expressed as conditions in a C-table. However, constraints should be time independent, which is not the case with subjection updates.

The most important use of constraints in a database with nulls is to eliminate null values. We will only consider constraints with Codd tables and V-tables. With C-tables the use of constraints leads to severe complications. In Figure 6.4

for instance we have that a room is never assigned to 2 visitors for the same day, and also, every visitor has only one room. Because of the complicated conditions, these constraints are not at all easy to verify.

Apart from using constraints to eliminate nulls, one can define new constraints that limit the use of nulls. One can forbid null-values for certain attributes, and one can require that if a tuple is non-null for some attribute it should also be non-null for some other attribute.

Definition 6.5 Let $\mathbf{T}$ be a table for R (Codd table or V-table), and let $\mathcal{F}$ be a set of fds for R. The table $\mathbf{T}$ is *permissible* with respect to $\mathcal{F}$ if some completion r of $\mathbf{T}$ satisfies $\mathcal{F}$. (A completion is an instance, obtained by replacing null values in $\mathbf{T}$ by elements of the domain of the corresponding attribute). A completion that satisfies $\mathcal{F}$ is a *permissible completion* under $\mathcal{F}$.

□

In order to test permissibility, we will fill in (i. e. replace by elements of the domain) as many nulls as possible, using information given by the fds. Consider the fd $X \rightarrow A$. Let t_1 and t_2 be two tuples in $\mathbf{T}$ such that $t_1[X]$ and $t_2[X]$ are equal and *definite*, i. e. they do not contain nulls. If $t_1[A] = @$ and $t_2[A] = a$ then we change $t_1[A]$ to a, since in any permissible completion of $\mathbf{T}$, $t_1[A]$ must be a to satisfy $X \rightarrow A$. This replacement rule is correct, but does not go far enough to detect whether a permissible completion exists or not. This is only possible with V-tables, but of course every Codd table can be easily converted to a V-table by giving all null-values different names.

Definition 6.6 Let $\mathbf{T}$ be a V-table for R, let $X \rightarrow A$ be an fd for R, and let t_1 and t_2 be tuples in $\mathbf{T}$ that agree on X. If t_1 and t_2 are both non-null on A, but $t_1[A] \neq t_2[A]$ then $\mathbf{T}$ has a *hard violation* of $X \rightarrow A$. If $t_1[A] \neq t_2[A]$ but at least one is null, then $\mathbf{T}$ has a *soft violation* of $X \rightarrow A$. Hard violations cannot be removed by filling in nulls, but soft violations can.

□

Assume all null values are x_i, for some number i. (We use this notation to be able to impose an order on the null values.) The fill-in rules for (marked) nulls then become:

1. If $t_1[A] = x_i$ and $t_2[A]$ is definite, change every occurrence of x_i in $\mathbf{T}$ to $t_2[A]$.
2. If $t_1[A] = x_i$ and $t_2[A] = x_j$ and $i \leq j$, change every occurrence of x_j to x_i.

The repeated application of these fill-in rules is very similar to the chase for tableaux. The values of the domains correspond to the distinguished variables and the null-values correspond to the undistinguished variables. A V-table however may have several different null-values in the same column, whereas a tableau may not.

The reader is invited to prove the following result:

Theorem 6.9 *A V-table* $\mathbf{T}$ *has a permissible completion under* $\mathcal{F}$ *iff the table which results from the exhaustive application of the fill-in rules does not have a hard violation of any fd of* $\mathcal{F}$.

□

An easy constraint on the use of nulls is the restriction that nulls are forbidden in the attributes of the primary key of a relation. This is usually necessary in order to be able to get complete answers to some queries. It does not seem very useful to give the database the information that "someone has left the hotel on July 16, but we do not know who".

Apart from this constraint, it is also wise to prevent null values from occurring in different columns at the same time.

Definition 6.7 An *existence constraint* is a statement of the form $X \searrow Y$ (read "X requires Y"). It means that if for a tuple t in the table $\mathbf{T}$ $t[X]$ is definite, then $t[Y]$ must be definite too.

□

The existence constraints are constraints which can be verified on each tuple separately. Indeed, a table satisfies an existence constraint if all its tuples satisfy this constraint. Although this is very different from the behavior of fds, the existence constraints have the same inference rules as fds.

While the verification of existence constraints is easy (both statically and after an update) there is some interaction between existence constraints and fds: when fds are used to fill nulls, inserting a tuple which satisfies the existence constraints, and such that the table still satisfies the fds after the insertion, filling nulls may cause some existence constraints to fail. This is just one example of the many open problems regarding incomplete databases with existing-but-unknown nulls.

6.4 Relations with No-Information Nulls

So far we have been trying to express as much knowledge about unknown values as possible. This is basically a good idea, since we want to keep the information as complete as possible. But the previous sections show that it is very difficult to answer queries correctly and to keep the database in a consistent state after updates. One of the problems with this approach is that we can disguise trivial selections, by using tautologies.

Zaniolo [117] has approached the introduction of null-values from the other end, by considering null-values which contain no information, i. e. nothing is known about the value, not even its existence. With existing-but-unknown values there always is the problem of detecting whether a null-value satisfies the conditions in a query, such as "List all the visitor numbers of visitors who leave no later than July 15, or who leave after July 15", because like in this query, the condition is a tautology and hence satisfied by all (including the unknown) values. Detecting tautologies is very difficult, and should not be necessary in a query answering system, and in fact, if we assume that *unknown* does not mean a *LEAV-DATE* exists (meaning that the visitor will eventually leave the hotel), then we cannot answer the query altogether, unless the question is rephrased as "List all the visitor numbers of visitors who for sure leave no later than July 15, or who leave after July 15", in which case one gets all the visitors with a known *LEAV-DATE* without having to realize that the condition is a tautology.

This approach has an immediate advantage: if we want to add an attribute *VIS-PHONE* to the relation *VISITORS* we can start by giving every visitor a "null" phone number. Under the no-information interpretation these nulls add no information to the relation, so it is harmless to introduce them here. It is not possible to complete the relation instance with existing-but-unknown null-values, because this would add information which (presumably) is not available at the time the relation is augmented with the extra attribute. So although the no-information nulls are much less expressive than existing-but-unknown nulls they can be useful in very basic situations where even the most complicated null-values (like in C-tables) cannot be used. We shall rebuild the relational database model (partially) and show that with the no-information nulls most relational operators can be easily generalized to relations with nulls.

In the sequel we shall denote the no-information null-value by **ni**, when it appears in text, and by "$-$" when it appears in tables, to be consistent with the notation of [117].

Definition 6.8 An X-value s is said to be *more informative* than a Y-value t if for each $B \in Y$, if $t[B] \neq \mathbf{ni}$ then $B \in X$ and $s[B] = t[B]$. If s and t are (whole) tuples we write $s \geq t$ to denote that s is more informative than t, which means that s must match t in each non-null value of t. If $s \geq t$ we also write $t \leq s$, and if $s \geq t$ and $t \geq s$ we say that s and t are *(information-wise) equivalent* and write $s \equiv t$.

□

Note that we can use different domains for s and t in the previous definition: consider the following tuples (some of which could appear in an instance of *VISITORS*, others have the extra *VIS-PHONE*):

$$\begin{aligned} t_1 &= (100, \mathit{Jones}, \mathit{Main\ Street}, \mathit{Pittsburg}, -) \\ t_2 &= (100, \mathit{Jones}, \mathit{Main\ Street}, \mathit{Pittsburg}, \mathit{USA}) \\ t_3 &= (100, \mathit{Jones}, \mathit{Main\ Street}, \mathit{Pittsburg}, \mathit{USA}, -) \\ t_4 &= (100, \mathit{Jones}, \mathit{Main\ Street}, \mathit{Pittsburg}, \mathit{USA}, 1234567) \end{aligned}$$

then $t_1 \leq t_2$, $t_2 \equiv t_3$, and $t_3 \leq t_4$.

In the sequel we use the terms *null*-tuple for a tuple containing only **ni**-values, *non-null* tuple for a tuple containing at least one non-**ni**-value, and *total* tuple for a tuple without **ni**-values.

Definition 6.9 A relation instance r_1 *subsumes* an instance r_2, denoted $r_1 \supseteq r_2$ if for each non-null tuple $t_2 \in r_2$ there is a tuple $t_1 \in r_1$ such that $t_1 \geq t_2$. r_1 and r_2 are *(information-wise) equivalent*, denoted $r_1 \equiv r_2$ if $r_1 \supseteq r_2$ and $r_2 \supseteq r_1$. □

Since $\equiv$ is an equivalence relation we can easily use the partitions of the universe of instances to define *representations*:

Definition 6.10 An *extended relation* (or *x-relation* for short) is an equivalence class under $\equiv$. The class of instances equivalent to r is denoted $\hat{r}$. r is called a *representation* of $\hat{r}$.

□

Thus $r_1 \equiv r_2$ iff $\hat{r}_1 = \hat{r}_2$, and if $r_1' \equiv r_1$ and $r_2' \equiv r_2$ then r_1' subsumes r_2' iff r_1 subsumes r_2. Therefore, when extending the notion of *subsumes* to x-relations, it becomes a real set-inclusion, i.ė. $\hat{r}_1 \supseteq \hat{r}_2$ iff r_1 subsumes r_2. We also use the notation $\hat{r}_1 \supset \hat{r}_2$ if $\hat{r}_1 \supseteq \hat{r}_2$ but $\hat{r}_1 \neq \hat{r}_2$.

Definition 6.11 A tuple t is said to *x-belong to*, or to be an *x-element of* $\hat{r}$, denoted $t \mathrel{\hat{\in}} \hat{r}$, if for some $r' \in \hat{r}$, $t \in r'$.

□

The $\hat{\in}$ relation can also be characterized as:

Theorem 6.10 *$t \mathrel{\hat{\in}} \hat{r}$ iff there exists a tuple $s \in r$ such that $s \geq t$.*

□

Thus a tuple t belongs to an x-relation iff its representation contains a tuple which is more informative than t. Also we will say that a tuple t x-belongs to r, denoted $t \mathrel{\hat{\in}} r$, if for some $s \in r$, $s \geq t$. There is no confusion between the two different usages of $\hat{\in}$ since $t \mathrel{\hat{\in}} \hat{r}$ iff $t \mathrel{\hat{\in}} r$.

Given a set of tuples $\{t_1, t_2, \ldots t_n\}$, one can obtain an x-relation $\widehat{\{t_1, t_2, \ldots, t_n\}}$ by eliminating all tuples that are less informative than some other tuples, and then extending all tuples with nulls to make them range over the same set of attributes. Using this notation we can define:

Definition 6.12 We define the following operations on instances:

$$\begin{array}{lll} \textit{union:} & \hat{r}_1 \cup \hat{r}_2 = \widehat{\{t \mid t \mathrel{\hat{\in}} \hat{r}_1 \text{ or } t \mathrel{\hat{\in}} \hat{r}_1\}} \\ \textit{x-intersection:} & \hat{r}_1 \mathbin{\hat{\cap}} \hat{r}_2 = \widehat{\{t \mid t \mathrel{\hat{\in}} \hat{r}_1 \text{ and } t \mathrel{\hat{\in}} \hat{r}_1\}} \\ \textit{difference:} & \hat{r}_1 - \hat{r}_2 = \widehat{\{t \mid t \mathrel{\hat{\in}} \hat{r}_1 \text{ and not } t \mathrel{\hat{\in}} \hat{r}_1\}} \end{array}$$

□

This definition leads to lots of nice properties of these generalizations of the union, intersection and difference of relations:

Theorem 6.11 *Let $\hat{r}_1' = \hat{r}_1$ and $\hat{r}_2' = \hat{r}_2$, then*

- $\hat{r}_1' \cup \hat{r}_2' = \hat{r}_1 \cup \hat{r}_2$.
- $\hat{r}_1' \mathbin{\hat{\cap}} \hat{r}_2' = \hat{r}_1 \mathbin{\hat{\cap}} \hat{r}_2$.
- $\hat{r}_1' - \hat{r}_2' = \hat{r}_1 - \hat{r}_2$.

If $\hat{r} \supseteq \hat{r}_1$ *and* $\hat{r} \supseteq \hat{r}_2$ *then* $\hat{r} \supseteq \hat{r}_1 \cup \hat{r}_2$.
If $\hat{r} \subseteq \hat{r}_1$ *and* $\hat{r} \subseteq \hat{r}_2$ *then* $\hat{r} \subseteq \hat{r}_1 \hat{\cap} \hat{r}_2$.
For any two x-relations $\hat{r}_1$ *and* $\hat{r}_2$ *we have* $(\hat{r}_1 - \hat{r}_2) \cup \hat{r}_2 = \hat{r}_1$. *If* $\hat{r} \cup \hat{r}_2 = \hat{r}_1$ *then* $\hat{r} \supseteq (\hat{r}_1 - \hat{r}_2)$.

□

In order to be able to really work with x-relations we define:

Definition 6.13 An instance r is a *minimal representation* for $\hat{r}$ if no proper subset of r is also a representation of $\hat{r}$.
A set of attributes W is called the *scope* of $\hat{r}$ if $\hat{r}$ can be represented by an instance with W as its set of attributes but not by an instance with a proper subset of W as its set of attributes.

□

Constructing a minimal representation is easy: one just removes the null tuple (if present) and all tuples which are less informative than any other tuple in r. Then we remove the attributes for which all tuples are **ni**, to obtain an instance over the scope of the x-relation. This process can be regarded as an extension of the process to make sure an instance does not contain duplicate tuples (in the relational model without nulls).

So far we have defined a very straightforward generalization of set-theoretic operations in instances. For query evaluation we also need operations like selection, projection and cartesian product or join.

Definition 6.14 Let θ be a relational operator, such as =, >, etc., and let k be a constant.

$$\begin{aligned}
\sigma(\hat{r}; A\theta B) &= \hat{\{}t \mid t \in r \text{ if } A\text{-total and } B\text{-total and } r[A]\theta r[B]\hat{\}} \\
\sigma(\hat{r}; A\theta k) &= \hat{\{}t \mid t \in r \text{ if } A\text{-total and } r[A]\theta r[B]\hat{\}} \\
\hat{r}_1 \times \hat{r}_2 &= \hat{\{}t_1 \vee t_2 \mid t_1 \in r_1 \text{ and } t_2 \in r_2 \text{ are not null}\hat{\}} \\
\hat{r}[X] &= \hat{\{}t[X] \mid t \in r\hat{\}}
\end{aligned}$$

□

The reader can easily verify that these operators reduce to the relational algebra when applied to instances without nulls, hence we do have a valid generalization of the relational algebra to relations with no-information nulls.

Although this generalization is nice in theory, we really want to find out what answers it gives to queries. Consider the following table:

SUPPLIER	*PART*
*s*1	*p*1
*s*1	*p*2
*s*1	–
*s*2	*p*1
*s*2	–
*s*3	–
*s*4	*p*4

Consider the following query: "List all suppliers who supply every part supplied by $s2$."

The reader is invited to show that the answer to that query is $\{-, p1\}$. This is assuming that the query reads as "List all suppliers who for sure supply every part supplied by $s2$". If we consider the existing-but-unknown interpretation of nulls, the answer to this query, given the same table, would be the empty instance. This is known as "Codd's paradox", since this means that "For sure, $s2$ does not supply all the parts $s2$ supplies."

Now, if we ask "List all parts supplied by $s1$ and not by $s2$, then the answer (given by the expression one would use with the normal relational algebra) is $\{p2\}$. So this actually answers "List all parts that are supplied by $s1$ for sure, but that are not for sure supplied by $s2$". Note that this answer does not say that we know for sure that $s2$ does not supply $p2$!

Let us conclude this section by remarking that both the existing-but-unknown and the no-information nulls make it necessary to rephrase queries using "for sure" or "maybe" in order to make them unambiguous. The straightforward generalization of the relational algebra may result in answers that were not intended by the user. The no-information interpretation has two advantages: it does not generate paradoxes like the existing-but-unknown interpretation, and it leads to a straightforward definition of a representation system which is capable of expressing the complete relational algebra.

6.5 The Weak Instance Model

In the previous sections we have assumed that incomplete information appears in a relation because one inserts incomplete tuples in a relation, or (in case of the no-information nulls only) because one changes the scheme by adding attributes. Under the *universal instance assumption*, (also called the universal relation assumption,) one can introduce incomplete information in a multi-relational database by changing one instance in such a way that some instance is no longer the projection (onto its set of attributes) of the join of all instances. Almost every insertion or deletion into only one relation causes a violation of the universal relation assumption.

To overcome this problem a new basis for universal relation interfaces is given by the *weak instance model*, by adding null-values to the universal instance. These null-values will then mean that a value does not exist. The concept of weak instance was introduced by Honeyman [65], as follows (translated into our terminology):

Definition 6.15 Let $DS = (PDS, DM, SDC)$ be a database scheme, where PDS is a family of relation schemes RS_i, (as in Definition 1.6), and where SDC expresses the universal relation assumption, i. e. there exists a relation scheme RS such that $RS_i = \Pi(RS, \Omega_i)$ for all i. Let $\Omega = \bigcup \Omega_i$. Let rs_i be an instance of RS_i (for all i). A set of tuples r over Ω is called a *weak instance RS* if r satisfies all constraints of the individual relations and of SDC and if $rs_i \subseteq \Pi(r; \Omega_i)$ for all i.

□

This definition is not practical, since it does not say how weak instances can be computed. The existence of a weak instance can be tested by means of a *representative instance*. The construction of a representative instance starts with a tableau over Ω, created by taking the union of the rs_i, extended by nulls (to obtain instances over Ω), which are initially different from one another. Then, the chase procedure is applied to this tableau, using the constraints to equate nulls and to promote nulls to constants. If the constraints are functional dependencies for instance, the chase procedure stops either because nothing changes anymore, or because it tries to identify two constants, in which case we say the chase produces a contradiction. Honeyman [65] has shown:

Theorem 6.12 *A database instance has a weak instance iff the corresponding representative instance is generated without encountering contradictions in the chase process.*

□

The universal relation assumption was introduced to simplify the construction of a relational interface: if a user needs a *window* (or *view*) onto some set of attributes, this can be easily achieved by performing a projection of the universal instance. Whereas the existence of a universal instance is a severe constraint, the existence of a weak instance is sufficient to produce this same *window function*. And although the weak instance may contain nulls, the individual relation instances do not.

The odd part of Definition 6.15 is that a weak instance may be arbitrarily large, because of the inclusions. Any superfluous information is of course useless.

Definition 6.16 Let $X \subseteq \Omega$. The *window* of a database instance on X is the set of tuples that appear in the projection on X of every weak instance of the database instance.

□

Theorem 6.13 *The window on X is identical to the X-total projection of the representative instance, that is, the instance obtained by projecting the representative instance onto X and then eliminating the tuples that contain nulls.*

□

What exactly is the meaning of the nulls in a representative instance? This becomes clear when we look at sentences of the logical theory for the weak instance model, given by Maier, Ullman and Vardi [78]. For every database instance, the theory has 5 kinds of sentences:

1. A set DB of atomic sentences describing the relations in the database.
2. A set INC of sentences saying that the relation instances are projections of the weak instance; these sentences are existentially quantified with respect to the attributes not appearing in the relation scheme.
3. A set CON of sentences saying that, for every $X \subseteq \Omega$, the instance over X contains the projection of the weak instance on X.
4. A set DIS of sentences stating that all elements are distinct.
5. A set DEP of first-order sentences representing SC and SDC (the sets of constraints).

Theorem 6.14 *A database instance satisfies the given constraints iff the corresponding theory is satisfiable.*

□

Theorem 6.15 *Let $X \subseteq \Omega$. The set of tuples over X, implied by the logical theory, is exactly the window over X.*

□

An important observation from this logical theory is that the set INC describes that the nulls in a weak instance represent existing values which are currently unknown. So the weak instance model does imply explicitly that the null values can only represent existing values. There is no way to express that a tuple has *no value* for some attributes, or that we don't know whether a tuple should have a value for some attribute or not.

Atzeni and De Bernardis [8] have redefined the weak instance model, to take into account the new meaning of null-values. The difference is most apparent in the following instance:

A	B	C
a_1	x_1	c_1
a_1	x_2	x_3

with the fds $A \rightarrow B$ and $B \rightarrow C$. The chase procedure for "unknown value"-nulls would first identify x_1 and x_2 and their equality would then be used to infer $c_1 = x_3$. With the "no information"-nulls x_1 and x_2 would still be identified, but there equality would not infer $c_1 = x_3$, since the existence of a value for x_1 or x_2 is uncertain.

Atzeni and De Bernardis showed that the theorems for the weak instance model (Theorems 6.13 and 6.12) remain valid with this new definition. The logical theories for the new model remain the same, except that the set of sentences INC is no longer present. The new logical theories still satisfy Theorems 6.14 and 6.15.

The theory of incomplete information, caused by combining several relation instances (which themselves are complete) into one database instance which does not satisfy the unrealistic universal relation assumption, is still under development, and several new definitions for the weak instance model (or similar models) are to be expected.

6.6 Exercises

6.1 Prove Corollary 6.1 formally.

6.2 Show that the selection operator used with Codd tables may be the *general selection.*

6.3 Evaluate $f(r) = \sigma(\Pi(\Pi(r; AC) \bowtie \Pi(r; AB); BC); B = b)$ on the C-table of Example 6.2.

6.4 Give counterexamples for the negative items of Theorem 6.8.

6.5 Give the exact update actions that are necessary to perform the evolution in the *stays* relation, described in Example 6.4.

6.6 Give an example to show that the table which results from the exhaustive application of the fill-in rules is not unique.

6.7 Prove Theorem 6.9.

6.8 Prove that the inference rules for fds are sound and complete for existence constraints.

6.9 Give an example which shows that inserting a tuple into a table can cause violation of an existence constraint, even is the tuple satisfies all given existence constraints, and the table with the new tuple still satisfies all fds.

6.10 Prove Theorem 6.13.

6.11 Construct a representative instance for Example 1.10 and explain the meaning of the introduced null values.

6.12 Prove more formally that $\hat{r}_1 \supseteq \hat{r}_2$ is a "real" set inclusion when r_1 subsumes r_2.

6.13 Show that Definition 6.11 and Theorem 6.10 are equivalent.

6.14 Prove the properties described in Theorem 6.11.

6.15 Show that every instance has an infinite number of minimal representations.

6.16 Show that the use of $\in$ instead of $\hat{\in}$ in Definition 6.14 is does not make an "information-wise" difference.

6.17 Show that in the *SUPPLIER, PART* example, the answer to the query "List all suppliers who supply every part supplied by $s2$" is indeed $\{-, p1\}$.

6.18 Describe the (5) sets of sentences of the logical theories for the weak instance model more formally.

Chapter 7

The Nested Relational Database Model

Up to this point, we have been dealing with the standard relational model introduced by Codd. Probably, one of the most fundamental assumptions made in this model is that data is represented in the form of flat tables; this is the so called *first normal form assumption.* In many practical circumstances, however, data is not represented as flat tables but rather in the form of hierarchically organized tables. For example consider the table shown in Figure 7.1. A row in that table represents a person, the set of his or her natural children and for each child, the set of his or her toys. In the relational model this table would be represented as shown in Figure 7.2. The argument made by many people is that the hierarchically organized table is a more natural representation of this data. So there is a need to represent and manipulate such data.

Certainly, hierarchically organized data has been dealt with by data practitioners. In fact, the hierarchical data model supports this data representation. The problem of the hierarchical model however, as contrasted with the relational model, stems from the fact that it is not equipped with high-level query languages such as the ones discussed for the relational model in Chapter 2. In this chapter we will see however that such query languages can be defined for hierarchically organized data, thus achieving the nice features attributed to the relational model for a more general data model.

7.1 Nested Relation Schemes and Instances

Basically we assume that we have an infinitely enumerable set U of *atomic attributes* and an infinitely enumerable set V of *atomic values.* All possible attribute names that can appear in the relations under consideration are supposed to be in U. A similar assumption is made for V. In this section, we explain how arbitrary attributes and values, nested relation schemes and nested relation instances are constructed from these.

First, we define an attribute. Attributes can either be atomic or composed. The latter ones are sets of attributes (which can be composed in turn).

PERSON	{*CHILD*	{*TOY*}}
John	Jim	Teddy Bear Monopoly
	Jenny	Cabbage Patch Doll Lazer Tag
Pam	Ann	Cabbage Patch Doll Hockey Stick Roller Skates
	Andy	Lego Building Blocks
	Dave	Trivial Pursuit
Tom	Steve	Lego Train Set

Figure 7.1: Example of a hierarchically organized table

PERSON	*CHILD*	*TOY*
John	Jim	Teddy Bear
John	Jim	Monopoly
John	Jenny	Cabbage Patch Doll
John	Jenny	Lazer Tag
Pam	Ann	Cabbage Patch Doll
Pam	Ann	Hockey Stick
Pam	Ann	Roller Skates
Pam	Andy	Lego
Pam	Andy	Building Blocks
Pam	Dave	Trivial Pursuit
Tom	Steve	Lego
Tom	Steve	Train Set

Figure 7.2: Relational representation of Figure 7.1

Definition 7.1 The set of all attributes $\mathcal{U}$ is the smallest set containing U such that for each finite subset X of $\mathcal{U}$ in which no atomic attribute appears more than once, $X \in \mathcal{U}$. An attribute of U is called an *atomic attribute*; an attribute of $\mathcal{U} \setminus U$ is called a *composed attribute*.

□

It is also possible to give a constructive definition of $\mathcal{U}$; see Exercise 7.1.

As in Chapter 1, we first define a *primitive nested relation scheme*:

Definition 7.2 A *primitive nested relation scheme* is a three-tuple

$$PNRS = (\Omega, \Delta, dom)$$

where

- Ω is a *composed attribute*, i.e. an element of $\mathcal{U} \setminus U$;
- Δ is a finite set of *domains*; each domain is a set of atomic values which may be infinite;
- *dom* is a function that associates with each atomic attribute a domain. For each atomic attribute, only the values of the corresponding domain may appear in the column that is headed by that attribute.

□

The definition of a *nested relation scheme* is now very straightforward:

Definition 7.3 A *nested relation scheme* (or briefly a nested relation) is a three-tuple

$$NRS = (PNRS, M, SC)$$

where

- *PNRS* is a *primitive nested relation scheme*;
- M is the *meaning* of the nested relation scheme expressed in a natural language;
- *SC* is a set of *nested relation constraints*.

Nested relation constraints will be discussed in Section 7.3. As for traditional "flat" relations, we shall often denote a nested relation scheme as a five-tuple $NRS = (\Omega, \Delta, dom, M, SC)$.

Example 7.1 Assume we want to store information about fathers, sons and their hobbies. A nested relation scheme that can be used for this purpose is $HOBBY\text{-}INFO = (\Omega, \Delta, dom, M, SC)$ with

- $\Omega = \{FATHER, \{SON, \{SON\text{-}HOBBY\}\}, \{FATHER\text{-}HOBBY\}\}$;
- $\Delta = \{$set of person names, set of hobby names$\}$;
- *dom* is straightforward;
- The meaning M of this nested relation scheme describes information about fathers, sons and their hobbies. A father can have several sons and hobbies, in term, a son may have several hobbies;

- the set SC includes constraints such as
  - a father can appear only once in the column corresponding to the *FATHER* attribute;
  - a son can appear only once in the column corresponding to the *SON* attribute.

□

Example 7.2 Assume further that we want to store information about the equipment needed for hobbies. A nested relation scheme that can be used for this purpose is *HOBBY-EQUIPMENT* $= (\Omega, \Delta, dom, M, SC)$ with

- $\Omega = \{HOBBY, \{EQUIPMENT, \{STORE, PRICE\}\}\}$;
- Δ = {set of hobby names, set of equipment names, set of store names, set of real numbers};
- *dom* is straightforward.;
- The meaning M of this nested relation scheme describes some information about the equipment necessary for hobbies, and its associated cost at various stores;
- the set SC includes constraints such as:
  - a hobby is only listed once under the *HOBBY* column;
  - a store has a unique price for a given equipment.

□

We introduced the nested relation scheme in order to specify the structure of nested relation instances. A nested relation instance can be viewed as a hierarchically organized table like the one in Figure 7.1. As such it is a set of rows the order of which is not important. Each row has several entries, one for each attribute in the scheme. Furthermore each entry must belong to the appropriate domain. If the attribute is atomic, the entry is an element of the domain associated with that attribute. If the attribute is composed, the entry is an instance over that attribute (remember a composed attribute is a scheme in itself). Before proceeding, we give some other examples of nested relation instances:

Example 7.3 Recall the flat relation instances shown in Figure 2.1 and Figure 2.2 respectively. In Figure 7.3 we show an alternative representation of this data using nested relation instances. For example the scheme of the first nested relation instance is a set of two attributes, the first of which is atomic whereas the other is composed. They are represented as *FLOOR* and $\{NUMBER\text{-}OF\text{-}BEDS, BATH?, RATE, \{ROOM\text{-}NUMBER\}\}$ respectively. The composed values corresponding to this composed attribute are nested relation instances over the nested relation scheme corresponding to this scheme.

□

In analogy with Chapter 1, we shall distinguish between sets of tuples satisfying only the requirements encoded in some primitive nested relation scheme

FLOOR	{*NUMBER-OF-BEDS*	*BATH?*	*RATE*	{*ROOM-NUMBER*}}
2	2	*true*	200	205
	3	*true*	300	206
3	1	*true*	160	301 305
	3	*true*	300	303 304 306
	3	*false*	150	302

ROOMMAID-NUMBER	{*ROOM-NUMBER*}
*M*1	205 301 302 303
*M*2	206 304 305 306

Figure 7.3: Examples of nested relation instances

and sets of tuples satisfying also the additional constraints in a relation scheme containing that primitive scheme. It should be clear by now that the notions of *value*, *tuple* and *possible nested relation instance* are so closely intertwined that it is easier to define them jointly:

Definition 7.4 The set $\mathcal{V}$ of all *values*, the set $\mathcal{T}_X$ of all *tuples* over $X \in \mathcal{U} \setminus U$, the set $\mathcal{PI}_X$ of all *possible nested relation instances* over $X \in \mathcal{U} \setminus U$ and the set $\mathcal{PI}$ of all *possible nested relation instances* are the smallest sets satisfying:

- $\mathcal{V} = V \cup \mathcal{PI}$;
- $\mathcal{PI} = \bigcup_{X \in \mathcal{U} \setminus U} \mathcal{PI}_X$;
- $\mathcal{PI}_X$ consists of all finite subsets of $\mathcal{T}_X$;
- $\mathcal{T}_X$ consists of all mappings t from X into $\mathcal{V}$, called tuples, satisfying $t(A) \in dom(A)$ for all atomic attributes $A \in X \cap U$ and $t(Y) \in \mathcal{PI}_Y$ for all composed attributes $Y \in X \setminus U$.

□

Again, it is possible to replace Definition 7.4 by a more constructive one (see Exercise 7.1). We now immediately have:

Definition 7.5 Let $NRS = (PNRS, M, SC)$ be a nested relation scheme.

- A *nested relation constraint* of the nested relation scheme NRS is represented by a boolean function that associates with every possible nested relation instance of $PNRS$ the value *true* or *false*. If that function associates the value *true* with a possible nested relation instance of $PNRS$, then we say that the possible relation instance satisfies the relation constraint.
- A *nested relation instance* of the relation scheme NRS is a possible nested relation instance of $PNRS$, that satisfies all the nested relation constraints of SC. The set of all nested relation instances of the scheme NRS is denoted as $\mathcal{I}_{NRS}$.

□

We also want to define *flat relation instances* in term of this definition:

Definition 7.6 A nested relation instance of the nested relation scheme $NRS = (\Omega, \Delta, M, dom, SC)$ is called a *flat relation instance* if $\Omega \subseteq U$.

□

In what follows we will mostly be concerned with the composed attribute Ω of a nested relation scheme $NRS = (\Omega, \Delta, dom, M, SC)$ and we will therefore often denote NRS by Ω. Consequently, we shall also write $\mathcal{I}_\Omega$ for $\mathcal{I}_{NRS}$ if the other components of the scheme are understood. Also, for reasons of convenience, we shall not bother about the domains (e. g. by assuming them all to be equal and sufficiently large).

The notions of nested database schemes, nested database instances, dynamic schemes and evolution, and the classification of constraints are defined in an analogous fashion as done in Chapter 1 for the ordinary relational model.

Example 7.4 Consider the nested relation schemes *HOBBY-INFO* and *HOBBY-EQUIPMENT* introduced in Example 7.1 and Example 7.2 respectively. In Figure 7.4 we show a nested relation instance of the *HOBBY-INFO* scheme and in Figure 7.5 we show a nested relation instance of the *HOBBY-EQUIPMENT* scheme.

FATHER	{*SON*	{*SON-HOBBY*}}	{*FATHER-HOBBY*}
Jones	Eric	Reading	Music
		Stamps	Reading
	Marc	Music	
		Tennis	
	John	Soccer	
		Stamps	
Miller	Henry	Soccer	Tennis
		Music	Stamps
	Joe	Hockey	Reading
		Soccer	

Figure 7.4: A nested relation instance over the *HOBBY-INFO* scheme

HOBBY	{*EQUIPMENT*	{*STORE*	*PRICE*}}
Stamps	Album	Sears	12.95
		Macys	14.95
	Magnifying Glass	Sears	6.50
		J.C. Penny	6.29
Soccer	Shoes	Kinnys	29.99
		Athlete's Foot	39.50
	Ball	Athlete's Foot	12.50
		Sears	7.99

Figure 7.5: A nested relation instance over the *HOBBY-EQUIPMENT* scheme

□

7.2 The Nested Relational Algebra

In this section, we define a query language, in the form of an algebra, for nested relation schemes and instances. This algebra was first introduced by Jaeschke and Scheck [67] for nested relations with one level of nesting and later generalized by Thomas and Fischer [103] and by Schek and Scholl [98] for arbitrary ones. Ozsoyoglu et al. [82] also introduced an algebraic query language to manipulate (one-level) nested relations but their language can not easily be generalized to arbitrary nested relation instances. Finally, it should be mentioned that Abiteboul and Bidoit [2] introduced an algebra, similar in spirit to the one of Schek and Scholl, but which can only manipulate a certain class of nested relations, the so called *hierarchical relations* studied at the end of this chapter.

Our algebra is very similar to the one of Thomas and Fischer and consists of the standard relational algebra, generalized to nested relations instances, plus two restructuring operators, the nest and the unnest operators. The nest operator takes as input a nested relation scheme or instance and produces a nested relation scheme or instance with one additional level of nesting. The unnest operator has the opposite effect. We illustrate these new operators in the following two examples.

Example 7.5 Reconsider Figure 7.4 showing a nested relation instance over the *HOBBY-INFO* scheme. Unnesting this instance over the composed attributes $\{SON, \{SON\text{-}HOBBY\}\}$ and $\{FATHER\text{-}HOBBY\}$ respectively, yields the instance shown in Figure 7.6.

□

Example 7.6 Consider the previous example. The result of projecting the nested relation instance shown in Figure 7.6 on $\{FATHER, FATHER\text{-}HOBBY\}$ and subsequently nesting this flat relation instance on $\{FATHER\}$ yields the instance shown in Figure 7.7. As can be seen, the nest operator groups together for each hobby those fathers who perform that hobby.

□

We now give a precise definition of the operators of the nested relational algebra and define the syntax and semantics of nested relation algebra expressions.

Definition 7.7 Let ω_1 and ω_2 be nested relation instances over the same scheme Ω:

- The *union* $\omega_1 \cup \omega_2$ is the standard set union of ω_1 and ω_2. Clearly, the scheme of $\omega_1 \cup \omega_2$ is Ω;
- The *difference* $\omega_1 \setminus \omega_2$ is the standard set difference of ω_1 and ω_2. Clearly, the scheme of $\omega_1 \setminus \omega_2$ is Ω.

Let ω_1 and ω_2 be nested relation instances over the schemes Ω_1 and Ω_2 respectively, and suppose that no atomic attribute appears both in Ω_1 and Ω_2.

FATHER	*SON*	{*SON-HOBBY*}	*FATHER-HOBBY*
Jones	Eric	Reading Stamps	Music
Jones	Eric	Reading Stamps	Reading
Jones	Marc	Music Tennis	Music
Jones	Marc	Music Tennis	Reading
Jones	John	Soccer Stamps	Music
Jones	John	Soccer Stamps	Reading
Miller	Henry	Soccer Music	Tennis
Miller	Henry	Soccer Music	Stamps
Miller	Henry	Soccer Music	Reading
Miller	Joe	Hockey Soccer	Tennis
Miller	Joe	Hockey Soccer	Stamps
Miller	Joe	Hockey Soccer	Reading

Figure 7.6: Example of the unnest operator

FATHER	*FATHER-HOBBY*
Jones	Music
Jones Miller	Reading
Miller	Tennis
Miller	Stamps

Figure 7.7: Example of the nest operator

- The *cartesian product* $\omega_1 \times \omega_2$ is a nested relation instance of the scheme $\Omega' = \Omega_1 \cup \Omega_2$ and equals

$$\{t \in \mathcal{T}_{\Omega'} \mid t[\Omega_1] \in \omega_1 \ \wedge \ t[\Omega_2] \in \omega_2\}$$

Let ω be a nested relation instance over the scheme Ω:

- Let $\Omega' \subseteq \Omega$. The *projection* $\Pi(\omega; \Omega')$ is a nested relation instance over the scheme Ω' and equals: $\{t[\Omega'] \mid t \in \omega\}$;
- Let $X \subseteq \Omega$. The *nesting* $\nu(\omega; X)$ is a nested relation instance over the scheme $\Omega' = (\Omega \setminus X) \cup \{X\}$ and equals

$$\{t \in \mathcal{T}_{\Omega'} | \exists t' \in \omega \colon t[\Omega \setminus X] = t'[\Omega \setminus X] \ \wedge$$
$$t(X) = \{t''[X] \mid t'' \in \omega \ \wedge \ t'[\Omega \setminus X] = t''[\Omega \setminus X]\}\}$$

- Let $X \in \Omega \setminus U$. The *unnesting* $\mu(\omega; X)$ is a nested relation instance over the scheme $\Omega' = (\Omega \setminus \{X\}) \cup X$ and equals

$$\{t \in \mathcal{T}_{\Omega'} \mid \exists t' \in \omega \colon t[\Omega \setminus \{X\}] = t'[\Omega \setminus \{X\}] \ \wedge \ t[X] \in t'(X)\}$$

Let φ be a permutation on U. It is straightforward to see that φ can be extended in the natural way to $\mathcal{U}$, to $\mathcal{I}$ and to $\mathcal{V}$:

- The *renaming* $\rho(\omega; \varphi)$ is the nested relation instance $\varphi(\omega)$. Clearly, the scheme of this nested relation instance is $\varphi(\Omega)$;
- Let $X, Y \in \Omega$ and suppose $\varphi(X) = Y$. The *selection* $\sigma(\omega; X = Y, \varphi)$ is a nested relation instance over the scheme Ω and equals

$$\{t \in \omega \mid \varphi(t(X)) = t(Y)\}$$

  When φ is understood we will write $\sigma(\omega; X = Y)$ instead of $\sigma(\omega; X = Y, \varphi)$.
- Let $X \in \Omega$ and let v be an appropriate value (i.e. $v \in dom(X)$ if $X \in U$ and $v \in \mathcal{I}_X$ in the other case). The *selection* $\sigma(\omega; X = v)$ or $\sigma(\omega; x = X)$ is a nested relation instance over the scheme Ω and equals

$$\{t \in \omega \mid \varphi(t(X)) = x\}$$

□

Note that the cartesian product is only defined for nested relation instances with completely "independent" schemes. This is actually not a serious restriction: it is indeed always possible to arrange that the schemes of the two instances have no atomic attributes in common by performing an appropriate renaming. Also notice that we did not define the join operation. The reason for the absence of the join operator in the nested relation algebra results from the observation that its semantics in the context of nested relation instances is unclear. To understand this, we would like the reader to reflect on what the meaning should be of joining a nested relation instance over the scheme $\{A, \{B\}\}$ with a nested relation instance over the scheme $\{\{A\}, B\}$.

We can now formally define a *nested algebra expression (nae)*:

Definition 7.8

- x, y, z, ... are naes;
- For all $\Omega \in \mathcal{U} \setminus U$ and for all $\omega \in \mathcal{I}_\Omega$, ω is an nae;
- For all naes, the basic operators of Definition 7.7 applied to these expressions, are also naes.

If $r, s, \ldots$ is a finite sequence of nested relation instances and $E(x, y, \ldots)$ is an nae with as many variables as there are instances, then $E(r, s, \ldots)$ is interpreted as the nested relation instance obtained by substituting every occurrence of a variable in $E(x, y, \ldots)$ by the corresponding nested relation instance, whenever this substitution makes sense, and undefined otherwise.

□

Example 7.7 In this example we give some examples of nested algebra expressions. Consider the nested relation instance over the scheme *HOBBY-INFO* shown in Figure 7.4.

- Get all father-son pairs. A nested algebra expression for this query is:

$$\Pi(\mu(\omega_1; \{SON, \{SON\text{-}HOBBY\}\}); \{FATHER, SON\})$$

- Get all fathers who play tennis. A nested algebra expression for this query is:

$$\Pi(\sigma(\mu(\omega_1; \{FATHER\text{-}HOBBY\}); FATHER\text{-}HOBBY = Tennis); \{FATHER\})$$

□

7.3 Constraints

It is possible to generalize some well-known types of (flat) relation constraints to nested relations, by allowing the equality symbol '=' to be interpreted for atomic as well as set-valued tuple components. For clarity, we redefine the notions of functional dependencies and multivalued dependencies in the context of nested relation instances. For more detail we recommend [49, 50, 51, 52, 67, 68, 79, 83, 93, 102, 103, 105, 107, 108].

Definition 7.9 Let ω be a set of tuples of the scheme Ω and let $X, Y \subseteq \Omega$. Then $X \rightarrow Y$ denotes a *functional dependency.* ω satisfies $X \rightarrow Y$ if and only if for all $t_1, t_2 \in \omega$: $t_1[X] = t_2[X] \Rightarrow t_1[Y] = t_2[Y]$.

□

Example 7.8 Consider the nested relation instance of the *HOBBY-INFO* scheme shown in Figure 7.4. This instance satisfies the fd $\{FATHER\} \rightarrow \{SON, \{SON\text{-}HOBBY\}, \{FATHER\text{-}HOBBY\}\}$.

□

Definition 7.10 Let ω be a set of tuples of the scheme Ω and let $X, Y \subseteq \Omega$. Then $X \rightarrow\rightarrow Y$ denotes a *multivalued dependency.* ω satisfies $X \rightarrow\rightarrow Y$ if and only for all $t, u \in \omega$ with $t[X] = u[X]$ there exists $v \in \omega$ such that $t[XY] = v[XY]$ and $u[X(\Omega \setminus Y)] = v[X(\Omega \setminus Y)]$.

□

Example 7.9 Consider the nested relation instance obtained in Example 7.5 and shown in Figure 7.6. This instance satisfies the mvd's $\{FATHER\} \rightarrow\rightarrow \{SON, \{SON\text{-}HOBBY\}\}$ and $\{FATHER\} \rightarrow\rightarrow \{FATHER\text{-}HOBBY\}$.

□

Constraints like join dependencies, inclusion dependencies, tuple and equality generating dependencies can be generalized to nested relation instances in a similar fashion. In the remainder of this section we will show how the nest and unnest operators are related to dependencies. The first theorem relates the nest operator to functional dependencies.

Theorem 7.1 *Let ω be a set of tuples of the scheme Ω and let $X \subseteq \Omega$. Then $\nu(\omega; X)$ satisfies the fd $(\Omega \setminus X) \rightarrow \{X\}$.*

Proof Nesting over X associates with each $(\Omega \setminus X)$ subtuple $t_{(\Omega \setminus X)}$ of ω the set of *all* the X subtuples of tuples of ω which agree with t on $(\Omega \setminus X)$. Hence, $\nu(\omega; X)$ satisfies the functional dependency $(\Omega \setminus X) \rightarrow \{X\}$.

□

In general, the nest operator does not commute.

Example 7.10 Consider the flat relation instance ω over the scheme $\{A, B\}$ shown in Figure 7.8. It can easily be verified that

$$\nu(\nu(\omega; \{A\}); \{B\}) \neq \nu(\nu(\omega; \{B\}); \{A\})$$

A	B
a_1	b_1
a_1	b_2
a_2	b_1

Figure 7.8: $\nu(\nu(\omega; \{A\}); \{B\}) \neq \nu(\nu(\omega; \{B\}); \{A\})$

□

To characterize when two nest operations commute, we need the notion of *weak multivalued dependencies*, introduced by Jaeschke and Schek [67] and further studied by Fischer, Thomas and Van Gucht [102, 50, 106, 107].

Definition 7.11 Let ω be a nested relation instance over the scheme Ω and let $X, Y \subseteq \Omega$. Then $X \twoheadrightarrow_w Y$ denotes a *weak multivalued dependency (wmvd)*. ω satisfies $X \twoheadrightarrow_w Y$ if and only for all $t, u, v \in \omega$ with $t[XY] = u[XY]$ and $u[X(\Omega \backslash Y)] = v[X(\Omega \backslash Y)]$ there exists $w \in \omega$ such that $t[X(\Omega \backslash Y)] = w[X(\Omega \backslash Y)]$ and $v[XY] = w[XY]$.

□

Example 7.11 Consider the flat relation instance ω defined over the scheme $\{A, B, C\}$ shown in Figure 7.9. This relation satisfies the wmvd $A \twoheadrightarrow_w B$.

A	B	C
a	b_1	c_1
a	b_1	c_2
a	b_2	c_1
a	b_2	c_2
a	b_3	c_3
a	b_3	c_4

Figure 7.9: A flat relation instance satisfying the wmvd $A \twoheadrightarrow_w B$

□

Regarding the notion of wmvd's there are several facts which are easy to verify:

- *If ω satisfies the wmvd $X \twoheadrightarrow_w Y$ then it also satisfies the WMVD $X \twoheadrightarrow_w (\Omega \setminus Y)$.* This follows immediately from the definition of wmvd's which is symmetric in Y and $(\Omega \setminus Y)$.
- *If ω satisfies the mvd $X \twoheadrightarrow Y$ then it also satisfies the wmvd $X \twoheadrightarrow_w Y$.* It can easily be verified that the conditions associated with the satisfaction of a mvd (see Definition 7.10) are stronger than those associated with the satisfaction of a wmvd (see Definition 7.11).

We can now state a characterization for when two nest operations commute.

Theorem 7.2 *Let ω be a nested relation instance over the scheme Ω and let $Y, Z \subseteq \Omega$ with $Y \cap Z = \emptyset$. Let $X = (\Omega \setminus (YZ))$. Then*

$$\nu(\nu(\omega; Y); Z) = \nu(\nu(\omega; Z); Y)$$

if and only if ω satisfies the wmvd $X \twoheadrightarrow_w Y$.

Proof We leave this proof to the reader. Proving this theorem will give you some insights in the properties of the nest operator.

□

Since mvds imply wmvds we have the following simple corollary to Theorem 7.2:

Corollary 7.1 *Let ω be a nested relation instance over the scheme Ω and let $Y, Z \subseteq \Omega$ with $Y \cap Z = \emptyset$. Let $X = (\Omega \setminus (YZ))$. If ω satisfies the mvd $X \rightarrow\rightarrow Y$ then*

$$\nu(\nu(\omega; Y); Z) = \nu(\nu(\omega; Z); Y)$$

□

Next, we study how certain dependencies are preserved by nest and unnest operations. These results will become useful in Section 7.5 where we introduce the notion of hierarchical instances. The following two lemmas indicate what happens when we perform certain nest operations on a nested relation instance satisfying a fd or a mvd.

Lemma 7.1 *Let ω be a nested relation instance over the scheme Ω and let $X, Y, Z \subseteq \Omega$ with $XY \cap Z = \emptyset$. Then*

1. *If ω satisfies the fd $X \rightarrow Y$ then $\nu(\omega; Z)$ satisfies the fd $X \rightarrow Y$.*
2. *If ω satisfies the mvd $X \rightarrow\rightarrow Y$ then $\nu(\omega; Z)$ satisfies the mvd $X \rightarrow\rightarrow Y$.* □

Proof

1. Immediate, since $\Pi(\omega; XY) = \Pi(\nu(\omega; Z); XY)$.
2. Let $W = \Omega \setminus (XYZ)$. We need to show that for any two tuples in $\nu(\omega; Z)$ of the form $< x, y, S, w >$ and $< x, y', S', w' >$, $\nu(\omega; Z)$ also contains a tuple of the form $< x, y', S, w >$. For each $z \in S$ and $z' \in S'$ we know from the definition of nesting, that $< x, y, z, w >$ and $< x, y', z', w' >$ are tuples of ω. Since $X \rightarrow\rightarrow Y$ is satisfied by ω, we also have $< x, y', z, w > \in \omega$. From this we can conclude that $\nu(\omega; Z)$ contains a tuple $< x, y, S'', w >$ with $S \subseteq S''$. Thus, we need only show that $S'' \subseteq S$. For $z'' \in S''$ and $z \in S$ we know that $< x, y', z'', w > < x, y, z, w >$ are tuples of ω. Since $X \rightarrow\rightarrow Y$ holds in ω, we also have $< x, y, z'', w > \in \omega$. Therefore, $z'' \in S$ and $S'' = S$. Hence $X \rightarrow\rightarrow Y$ holds in $\nu(\omega; Z)$.

□

Lemma 7.2 *Let ω be a nested relation instance over the scheme Ω and let $X, Y, Z \subseteq \Omega$ with $X \cap Y = \emptyset$ and $Z \subseteq Y$. Then*

1. *If ω satisfies the mvd $X \rightarrow\rightarrow Y$ then $\nu(\omega; Z)$ satisfies the mvd $X \rightarrow\rightarrow (Y \setminus Z)\{Z\}$.*
2. *If ω satisfies the mvd $X \rightarrow\rightarrow Y$ then $\nu(\omega; Y)$ satisfies the fd $X \rightarrow \{Y\}$.*

Proof We leave this proof to the reader.

□

The last two lemmas of this section indicate what happens when we perform certain unnest operations on a nested relation instance satisfying a fd or a mvd. Notice how these two lemmas and the previous two lemmas correspond.

Lemma 7.3 *Let ω be a nested relation instance over the scheme Ω, let $X, Y \subseteq \Omega$ and let $Z \in \Omega \setminus U$ such that $Z \notin XY$. Then*

1. *If ω satisfies the fd $X \rightarrow Y$ then $\mu(\omega; Z)$ satisfies the fd $X \rightarrow Y$.*
2. *If ω satisfies the mvd $X \rightarrow\rightarrow Y$ then $\mu(\omega; Z)$ satisfies the mvd $X \rightarrow\rightarrow Y$.*

Proof

1. Immediate, since $\Pi(\omega; XY) = \Pi(\mu(\omega; Z); XY)$.
2. Let $W = \Omega \setminus (XYZ)$. We need to show that for any two tuples in $\mu(\omega; Z)$ of the form $< x, y, z, w >$ and $< x, y', z', w' >$, $\mu(\omega; Z)$ also contains a tuple of the form $< x, y', z, w >$. By the definition of unnesting on Z we know that ω contains tuples $< x, y, S, w >$ and $< x, y', S', w' >$ such that $z \in S$ and $z' \in S'$ respectively. Since $X \rightarrow\rightarrow Y$ holds in ω, we have $< x, y', S, w > \in \omega$. Then unnesting on Z yields $< x, y', z, w > \in \omega$.

□

Lemma 7.4 *Let ω be a nested relation instance over the scheme Ω, let $X, Y \subseteq \Omega$ and let $Z \in Y$. Then*

- *If ω satisfies the mvd $X \rightarrow\rightarrow Y$ then $\mu(\omega; Z)$ satisfies the mvd $X \rightarrow (Y \setminus \{Z\}) \cup Z$.*
- *If ω satisfies the fd $X \rightarrow \{Z\}$ then $\mu(\omega; Z)$ satisfies the mvd $X \rightarrow\rightarrow Z$.*

Proof We leave this proof to the reader.

□

7.4 The Expressiveness of the Nested Relational Algebra

In this section we present some of the basic algebraic properties of the nested algebra. In particular we study the properties of the nest and unnest operations and use these properties to analyze the expressiveness of the nested algebra. As a result, we will see how to write complex queries involving nested relation instances succinctly. We recommend [1, 2, 24, 63, 62, 64, 82, 88, 93, 99, 98, 102, 103, 105, 106, 109] for more details.

The first theorem states that the unnest operator is the left inverse of the nest operator.

Theorem 7.3 *Let ω be a nested relation instance over the scheme Ω and let $X \subseteq \Omega$. Then*

$$\mu(\nu(\omega; X); X) = \omega$$

Proof Trivial consequence of the definition of the nest and unnest operators.

□

Hence no information is lost after nesting. However unnesting followed by renesting does not always preserve a nested relation instance. Consider the following example:

Example 7.12 Consider the nested relation instance ω defined over the scheme $\{A, \{B\}\}$ shown in Figure 7.10. Now consider the expression $\nu(\mu(\omega; \{B\}); \{B\})$

A	$\{B\}$
a_1	b_1
a_1	b_2
a_2	

Figure 7.10: The nested relation instance ω

the result of which is shown in Figure 7.11. Clearly, $\nu(\mu(\omega; \{A\}); \{A\}) \neq \omega$,

A	$\{B\}$
a_1	b_1 b_2

Figure 7.11: $\nu(\mu(\omega; \{A\}); \{A\})$

which shows that the nest operator is not the left inverse of the unnest operator. □

As should be clear from the example, there are two reasons why the unnest operator can lose information:

- A tuple may have an emptyset-valued component on the component over which the unnest occurs;
- More than one tuple may agree on all the components outside the one over which the unnest occurs.

In fact, the following theorem characterize when the nest operator is the left inverse of the unnest operators in terms of these two reasons.

Theorem 7.4 *Let ω be a nested relation instance over the scheme Ω and let $X \in \Omega$. Then*

$$\nu(\mu(\omega; X); X) = \omega$$

if and only if:

- *for all $t \in \omega$: $t(X) \neq \emptyset$;*
- *The functional dependency $(\Omega \setminus \{X\}) \rightarrow \{X\}$ is satisfied by ω.*

Proof We leave this proof to the reader. We recommend you to consult Theorem 7.1. Proving this theorem will give you some insights in how the nest and unnest operators are related. □

Since the properties specified in the previous theorem are not generally true for arbitrary nested relation instances, but it may be necessary to perform operations at lower levels in such nested relation instances, we need to provide mechanisms to ensure that such operations can be performed safely. To do so, we introduce two new operators.

Definition 7.12 Let ω be a nested relation instance over the scheme Ω and let $X \in \Omega \setminus U$.

- Let φ be a permutation on U such that $\varphi(X)$ has no atomic attributes in common with Ω. Then the *tag operation* $\theta(\omega; X, \varphi)$ is a nested relation instance over the scheme $\Omega' = \Omega \cup \{\varphi(X)\}$ and equals

$$\{t \in \mathcal{T}_{\Omega'} \mid \exists t' \in \omega : t[\Omega] = t' \ \wedge \ t(\varphi(X)) = \varphi(t'(X))\}$$

- The *empty-component operator*, $\phi(\omega; X)$ is a nested relation instance over the scheme Ω and equals

$$\{t \in \omega \mid t(X) = \emptyset\}$$

□

We leave it as an exercise to prove that these two operators can be expressed in the nested algebra. The importance of the tag and empty-component operators can be seen in the following theorem which shows that an unnest operation can be performed safely if one tags the nested relation instance first and furthermore keeps the tuples with empty-valued components.

Theorem 7.5 *Let ω be a nested relation instance over the scheme Ω and let $X \in \Omega$. Let φ be a permutation on U such that $\varphi(X)$ has no atomic attributes in common with Ω. Then*

$$\omega = \Pi(\nu(\mu(\theta(\omega; X, \varphi); X); X); \Omega) \ \cup \ \phi(\omega; X)$$

Proof Consider the nested relation instance

$$\omega' = \theta(\omega; X, \varphi) \setminus \phi(\theta(\omega; X, \varphi))$$

Clearly,

$$\omega = \Pi(\omega'; \Omega) \ \cup \ \phi(\omega; X)$$

So to show that the theorem is correct we need to show that

$$\omega' = \nu(\mu(\omega'; X); X)$$

Clearly for each $t' \in \omega'$, $t'(X) \neq \emptyset$. Furthermore, by the definition of the the tag operator, the functional dependency $(\Omega' \setminus \{X\}) \rightarrow \{X\}$ is satisfied by ω'. Hence by Theorem 7.4

$$\omega' = \nu(\mu(\omega'; X); X)$$

□

To further illustrate the expressive power of the nested algebra we define useful selection operations and show how they can be expressed in terms of the tag operator, the empty-component operators and other operators of the nested relational algebra.

Definition 7.13 Let ω be a nested relation instance over the scheme Ω, let $X, Z \in \Omega \setminus U$, $Y \subseteq \Omega$, $z \in \mathcal{I}_Z$ and $v \in \mathcal{T}_Z$. Let φ and ψ be permutations on U such that $\varphi(X) = Z$ and $\psi(\{Y\}) = Z$. We define

- $\sigma(\omega; X \subseteq Z, \varphi) = \{t \in \omega \mid \varphi(t(X)) \subseteq t(Z)\}$;
- $\sigma(\omega; z \subseteq Z) = \{t \in \omega \mid z \subseteq t(Z)\}$;
- $\sigma(\omega; Z \subseteq z) = \{t \in \omega \mid t(Z) \subseteq z\}$;
- $\sigma(\omega; Y \in Z, \psi) = \{t \in \omega \mid \psi(t[Y]) \in t(Z)\}$;
- $\sigma(\omega; v \in Z) = \{t \in \omega \mid v \in t(Z)\}$;
- $\sigma(\omega; X \cap Z = \emptyset, \varphi) = \{t \in \omega \mid \varphi(t(X)) \cap t(Z) = \emptyset\}$;
- $\sigma(\omega; z \cap Z) = \{t \in \omega \mid z \cap t(Z) = \emptyset)$;

□

Lemma 7.5 *The operations described in Definition 7.13 can be expressed in the nested relational algebra.*

Proof We leave it as an exercise to the reader to show that these selection operations can be expressed in the nested relational algebra.

□

Thus far, we have only looked at selection operations that involve the "top-level" attributes of the scheme of a nested relation instance. Next, we show that we are not restricted to that, by studying how to perform selection operations that involve attributes at different levels in nested relation instances.

Definition 7.14 Let ω be a nested relation instance over the scheme Ω. Let $(X_1, X_2, \ldots, X_p)$, $p \geq 1$, and $(Y_1, Y_2, \ldots, Y_q)$, $q \geq 1$, be sequences of attributes such that:

- there exists a permutation φ on U such that $\varphi(X_p) = Y_q$;
- $X_{i+1} \in X_i$ for all i, $1 \leq i \leq p-1$;
- $Y_{j+1} \in Y_j$ for all j, $1 \leq j \leq q-1$;
- X_1 and Y_1 are elements of Ω.

Then $\sigma(\omega; X_p = Y_q, \varphi)$ is a nested relation instance over the scheme Ω and equals

$$
\begin{aligned}
\{t \in \omega \mid \exists r_1 \exists r_2 \ldots \exists r_p\ \exists s_1 \exists s_2 \ldots \exists s_q \\
t = r_1 \ \wedge\ r_2 \in r_1(X_1) \ \wedge\ \ldots\ \wedge\ r_p \in r_{p-1}(X_{p-1}) \ \wedge \\
t = s_1 \ \wedge\ s_2 \in s_1(Y_1) \ \wedge\ \ldots\ \wedge\ s_q \in s_{q-1}(Y_{q-1}) \ \wedge \\
\varphi(r_p(X_p)) = s_q(Y_q)\}
\end{aligned}
$$

□

It should be noticed that if p and q are equal to 1, we have the selection operation defined in Definition 7.7.

Lemma 7.6 *Let ω be a nested relation instance over the scheme Ω. Then $\sigma(\omega; X_p = Y_q, \varphi)$ can be expressed in the nested relational algebra.*

Proof We leave the proof of this lemma as an exercise to the reader. □

Similar selection operations involving '$\in$', '$\subseteq$', or constants can be defined and shown to be expressible in the nested relational algebra.

Example 7.13 Consider the nested relation instance ω defined over the scheme *HOBBY-INFO* shown in Figure 7.4.

- Suppose we want to retrieve fathers who do not share a hobby with their sons. A nested algebra expression for this query is:

$$\Pi(\sigma(\omega; \{\mathit{FATHER\text{-}HOBBY}\} \cap \{\mathit{SON\text{-}HOBBY}\} = \emptyset); \{\mathit{FATHER}\})$$

- Suppose we want the father-son pairs such that the father's hobbies are contained in the son's hobbies. A nested algebra expression for this query is:

$$\Pi(\sigma(\mu(\omega; \{\mathit{SON}, \{\mathit{SON\text{-}HOBBY}\}\}); \mathit{FATHER\text{-}HOBBY}\} \subseteq \{\mathit{SON\text{-}HOBBY}\}); \{\mathit{FATHER}, \mathit{SON}\})$$

□

Thus far, we have shown how we can express powerful selection operations in the nested algebra. We leave it as an exercise to the reader to show that similarly, one can extend the definition of operators such as unnest and project so that they operate at any level of nested relation instances.

7.5 Hierarchical Instances

In most database applications only particular kinds of nested relation instances are used. These nested relation instances have become known as hierarchical instances. A hierarchical instance has the property that for the instance and each of its sub-instances, the atomic attributes of the associated composed attribute form a superkey for that instance or sub-instance. Hierarchical instances were studied in detail by Bancilhon et al. [12] and Abiteboul and Bidoit [2]. Later work on hierarchical instances was done by Roth et.al. [93] and Van Gucht and Fischer [109].

Definition 7.15 Let $\Omega \in \mathcal{U} \setminus U$. We denote by $\kappa(\Omega)$ the set $\Omega \cap U$. □

We are now ready to define hierarchical instances.

Definition 7.16 A nested relation instance ω defined over the scheme Ω is called a *hierarchical instance* if and only if

- ω satisfies the fd $\kappa(\Omega) \rightarrow \Omega$, i.e. $\kappa(\Omega)$ is a superkey for ω;
- For all $t \in \omega$ and for all $X \in \Omega \setminus U$, $t(X)$ is a hierarchical instance.

□

It should be noted that for obvious reasons, flat relation instances are also hierarchical instances.

Example 7.14 The nested relation instances described in Figures 7.3, 7.4 and 7.5 are examples of hierarchical instances, whereas the nested relation instance described in Figure 7.10 is not a hierarchical instance.

□

There is a strong link between hierarchical instances, multivalued dependencies and acyclic join dependencies.

Example 7.15 Consider the hierarchical instance ω defined over the scheme $(\{A, \{B\}, \{C, \{D\}, \{E\}\}\})$ shown in Figure 7.12. In Figure 7.13 we show the flat relation instance obtained by completely unnesting this hierarchical instance. It can easily be verified that this instance satisfies the mvd's:

$$\begin{array}{rcl} A & \twoheadrightarrow & B \\ A & \twoheadrightarrow & CDE \\ AC & \twoheadrightarrow & D \\ AC & \twoheadrightarrow & E \end{array}$$

Furthermore, it can be verified that this set of mvd's is equivalent to the acyclic join dependency $AB \bowtie ACD \bowtie ACE$. In Figure 7.14 we show how the flat relation instance of Figure 7.13 is decomposed according to this join dependency. We leave it as an exercise for the reader to reconstruct the original hierarchical instance from these three flat relation instances.

A	$\{B\}$	$\{C$	$\{D\}$	$\{E\}\}$
a_1	b_1	c_1	d_1	e_1
	b_2			e_2
		c_2	d_2	e_1
			d_3	e_3
a_2	b_3	c_3	d_2	e_1
				e_4

Figure 7.12: A hierarchical instance

□

A	B	C	D	E
a_1	b_1	c_1	d_1	e_1
a_1	b_1	c_1	d_1	e_2
a_1	b_1	c_2	d_2	e_1
a_1	b_1	c_2	d_2	e_3
a_1	b_1	c_2	d_3	e_1
a_1	b_1	c_2	d_3	e_3
a_1	b_2	c_1	d_1	e_1
a_1	b_2	c_1	d_1	e_2
a_1	b_2	c_2	d_2	e_1
a_1	b_2	c_2	d_2	e_3
a_1	b_2	c_2	d_3	e_1
a_1	b_2	c_2	d_3	e_3
a_2	b_3	c_3	d_2	e_1
a_2	b_3	c_3	d_2	e_4

Figure 7.13: Flat relation instance obtained by completely unnesting the hierarchical instance in Figure 7.12

A	B
a_1	b_1
a_1	b_2
a_2	b_3

A	C	D
a_1	c_1	d_1
a_1	c_2	d_2
a_1	c_2	d_3
a_2	c_3	d_4

A	C	D
a_1	c_1	e_1
a_1	c_1	e_2
a_1	c_2	e_1
a_1	c_2	e_3
a_2	c_2	e_3
a_2	c_3	e_1

Figure 7.14: Flat relation instances obtained by decomposing the the relation instance of Figure 7.13 according to the jd $AB \bowtie ACD \bowtie ACE$

In the remainder of this section we formalize the connection between hierarchical instances and certain acyclic flat relational databases. To do so we need to redirect the attention of the reader to Section 7.3 where we established properties (Theorem 7.2) about the commutativity of the nest operation as well as discussed the relationship between fds, mvds and the nest and unnest operators (Lemma 7.1, Lemma 7.2, Lemma 7.3 and Lemma 7.4). In addition to these results we show in the following theorem how hierarchical instances, the nest and unnest operators, and mvds are related at the "top" level.[1]

Theorem 7.6 *Let ω be a hierarchical instance over scheme Ω and let $Y \in \Omega \setminus U$. Then*

1. *$\mu(\omega; Y)$ satisfies the mvd $\kappa(\Omega) \rightarrow\rightarrow Y$;*
2. *$\mu(\omega; Y)$ is a hierarchical instance;*
3. *$\nu(\mu(\omega; Y); Y) = \omega$.*

Proof

1. Since ω is a hierarchical instance, it satisfies the fd $\kappa(\Omega) \rightarrow \Omega$. Hence in particular the fd $\kappa(\Omega) \rightarrow \{Y\}$. It follows from Lemma 7.4 that $\mu(\omega; Y)$ satisfies the mvd $\kappa(\Omega) \rightarrow\rightarrow Y$.
2. Left to the reader. As part of the proof we recommend you to consult Lemma 7.3.
3. This follows from the footnote, the definition hierarchical instances and Theorem 7.4.

□

We are almost ready to give a characterization of hierarchical instances in terms of multivalued dependencies or acyclic join dependencies. But first we need a result concerning the commutativity of the unnest operator as well as some additional definitions.

Theorem 7.7 *Let ω be a nested relation instance over the scheme Ω and let $X, Y \in \Omega \setminus U$. Then*

$$\mu(\mu(\omega; X); Y) = \mu(\mu(\omega; Y); X)$$

Proof Straightforward consequence of the definition of the unnest operator. □

Definition 7.17 Let ω be a nested relation instance over the scheme. Then $\mu^*(\omega)$ is a flat relation instance defined as

- ω if ω is a flat relation instance;
- $\mu^*(\mu(\omega; X))$ where $X \in \Omega \setminus U$ otherwise.

□

[1] To make our discussion simpler, we will assume from now on that hierarchical instances have no tuples or sub-tuples with empty-valued components.

It follows from Theorem 7.7 which states that the order of unnesting is immaterial that this is a sound definition. In the following definition we indicate how we can associate and important family of mvds with each composed attribute.

Definition 7.18 Let Ω be a composed attribute, i.e. an element of $\mathcal{U} \setminus U$.

- Then $\varepsilon(\Omega)$, i.e. all the atomic attributes appearing in Ω, is defined as
  - Ω if $\Omega \subset U$;
  - $\kappa(\Omega) \bigcup_{X \in \Omega \setminus U}(\varepsilon(X))$.
- Now $MVD(\Omega)$ is defined as
  - The empty set if $\Omega \subset U$;
  - The set of mvd's

$$\{\kappa(\Omega) \rightarrow\!\!\!\rightarrow \varepsilon(X) \mid X \in \Omega \setminus U\} \cup$$
$$\{(\kappa(\Omega) \cup Y) \rightarrow\!\!\!\rightarrow Z \mid Y \rightarrow\!\!\!\rightarrow Z \in mvd(X) \ \wedge \ X \in \Omega \setminus U\}$$

- and $JD(\Omega)$ is defined as

$$\bowtie_{(X \rightarrow\!\!\!\rightarrow Y) \in MVD(\Omega)} (XY)$$

□

We finally have all the definitions and results to characterize hierarchical instances in terms of flat relation instances satisfying certain multivalued or join dependencies.

Theorem 7.8 *Let ω be a nested relation instance over the scheme Ω. The following statements are equivalent:*

- *ω is a hierarchical instance;*
- *$\mu^*(\omega)$ satisfies the mvd's in $MVD(\Omega)$;*
- *$\mu^*(\omega)$ satisfies the join dependency $JD(\Omega)$.*

Proof Consult [109]. In their proof, the results described in Section 7.3 are used.

□

7.6 Exercises

7.1 Give a constructive definition of the set $\mathcal{U}$ of all attributes in Definition 7.1. Also, give a constructive definition of the set $\mathcal{V}$ of all values in Definition 7.4.

7.2 If t is a tuple and X a composed attribute, we sometimes write $t(X)$ and sometimes $t[X]$. Explain the difference.

7.3 Let ω_1 be the nested relation instance defined over the scheme *HOBBY-INFO* shown in Figure 7.4 and let ω_2 be the nested relation instance defined over the scheme *HOBBY-INFO* shown in Figure 7.5. Write nested algebra expressions using only the basic operators introduced in Definition 7.7 for the following queries:

- Get all the sons who have a father that play soccer.
- Get all fathers and sons who share a hobby. Make sure that you group the sons into a set.
- Find the stores that sell magnifying glasses.
- List all the equipment that Sears is selling.
- List for each store the equipment that it sells.
- List the stores where John can shop to get the equipment for his hobbies.
- Find all sons who share a hobby with a brother.
- Find all sons who do not share a hobby their father.

7.4 In Chapter 2 we described besides the relational algebra also the relational calculus and a version of *SQL*. Describe a calculus and an extension of *SQL* as query languages for nested relation instances. Are your query languages equivalent to the nested relational algebra? (Since this is a non-trivial exercise, we refer to [1, 88, 90, 92].)

7.5 Show how the nested relation instances shown in Figure 7.3 can be obtained from the flat relation instances shown in Figure 2.1 and Figure 2.2.

7.6 In this chapter we have studied when certain operators such as the nest and unnest operator commute. Characterize when the nest operator (respectively the unnest) commutes with the union, difference, cartesian product, the projection and the selection operators. (Since this is a non-trivial exercise, we refer to [102, 103].)

7.7 Show that the relation instance in Figure 7.8 does not satisfy the wmvd $\emptyset \twoheadrightarrow_w A$.

7.8 Give an example of a relation instance which satisfies a wmvd but not the corresponding mvd.

7.9 Prove Theorem 7.2 which gives a characterization for when two nest operations permute.

7.10 Define an axiom system for wmvd's and a mixed axiom system for mvd's and wmvd's (Since this is a non-trivial exercise we refer to [50, 51].)

7.11 Prove Lemma 7.2.

7.12 Prove Lemma 7.4.

7.13 Prove Theorem 7.4.

7.14 Consider the tag and empty-component operators introduced in Definition 7.12. Prove that these operators can be expressed in the nested algebra introduced in Definition 7.7

7.15 Prove Lemma 7.5.

7.16 Prove Lemma 7.6.

7.17 Using the operators introduced in Section 7.4, give a nested algebra expression for each of the queries described in Exercise 7.1.

7.18 In Section 7.4 we showed how one can express powerful selection operations in the nested algebra. Show that similarly, one can extend the definition of operators such as unnest and project so that they operate at any level of nested relation instances.

7.19 Consider the operator which generates for a given nested relation instance all the subsets of that nested relation instance. Call this operator the powerset operator.

- Prove that the powerset operator can not be expressed by a nested relational algebra expressions.
- Prove that if one augments the nested relational algebra with the powerset operator that it is possible to express the transitive closure of a binary (flat) relation. (Since these are non-trivial exercises we refer to [1, 62, 64, 88].)

7.20 Complete the proof of Theorem 7.6.

7.21 Show that the definition of $\mu^*(\omega)$ introduced in Definition 7.17 is sound.

7.22 A fundamental property of the query languages for the relational model is that they map flat relation instances into flat relation instances. A similar property is true for the nested relational algebra and nested relation instances. Now, consider hierarchical instances.

- Which operators of the nested relational algebra map hierarchical instances into hierarchical instances?
- Which operators of the nested relational algebra do not map hierarchical instances into hierarchical instances?
- Suggest replacements for those operators which violate the closure property mentioned above such that the closure property for hierarchical instances becomes satisfied (you may want to consult [2, 93, 109]).

7.23 Consider the nested relation scheme *HOBBY-INFO* and *HOBBY-EQUIPMENT* shown in Example 7.1 and Example 7.2 respectively. Determine *MVD*(*HOBBY-INFO*), *MVD*(*HOBBY-EQUIPMENT*), *JD*(*HOBBY-INFO*) and *JD*(*HOBBY-EQUIPMENT*). Consider the nested relation instances shown in Figure 7.4 and Figure 7.5. Verify Theorem theo-7.8 for these nested relation instances.

7.24 Prove Theorem 7.8. (Since this is a non-trivial exercise, we refer to [109].)

Chapter 8

Updates

In this chapter we describe some problems and some important results about updates in a database. Most databases are very dynamic in the sense that regularly their contents or their instances change. These updates are described by the user in some language. It is not the aim of this chapter to describe such a language. Nor is it the aim to give a complete overview over the expressive power of such a language. We will discuss a very elegant and easy formalism that can only express a rather small class of updates. This formalism mainly includes transactions, which are sequences of insertions, deletions and modifications.

In this chapter we only use one relation scheme $RS = (\Omega, \Delta, dom, M, SC)$. A generalization to a database with more relations is straightforward. We suppose that every $dom(A)$ is infinite.

The contents of this chapter is mainly related to two papers of S. Abiteboul, A. Karabeg, D. Karabeg, K. Papakonstantinou and V. Vianu [4, 70].

8.1 Transactions

As we mentioned earlier there are three kinds of updates : insertions, deletions and modifications. In each case a set of tuples has to be indicated that will be inserted, deleted or modified. Therefore we use the conditions.

Definition 8.1 A *condition* is an expression of the form $A = a$ or $A \neq a$, where A is an attribute of Ω and a is an element of $dom(A)$. $A = a$ and $A \neq a$ are called conditions corresponding to the attribute A. A tuple t satisfies $A = a$ iff $t(A) = a$. It satisfies $A \neq a$ iff $t(A) \neq a$.

□

In many cases a tuple has to satisfy more conditions. Therefore we use a set of conditions.

Definition 8.2 A tuple satisfies the set of conditions C iff it satisfies every condition in C.

□

Note that no tuple satisfies the set $\{A = a, A \neq a\}$. Note also that, if $a \neq b$, the sets $\{A = a, A \neq b\}$ and $\{A = a\}$ are satisfied by the same tuples. Clearly every set of tuples satisfies the empty set of conditions.

The class of updates we discuss is very limited. Most database systems include a wider class. The techniques we use are however generalizable to a larger class of updates.

We are now ready to define the three kinds of updates that we will consider. First we define their syntax.

Definition 8.3 Let r be a set of tuples of RS, or a *variable* representing a set of tuples of RS. A *deletion* is an expression of the form $Del(C, r)$, where C is a set of conditions. An *insertion* is an expression of the form $Ins(C, r)$, where C is a set of conditions containing only conditions of the form $A = a$. Furthermore C contains exactly one condition of the form $A = a$, for every attribute A in Ω. A *modification* is an expression of the form $Mod(C, C', r)$, where C and C' are both sets of conditions, such that for each attribute A of Ω holds that C and C' have the same conditions corresponding to A or that there is exactly one condition corresponding to A in C'. This condition must have the form $A = a$. An *action* is a deletion, an insertion or a modification.

□

Example 8.1 Suppose that $\Omega = \{A, B, C, D\}$ and that $a, a' \in dom(A)$, $b, b' \in dom(B)$, $c, c' \in dom(C)$, $d \in dom(D)$.

$Mod(\{B \neq b, C \neq c\}, \{B \neq b, C = c', D = d\}, r)$
$Mod(\{B \neq b', B = b, A = a\}, \{A = a', B \neq b', B = b, C = c\}, r)$

are modifications. On the other hand

$Mod(\{A = a, B = b\}, \{B = b'\}, r)$
$Mod(\{B \neq b, A = a\}, \{A = a'\}, r)$
$Mod(\{A = a, B = b, D \neq d\}, \{C = c\}, r)$

are not modifications.

□

$Del(C, r)$ indicates the set of tuples r except those that satisfy C. $Ins(C, r)$ indicates the set of tuples r augmented with the only tuple that satisfies C. $Mod(C, C', r)$ needs more comment. Note first that there are four kinds of attributes in Ω :

- those which do not appear in C nor in C';
- those which appear in both C and C' and have the same corresponding conditions in C and C';
- those which appear in both C and C' and have a different corresponding condition in C and C'. There is exactly one corresponding condition (of the form $A = a$) in C';
- those which only appear in C'. There is exactly one corresponding condition (of the form $A = a$) in C'.

$Mod(C, C', r)$ indicates the set of tuples r where all the tuples that satisfy C are modified each, such that they satisfy C' afterwards.

Definition 8.4 $Del(C,r) = r - \{t \mid t \text{ satisfies } C\}$
$Ins(C,r) = r \cup \{t \mid t \text{ satisfies } C\}$
$Mod(C,C',r) = r - \{t \mid t \text{ satisfies } C\} \cup \{t \mid \exists t' \in r, (t' \text{ satisfies } C \text{ and } t(A) = t'(A)$ if no $A = a$ belongs to C' and $t(A) = a$ if $A = a$ belongs to $C')\}$.

□

r

A	B
a	b
a	a

r_1

A	B
a	b
a	a
b	b

r_2

A	B
a	a

r_3

A	B
a	b

r_4

A	B
a	b
b	a

Figure 8.1: Some Actions

Example 8.2 Verify the following equations in Figure 8.1 :

$Ins(\{A = b, B = b\}, r) = r_1$
$Ins(\{A = a, B = b\}, r) = r$
$Del(\{B = b\}, r) = r_2$
$Del(\{B \neq c, B \neq b\}, r) = r_3$
$Mod(\{B \neq b\}, \{B \neq b, A = b\}, r) = r_4$
$Mod(\{B \neq b\}, \{B = b\}, r) = r_3$

□

In most practical applications an update is a sequence of insertions, deletions and modifications. This will be called a transaction.

Definition 8.5 A *transaction* is an expression of the form

Transaction $< identifier > (fp);$

$r_1 := a_1; r_2 := a_2; ...; r_n := a_n;$

end;

where $< identifier >$ is the name of the transaction, fp is the formal parameter, representing a set of tuples, the a_j are actions, and the r_j are variables representing sets of tuples. A transaction is called by writing down its name followed by the actual parameter between brackets. The set of tuples that is represented by the call of the transaction, is the value of r_n, that results from substituting the formal parameter by the actual parameter and substituting r_1 by the value of a_1, r_2 by a_2, etc.

□

Example 8.3 Consider the relation *ROOMS* of Example 1.2 of Chapter 1 and suppose we want to describe the following transaction : Put a bath in every room, make the rate for each two-bed room 200 and for each three-bed room 300, add the two-bed room 502, on the fifth floor, with a bath and a rate of 200. Finally delete all the rooms on the first floor. This can be expressed by

Transaction $ROOM_{UPDATE}(r);$

$r_1 := Mod(\emptyset, \{BATH? = true\}, r);$

$r_2 := Mod(\{NUMBER\text{-}OF\text{-}BEDS = 2\},$
$\{RATE = 200, NUMBER\text{-}OF\text{-}BEDS = 2\}, r_1);$

$r_3 := Mod(\{NUMBER\text{-}OF\text{-}BEDS = 3\},$
$\{RATE = 300, NUMBER\text{-}OF\text{-}BEDS = 3\}, r_2);$

$r_4 := Ins(\{ROOM\text{-}NUMBER = 502, NUMBER\text{-}OF\text{-}BEDS = 2,$
$BATH? = true, FLOOR = 5, RATE = 200\}, r_3);$

$r_5 := Del(\{FLOOR = 1\}, r_4);$

end;

□

8.2 Equivalent Transactions

Clearly, some transactions have the same effect, i.e. for some transactions T and T' we have that $T(r) = T'(r)$ for every set of tuples r of RS. Such transactions are called equivalent.

Definition 8.6 The transactions are called *equivalent* iff for every set of tuples r of RS holds that $T(r) = T'(r)$. An insertion (deletion, modification) is called equivalent to the transaction T iff for every set of tuples r of RS holds that $T(r) = Ins(C, r)$ $(T(r) = Del(C, r)$, $T(r) = Mod(C, C', r))$.

□

Example 8.4 Suppose that $\Omega = \{A, B\}$ and that $a, a' \in dom(A)$ and $b, b' \in dom(B)$. The following transactions are all equivalent:

Transaction $T_1(r)$;
$r_1 := Ins(\{A = a, B = b\}, r)$;
$r_2 := Mod(\{A = a\}, \{A = a'\}, r_1)$;
$r_3 := Mod(\{B = b\}, \{B = b'\}, r_2)$;
end;
Transaction $T_2(r)$;
$r_1 := Ins(\{A = a, B = b\}, r)$;
$r_2 := Mod(\{B = b\}, \{B = b'\}, r_1)$;
$r_3 := Mod(\{A = a\}, \{A = a'\}, r_2)$;
end;
Transaction $T_3(r)$;
$r_1 := Mod(\{A = a\}, \{A = a'\}, r)$;
$r_2 := Ins(\{A = a', B = b\}, r_1)$;
$r_3 := Mod(\{B = b\}, \{B = b'\}, r_2)$;
end;
Transaction $T_4(r)$;
$r_1 := Mod(\{A = a\}, \{A = a'\}, r)$;
$r_2 := Mod(\{B = b\}, \{B = b'\}, r_1)$;
$r_3 := Ins(\{A = a', B = b'\}, r_2)$;
end;
Transaction $T_5(r)$;
$r_1 := Mod(\{B = b\}, \{B = b'\}, r)$;
$r_2 := Ins(\{A = a, B = b'\}, r_1)$;
$r_3 := Mod(\{A = a\}, \{A = a'\}, r_2)$;
end;
Transaction $T_6(r)$;
$r_1 := Mod(\{B = b\}, \{B = b'\}, r)$;
$r_2 := Mod(\{A = a\}, \{A = a'\}, r_1)$;
$r_3 := Ins(\{A = a', B = b'\}, r_2)$;
end;

□

We need a general algorithm to decide whether two given transactions are equivalent. It consists in considering a number of sets that contain only one tuple. If the value of the transactions for each of these sets is equal we deduce that the transactions are equivalent. This algorithm will be polynomial in the number of actions in the transactions.

First we define the single-tuple sets we need. They are called domain-sets. Their tuple only contains values that appear somewhere in T and a special value ϖ_A for each attribute A.

Definition 8.7 Let T be a transaction, and A be an attribute. $dom_T(A)$ is the set of all values of $dom(A)$ that appear in some condition that corresponds to A and that is in some action of T. Let ϖ_A be an arbitrary but fixed element of $dom(A) - dom_T(A)$. The tuple t is called a ***domain-tuple*** of T iff for each A, $t(A) \in dom_T(A) \cup \{\varpi_A\}$. A set is called a ***domain-set*** of T iff it only contains one domain-tuple of T.

□

Consider the first transaction of Example 8.4. $dom_{T_1}(A) = \{a, a'\}$ and $dom_{T_1}(B) = \{b, b'\}$. Hence T_1 has $3 * 3 = 9$ domain-sets. In Example 8.3 there are $2 * 3 * 2 * 3 * 3 = 108$ domain-sets.

Two important properties of transactions are proved in the next two lemmas. They are used in the decision algorithm of the equivalence.

Lemma 8.1 For every transaction T holds that $T(r_1) \cup T(r_2) = T(r_1 \cup r_2)$.
Proof Here, we only prove that $Del(C, r_1) \cup Del(C, r_2) = Del(C, r_1 \cup r_2)$. The proof of $Ins(C, r_1) \cup Ins(C, r_2) = Ins(C, r_1 \cup r_2)$ and of $Mod(C, C', r_1) \cup Mod(C, C', r_2)$
$= Mod(C, C', r_1 \cup r_2)$ is left as an exercise. Clearly from these three equations follows that $T(r_1) \cup T(r_2) = T(r_1 \cup r_2)$. Suppose that $t \in Del(C, r_1) \cup Del(C, r_2)$, then it belongs to $Del(C, r_1)$ or to $Del(C, r_2)$. This means that t belongs to r_1 and does not satisfy C, or that it belongs to r_2 and does not satisfy C. Hence t belongs to $r_1 \cup r_2$ and it does not satisfy C, which induces that $t \in Del(C, r_1 \cup r_2)$. Clearly, inversely $t \in Del(C, r_1 \cup r_2)$ induces $t \in Del(C, r_1) \cup Del(C, r_2)$, which completes the proof.

□

Lemma 8.2 Let ϕ be a permutation on $dom(A)$ such that $\phi(a) = a$ for each $a \in dom_T(A)$. ϕ can be extended to tuples as follows: $\phi(t)(A) = \phi(t(A))$ and $\phi(t)(B) = t(B)$ for each $B \neq A$. ϕ can be extended to sets of tuples in a natural way. For every transaction holds $T(\phi(\{t\})) = \phi(T(\{t\}))$.
Proof We prove that $Del(C, \phi(\{t\})) = \phi(Del(C, \{t\}))$. The proof of $Ins(C, \phi(\{t\})) = \phi(Ins(C, \{t\}))$ and of $Mod(C, C', \phi(\{t\})) = \phi(Mod(C, C', \{t\}))$ is left as an exercise. Clearly from these three equations follows that $T(\phi(\{t\})) = \phi(T(\{t\}))$. Suppose that $t' \in Del(C, \phi(\{t\}))$, then $t' = \phi(t)$ and t' does not satisfy C. Since $\phi(a) = a$ for each $a \in dom_T(A)$ and by the definition of ϕ, t does not satisfy C inducing that it belongs to $Del(C, \{t\})$, so t' belongs to $\phi(Del(C, \{t\}))$. Clearly, inversely, $t' \in \phi(Del(C, \{t\}))$ induces $t' \in Del(C, \phi(\{t\}))$, which completes the proof.

□

We are now ready to describe and prove an algorithm to detect whether two given transactions are equivalent. The time complexity of this algorithm is polynomial.

Algorithm 8.1 *Detection of Equivalent Transactions*
Input: Two transactions T and T'.

Output: T and T' are equivalent or not.

Method: Take for every attribute A a fixed value ϖ_A of $dom(A) - dom_T(A) - dom_{T'}(A)$. T and T' are equivalent iff for every domain-set r holds that $T(r) = T'(r)$.

□

Theorem 8.1 Algorithm 8.1 is correct and has polynomial time complexity.
Proof Clearly if T is equivalent to T' then $T'(r) = T(r)$ for every domain-set r. On the other hand, for every possible tuple t there is a domain-tuple t' such that we can obtain t from t' using only permutations that we introduced in Lemma 8.2. Hence, if $T'(r) = T(r)$ for every domain-set r, then by Lemma 8.2 we have for every tuple t that $T(\{t\}) = T'(\{t\})$. By Lemma 8.1 T is equivalent to T'. Since there are only a polynomial number of domain-sets, the time complexity of the algorithm is polynomial.

□

Example 8.5 Consider the transactions T_1 and T_2 of Example 8.4

Transaction $T_1(r)$;
$r_1 := Ins(\{A = a, B = b\}, r)$;
$r_2 := Mod(\{A = a\}, \{A = a'\}, r_1)$;
$r_3 := Mod(\{B = b\}, \{B = b'\}, r_2)$;
end;
Transaction $T_2(r)$;
$r_1 := Ins(\{A = a, B = b\}, r)$;
$r_2 := Mod(\{B = b\}, \{B = b'\}, r_1)$;
$r_3 := Mod(\{A = a\}, \{A = a'\}, r_2)$;
end;

There are 9 domain-sets. We have

- $T_1(\{(a, b)\}) = \{(a', b')\} = T_2(\{(a, b)\})$
- $T_1(\{(a, b')\}) = \{(a', b')\} = T_2(\{(a, b')\})$
- $T_1(\{(a, \varpi_B)\}) = \{(a', b'), (a', \varpi_B)\} = T_2(\{(a, \varpi_B)\})$
- $T_1(\{(a', b)\}) = \{(a', b')\} = T_2(\{(a', b)\})$
- $T_1(\{(a', b')\}) = \{(a', b')\} = T_2(\{(a', b')\})$
- $T_1(\{(a', \varpi_B)\}) = \{(a', b'), (a', \varpi_B)\} = T_2(\{(a', \varpi_B)\})$
- $T_1(\{(\varpi_A, b)\}) = \{(a', b'), (\varpi_A, b')\} = T_2(\{(\varpi_A, b)\})$
- $T_1(\{(\varpi_A, b')\}) = \{(a', b'), (\varpi_A, b')\} = T_2(\{(\varpi_A, b')\})$
- $T_1(\{(\varpi_A, \varpi_B)\}) = \{(a', b'), (\varpi_A, \varpi_B)\} = T_2(\{(\varpi_A, \varpi_B)\})$

Hence T_1 is equivalent to T_2.

Consider

Transaction $T_7(r)$;

$r_1 := Mod(\{B = b\}, \{B = b'\}, r)$;

$r_2 := Mod(\{A = a\}, \{A = a'\}, r_1)$;

$r_3 := Ins(\{A = a, B = b\}, r_2)$;

end;.

T_1 is not equivalent to T_7 since $T_1(\{(a', b')\}) = \{(a', b')\}$ and $T_7(\{(a', b')\}) = \{(a, b), (a', b')\}$.

□

8.3 Dynamic Relation Constraints

Let us first extend the definition of transaction to include parameters for domain values.

Definition 8.8 A *parameterized transaction* is an expression of the form

Transaction $< identifier > (fp; v_1, ..., v_l)$;

$r_1 := a_1; r_2 := a_2; ...; r_n := a_n$;

end;

where $< identifier >$ is the name of the transaction, fp is a formal parameter, representing a set of tuples, the v_i are formal parameters for values, the a_j are generalized actions in the sense that they can use formal parameters for values instead of domain values, and the r_j are variables representing sets of tuples. The transaction is called by writing down its name followed by the actual parameters between brackets. The set of tuples that is represented by the call of the transaction, is the value of r_n, that results from substituting the formal parameters by the corresponding actual parameters and substituting r_1 by the value of a_1, r_2 by a_2, etc.

□

Example 8.6 Consider the relation *ROOMS* of Example 1.2 of Chapter 1 and suppose we want to describe the following parameterized transaction : Put a bath in every room, make the rate for each two-bed room rt_1 and for each three-bed room rt_2, add the two-bed room *room* on the fifth floor, with a bath and a rate of rt_{room}. Finally delete all the rooms on the first floor. This can be expressed by

Transaction $PAR\text{-}ROOM\text{-}UPDATE(r; rt_1, rt_2, room, rt_{room})$;

$r_1 := Mod(\emptyset, \{BATH? = true\}, r)$;

$r_2 := Mod(\{NUMBER\text{-}OF\text{-}BEDS = 2\},$
$\{NUMBER\text{-}OF\text{-}BEDS = 2, RATE = rt_1\}, r_1)$;

$r_3 := Mod(\{NUMBER\text{-}OF\text{-}BEDS = 3\},$
$\{NUMBER\text{-}OF\text{-}BEDS = 3, RATE = rt_2\}, r_2)$;

$r_4 := Ins(\{ROOM\text{-}NUMBER = room, NUMBER\text{-}OF\text{-}BEDS = 2,$
$BATH? = true, FLOOR = 5, RATE = rt_{room}\}, r_3);$
$r_5 := Del(\{FLOOR = 1\}, r_4);$
end.

The transaction of Example 8.3 is now described by the call
PAR-ROOM-UPDATE$(r; 200, 300, 502, 200)$;

□

In Chapter 1 we defined dynamic relation constraints as constraints that are represented by a function that associates *true* or *false* with each sequence of relation instances of RS. We said that a sequence of relation instances satisfies a dynamic relation constraint if the representing function returns *true* for that sequence. In this section we will discuss dynamic relation constraints where the transition between instances is described by transactions.

In general, the system has to verify all the static constraints after each update. In most cases however, not all the static constraints have to be verified, but still this verification is a very time consuming activity, which we want to reduce as much as possible. We can wonder in which cases we do not have to verify the static constraints at all. Indeed, the constraints that are consequences of the dynamic constraints have not to be verified, if the dynamic constraints hold. And in a well-designed system the latter holds as a consequence of the update-tools we use.

We will discuss some special cases of the above general problem: How can we restrict the transactions such that a set of functional dependencies that holds before, still holds after the restricted transactions? Furthermore every instance (where a given set of functional dependencies holds) has to be reachable by restricted transactions from the empty instance. This set of restricted transactions will be rich enough to describe every instance, but not too rich to violate the given dependencies.

Example 8.7 Consider the relation *TEACH* that has three attributes *TEACHER, STUDENT, COURSE* and that describes teachers teaching courses to students. The constraints require that each student is given a course only by one teacher. This is represented by the functional dependency $\{STUDENT, COURSE\} \to TEACHER$. Consider the following parameterized transactions *NEW* and *FIN*:

Transaction $NEW(r; t, s, c)$;
$r_1 := Del(\{STUDENT = s, COURSE = c\}, r);$
$r_2 := Ins(\{TEACHER = t, STUDENT = s, COURSE = c\}, r_1);$
end;

Transaction $FIN(r; t, s, c)$;
$r_1 := Del(\{TEACHER = t, STUDENT = s, COURSE = c\}, r);$
end;

It can be very easily verified that whenever the functional dependency {*STUDENT,COURSE*} → *TEACHER* is satisfied in r, it is also satisfied in $NEW(r;t,s,c)$ and in $FIN(r;t,s,c)$, for every value of t, s and c. Furthermore, every instance (that satisfies the functional dependency) can be expressed by a sequence of calls of *NEW* on the empty instance.

□

We now give the exact definition of a set of constraints that can be specified by a set of parameterized transactions.

Definition 8.9 A set of constraints SC is called to be *specified* by a set of parameterized transactions SPT iff

- whenever a set of tuples r satisfies all the constraints of SC, then the value of each call of a parameterized transaction (with arbitrary actual parameters for domain values) of SPT satisfies all the constraints of SC;
- every finite instance where the constraints of SC hold can be obtained from the empty set by calling only parameterized transactions of SPR.

□

In Example 8.7 clearly the functional dependency {*STUDENT,COURSE*} → *TEACHER* can be specified by both {*NEW*, *FIN*} and {*NEW*}.

Theorem 8.2 Every set of functional dependencies is specified by a set of parameterized transactions.

Proof Let $\{A_1, ...A_n\}$ be the set of attributes, and let the given set $FD = \{fd_1, ..., fd_k\}$ of functional dependencies contain k elements. We only consider functional dependencies with one attribute on the right. The general case can be trivially reduced to this case. We construct a set that contains only one parameterized transaction, namely $T(r_0; x_1, ..., x_n)$. Let fd_m be the functional dependency $\{A_{m_1}, ..., A_{m_{p_m}}\} \rightarrow A_m$. We add $r_m := Del(\{A_{m_1} = x_{m_1}, ..., A_{m_{p_m}} = x_{m_{p_m}}, A_m \neq x_m\}, r_{m-1})$; to the definition of $T(r_0; x_1, ..., x_n)$. Finally add $r_{k+1} := Ins(\{A_1 = x_1, ..., A_n = x_n\}, r_k)$;. One can easily verify that the set FD is specified by $\{T(r_0; x_1, ..., x_n)\}$.

□

Example 8.8 Let $\Omega = \{A, B, C, D, E\}$ and let $FD = \{AB \rightarrow CD, C \rightarrow E, CE \rightarrow A\}$. FD is specified by the following parameterized transaction.

Transaction $T(r_0; a, b, c, d, e)$;
$r_1 := Del(\{A = a, B = b, C \neq c\}, r_0)$;
$r_2 := Del(\{A = a, B = b, D \neq d\}, r_1)$;
$r_3 := Del(\{C = c, E \neq e\}, r_2)$;
$r_4 := Del(\{C = c, E = e, A \neq a\}, r_3)$;
$r_5 := Ins(\{A = a, B = b, C = c, D = d, E = e\}, r_4\})$;
end;

□

We proved above that every set of functional dependencies can be specified by a set of parameterized transactions. Not every class of dependencies has this property. In the next theorem we prove that the set of multivalued dependencies cannot be specified by a set of parameterized transactions.

Theorem 8.3 A set of non-trivial multivalued dependencies cannot be specified by a set of parameterized transactions.

Proof Consider the multivalued dependency $\emptyset \rightarrow\rightarrow \{A, B\}$. For every n and m there is an instance r that satisfies the multivalued dependency and that contains $n*m$ tuples. An insertion of a tuple can require $(n+m-1)$ other insertions. Since every transaction has only a finite number of actions, this unbounded number of insertions cannot be included in one transaction, which proves the theorem. □

8.4 Axiomatization of Equivalence of Transactions

In this final section we define independent sets of conditions. We then give a number of rules for transforming transactions in equivalent transactions.

Definition 8.10 Two sets of conditions C and C' are called *independent* iff no tuple satisfies both C and C'.

□

Example 8.9 Let $a \neq b \in dom(A)$. Consider $C_1 = \{A = a\}$, $C_2 = \{A \neq a\}$ and $C_3 = \{A = b\}$. C_1 and C_2 are independent. So are C_1 and C_3. But C_2 and C_3 are not independent.

□

We describe now 18 general examples of equivalent transactions. They indicate 18 different rules to transform transactions into equivalent transactions. Some of them are obvious. Others are explained. E12-E18 have to be verified by the reader.

E1

Transaction $T_1(r); r_1 := Mod(C, C, r);$ **end**;

is equivalent with the identity. Indeed T_1 does not modify any tuple.

E2

Transaction $T_1(r); r_1 := Ins(C, r); r_2 := Del(C, r_1);$ **end**;

is equivalent to

Transaction $T_2(r); r_1 := Del(C, r);$ **end**;

The tuple that is deleted by T_2 is first inserted by T_1, before being deleted.

E3

Transaction $T_1(r); r_1 := Del(C, r); r_2 := Ins(C, r_1);$ **end**;

is equivalent to

Transaction $T_2(r); r_1 := Ins(C, r);$ **end**;

The tuple that is inserted by T_2 is first deleted by T_1, before being inserted.

E4

Transaction $T_1(r); r_1 := Mod(C_1, C_2, r); r_2 := Ins(C_2, r_1);$ **end;**
is equivalent to
Transaction $T_2(r); r_1 := Del(C_1, r); r_2 := Ins(C_2, r_1);$ **end;**
In both cases, first the tuples satisfying C_1 are deleted. Then the tuple that satisfies C_2 is inserted.

E5

Transaction $T_1(r); r_1 := Ins(C_1, r); r_2 := Mod(C_1, C_2, r_1);$ **end;**
is equivalent to
Transaction $T_2(r); r_1 := Ins(C_2, r); r_2 := Mod(C_1, C_2, r_1);$ **end;**

E6

Transaction $T_1(r); r_1 := Del(C_1, r); r_2 := Mod(C_1, C_2, r_1);$ **end;**
is equivalent to
Transaction $T_2(r); r_1 := Del(C_1, r);$ **end;**

E7

Transaction $T_1(r); r_1 := Mod(C_1, C_2, r); r_2 := Del(C_2, r_1);$ **end;**
is equivalent to
Transaction $T_2(r); r_1 := Del(C_1, r); r_2 := Del(C_2, r_1);$ **end;**

E8

Transaction $T_1(r); r_1 := Ins(C_1, r); r_2 := Ins(C_2, r_1);$ **end;**
is equivalent to
Transaction $T_2(r); r_1 := Ins(C_2, r); r_2 := Ins(C_1, r_1);$ **end;**

E9

Transaction $T_1(r); r_1 := Del(C_1, r); r_2 := Del(C_2, r_1);$ **end;**
is equivalent to
Transaction $T_2(r); r_1 := Del(C_2, r); r_2 := Del(C_1, r_1);$ **end;**

E10

Transaction $T_1(r); r_1 := Mod(C_1, C_2, r); r_2 := Mod(C_2, C_3, r_1);$ **end;**
is equivalent to
Transaction $T_2(r); r_1 := Mod(C_1, C_3, r); r_2 := Mod(C_2, C_3, r_1);$ **end;**

E11

Transaction $T_1(r); r_1 := Ins(C_1, r); r_2 := Del(C_2, r_1);$ **end;**
is equivalent to
Transaction $T_2(r); r_1 := Del(C_2, r); r_2 := Ins(C_1, r_1);$ **end;**,
if C_1 and C_2 are independent.

E12

Transaction $T_1(r); r_1 := Ins(C_1, r); r_2 := Mod(C_2, C_3, r_1);$ **end;**
is equivalent to
Transaction $T_2(r); r_1 := Mod(C_2, C_3, r); r_2 := Ins(C_1, r_1);$ **end;**,
if C_1 and C_2 are independent.

E13

Transaction $T_1(r); r_1 := Mod(C_1, C_2, r);$ **end**;

is equivalent to

Transaction $T_2(r); r_1 := Mod(C_1, C_2, r); r_2 := Del(C_1, r_1);$ **end**;,

if C_1 and C_2 are independent.

E14

Transaction $T_1(r); r_1 := Del(C_1, r); r_2 := Mod(C_2, C_3, r_1);$ **end**;

is equivalent to

Transaction $T_2(r); r_1 := Mod(C_2, C_3, r); r_2 := Del(C_1, r_1);$ **end**;,

if C_1 and C_2 are independent and C_1 and C_3 are independent.

E15

Transaction $T_1(r); r_1 := Mod(C_1, C_2, r); r_2 := Mod(C_3, C_4, r_1);$ **end**;

is equivalent to

Transaction $T_2(r); r_1 := Mod(C_3, C_4, r); r_2 := Mod(C_1, C_2, r_1);$ **end**;,

if C_2 and C_3 are independent, C_1 and C_4 are independent and C_1 and C_3 are independent.

E16

Transaction $T_1(r)$;
$r_1 := Del(C_3, r);$
$r_2 := Mod(C_1, C_3, r_1);$
$r_3 := Mod(C_2, C_1, r_2);$
$r_4 := Mod(C_3, C_2, r_3);$
end;

is equivalent to

Transaction $T_1(r)$;
$r_1 := Del(C_3, r);$
$r_2 := Mod(C_2, C_3, r_1);$
$r_3 := Mod(C_1, C_2, r_2);$
$r_4 := Mod(C_3, C_1, r_3);$
end;

if C_1, C_2 and C_3 are mutually independent.

E17

Transaction $T_1(r)$;
$r_1 := Del(C_1, r);$
$r_2 := Mod(C_2, C_1, r_1);$
$r_3 := Mod(C_3, C_2, r_2);$
$r_4 := Mod(C_4, C_3, r_3);$
$r_5 := Mod(C_2, C_4, r_4);$
end;

is equivalent to

Transaction $T_1(r)$;

$r_1 := Del(C_1, r)$;

$r_2 := Mod(C_3, C_1, r_1)$;

$r_3 := Mod(C_4, C_3, r_2)$;

$r_4 := Mod(C_1, C_4, r_3)$; iip$r_5 := Mod(C_2, C_1, r_4)$;

end;

if C_1, C_2, C_3 and C_4 are mutually independent.

E18

Transaction $T_1(r)$;

$r_1 := Del(C_1, r)$;

$r_2 := Mod(C_2, C_1, r_1)$;

$r_3 := Mod(C_3, C_2, r_2)$;

$r_4 := Mod(C_1, C_3, r_3)$;

$r_5 := Mod(C_3, C_1, r_4)$;

$r_6 := Mod(C_4, C_3, r_5)$;

$r_7 := Mod(C_1, C_4, r_6)$;

end;

is equivalent to

Transaction $T_1(r)$;

$r_1 := Del(C_1, r)$;

$r_2 := Mod(C_4, C_1, r_1)$;

$r_3 := Mod(C_2, C_4, r_2)$;

$r_4 := Mod(C_1, C_2, r_3)$;

$r_5 := Mod(C_2, C_1, r_4)$;

$r_6 := Mod(C_3, C_2, r_5)$;

$r_7 := Mod(C_1, C_3, r_6)$;

end;

if C_1, C_2, C_3 and C_4 are mutually independent.

The general examples above can be considered as rules to transform transactions in equivalent transactions. For instance we can use E3 to transform

Transaction $T_1(r)$;

$r_1 := Del(\{A = a, B = b\}, r)$;

$r_2 := Ins(\{A = a, B = b\}, r_1)$;

$r_3 := Del(\{B \neq b\}, r_2)$;

end;

into the equivalent

Transaction $T_2(r)$;

$r_1 := Ins(\{A = a, B = b\}, r)$;

$r_2 := Del(\{B \neq b\}, r_1)$;

end;

Let T_1 and T_2 be two equivalent transactions with mutually independent sets of conditions. It can be proved that one can transform T_1 into T_2 by these rules [70].

8.5 Exercises

8.1 Indicate which of the following expressions are insertions or deletions. Give their value, r being the set of tuples of Figure 8.1

- $Ins(\{A = b, B = a\}, r)$
- $Ins(\{B = b\}, r)$
- $Ins(\{A = a, A = b, B = b\}, r)$
- $Ins(\{A = a, A \neq b, B = b\}, r)$
- $Ins(\{A = b, B = c\}, r)$
- $Ins(\emptyset, r)$
- $Del(\{A = a, A \neq b\}, r)$
- $Del(\{A = a, B \neq a\}, r)$
- $Del(\{B \neq b, B \neq c\}, r)$
- $Del(\{A \neq a\}, r)$
- $Del(\{A = a, B = b\}, r)$
- $Del(\{A = a, A = b\}, r)$
- $Del(\{B = a\}, r)$
- $Del(\emptyset, r)$

8.2 Indicate which of the following expressions are modifications. Give their value, r being the set of tuples of Figure 8.1

- $Mod(\{A = a\}, \{A = a, B = b\}, r)$
- $Mod(\{A = a\}, \{A = a\}, r)$
- $Mod(\{A \neq a\}, \{A = b\}, r)$
- $Mod(\{A \neq a\}, \{A \neq a, A = b\}, r)$
- $Mod(\{A \neq a, A \neq b\}, \{A = c\}, r)$
- $Mod(\emptyset, \emptyset, r)$
- $Mod(\emptyset, \{A = a\}, r)$
- $Mod(\emptyset, \{A \neq a\}, r)$
- $Mod(\{A = a\}, \emptyset, r)$
- $Mod(\{A = a\}, \{A = a\}, r)$
- $Mod(\{A = a\}, \{A \neq a\}, r)$
- $Mod(\{A \neq a\}, \emptyset, r)$

- $Mod(\{A \neq a\}, \{A = a\}, r)$
- $Mod(\{A \neq a\}, \{A \neq a\}, r)$
- $Mod(\{A = a\}, \{B = b\}, r)$
- $Mod(\{A \neq a\}, \{A \neq a, B \neq b\}, r)$
- $Mod(\{A \neq a\}, \{A \neq a, B = b, B = c\}, r)$
- $Mod(\{A = a, B \neq b\}, \{B = b\}, r)$
- $Mod(\{A = a, B \neq b\}, \{A = a, B = b\}, r)$

8.3 Describe in English some insertions, deletions and modifications we cannot express in the formalism of this chapter.

8.4 Can you find an insertion such that for every set of tuples r of *RS* holds $Ins(C, r) = r$? Answer the same question for the deletion and the modification.

8.5 Consider the relation *ROOMS* of Example 1.2 of Chapter 1. Describe the following updates by transactions, if possible :

- put a bath in every room that costs 200 or 300;
- add the two-bed rooms 506 and 507, both on the fifth floor, with a bath and a rate of 400;
- delete all the rooms that have no bath or that have only one bed;
- delete all the rooms that have no bath and have only one bed;
- delete all rooms, except those with one or two beds;
- double the rate of the rooms with bath;
- delete all the rooms that are lower than the fifth floor;
- put the rate of the rooms with a bath to 100 times the number of beds, and put the rate of the rooms without a bath to 50 times the number of beds (suppose there are maximum three beds in a room);
- renumber the floors, floor i becomes floor $i + 1$.

8.6 Prove that no transaction that only contains deletions and modifications is equivalent to an insertion.

8.7 Given a deletion. Is there a transaction that only contains insertions and modifications equivalent to the given deletion?

8.8 Given a modification. Is there a transaction that only contains insertions and deletions equivalent to the given modification?

8.9 Give 10 different transactions, each being equivalent to the 6 transactions of Example 8.4.

8.10 Express the number of domain-sets in terms of the number of elements of $dom_T(A)$, for every attribute A.

8.11 Prove that

$$Ins(C, r_1) \cup Ins(C, r_2) = Ins(C, r_1 \cup r_2)$$

and that

$$Mod(C, C', r_1) \cup Mod(C, C', r_2) = Mod(C, C', r_1 \cup r_2).$$

8.12 Prove that

$$Ins(C, \phi(\{t\})) = \phi(Ins(C, \{t\}))$$

and that

$$Mod(C, C', \phi(\{t\})) = \phi(Mod(C, C', \{t\})).$$

8.13 Let $\Omega = \{A, B\}$. Verify by Algorithm 8.1 which of the following transactions are equivalent :

Transaction $T_1(r)$;
$r_1 := Ins(\{A = a_1, B = b_1, C = c_1\}, r)$;
$r_2 := Mod(\{A \neq a_2, B = b_1\}, \{A = a_2, B = b_1\}, r_1)$;
$r_3 := Del(\{A = a_2, B = b_1\}, r_2)$;
end;

Transaction $T_2(r); r_1 := Mod(\emptyset, \emptyset, r);$ **end**;

Transaction $T_3(r)$;
$r_1 := Mod(\{A = a_1, B = b_1\}, \{A = a_2, B = b_1\}, r)$;
$r_2 := Del(\{A = a_2, B = b_1\}, r_1)$;
end;

Transaction $T_4(r)$;
$r_1 := Ins(\{A = a_1, B = b_1\}, r)$;
$r_2 := Ins(\{A = a_2, B = b_2\}, r_1)$;
$r_3 := Del(\{A = a_1, B = b_1\}, r_2)$;
$r_4 := Del(\{A = a_2, B = b_2\}, r_3)$;
end;

Transaction $T_5(r)$;
$r_1 := Mod(\{A = a_1\}, \{A = a_2\}, r)$;
$r_2 := Mod(\{A = a_2\}, \{A = a_1\}, r_1)$;
end;

Transaction $T_6(r)$;
$r_1 := Mod(\{A \neq a_1\}, \{A = a_2\}, r)$;
$r_2 := Del(\{A = a_2\}, r_1)$;
end;

Transaction $T_7(r); r_1 := Del(\{A = a_1\}, r);$ **end**;

8.14 Let $\Omega = \{A, B, C\}$. Verify by Algorithm 8.1 whether the two following transactions are equivalent:

Transaction $T_1(r)$;
$r_1 := Ins(\{A = a_1, B = b_3, C = c_1\}, r)$;
$r_2 := Mod(\{A \neq a_1, B = b_1, C \neq c_1\}, \{A \neq a_1, B = b_2, C \neq c_1\}, r_1)$;
$r_3 := Mod(\{A \neq a_2, B \neq b_2, C = c_1\}, \{A \neq a_2, B \neq b_2, C = c_2\}, r_2)$;
$r_4 := Del(\{B = b_2\}, r_3)$;
end;

Transaction $T_2(r)$;

$r_1 := Mod(\{A \neq a_1, B = b_1, C \neq c_1\}, \{A \neq a_1, B = b_2, C \neq c_1\}, r)$;

$r_2 := Del(\{B = b_2\}, r_1)$;

$r_3 := Ins(\{A = a_1, B = b_3, C = c_1\}, r_2)$;

$r_4 := Mod(\{A \neq a_2, B \neq b_2, C = c_1\}, \{A \neq a_2, B \neq b_2, C = c_2\}, r_3)$;

end;

8.15 Can a set of inclusion dependencies be specified by a set of parameterized transactions?

8.16 Let $\Omega = \{A, B, C\}$. Find a set of parameterized transactions that specifies the set $\{AB \rightarrow A, A \rightarrow AB\}$.

8.17 Let $\Omega = \{A, B, C, D, E\}$. Find a set of parameterized transactions that specifies the set $\{AB \rightarrow CD, C \rightarrow DE, D \rightarrow A, AE \rightarrow B, CB \rightarrow A\}$.

8.18 Consider the relation *ROOMS* of Example 1.2 of Chapter 1, with the only constraint that no floor contains more than two rooms. Can this constraint be specified by a set of parameterized transactions?

8.19 Consider the relation *ROOMS* of Example 1.2 of Chapter 1. Which of the constraints of SC can be specified by a set of parameterized transactions?

8.20 Let $a \neq b \in dom(A) \cap dom(B)$. Consider the following 7 sets of conditions. Which of the possible 21 pairs are independent?

- $C_1 = \{A = a, B = b\}$
- $C_2 = \{A \neq a\}$
- $C_3 = \{A = b, B \neq b\}$
- $C_4 = \{B \neq b\}$
- $C_5 = \{A \neq a, B \neq b\}$
- $C_6 = \{A = b, B = a\}$
- $C_7 = \{A = a\}$

8.21 Give examples to prove the necessity of the independency in E11.

8.22 Prove E12 - E18.

8.23 Give examples to prove the necessity of the independency in E12-E18.

Bibliography

[1] Abiteboul S., C. Beeri, On the Power of Languages for the Manipulation of Complex Objects. *INRIA Technical Report* 846, May 1988.

[2] Abiteboul S., N. Bidoit, Non First Normal Form Relations: An Algebra Allowing Data Restructuring. *Journal of Computer and System Sciences* **33:3**, pp. 361–393, December 1986.

[3] Abiteboul S., G. Grahne, Update Semantics for Incomplete Databases. *Proceedings* 11th *VLDB*, pp. 1–12, Stockholm, 1985.

[4] Abiteboul S., V. Vianu, Transactions and Integrity Constraints. *Proceedings* 4th *Symposium on Principles of Database Systems*, pp. 193–204, Portland, OR, 1985.

[5] Aho A., C. Beeri, J.D. Ullman, The Theory of Joins in Relational Databases. *Proceedings* 18th *Symposium on Foundations of Computer Science*, pp. 107–113, Providence, RI, 1977.

[6] Aho A., Y. Sagiv, J.D. Ullman, Equivalence among Relational Expressions. *Transactions on Database Systems* **4:4**, pp. 435–454, December 1979.

[7] Armstrong W.W., Dependency Structures of Data Base Relationships. *Proceedings IFIP*, North-Holland, Amsterdam, pp. 580–583, 1974.

[8] Atzeni P., M.C. De Bernardis, A New Basis for the Weak Instance Model. *Proceedings* 6th *Symposium on Principles of Database Systems*, pp. 79–86, San Diego, 1987.

[9] Atzeni P., D.S. Parker, Properties of Acyclic Database Schemes: an Analysis. *Proceedings XP2 Workshop on Relational Database Theory*, Pennsylvania State University, Philadelphia, 1981.

[10] Ausiello G., A. D'Atri, M. Moscarini, Minimal Coverings of Acyclic Database Schemata. *Advances in Database Theory II*, H. Gallaire, J. Minker, J.-M. Nicolas, eds., pp. 27–52, Plenum Press, New York, 1983.

[11] Ausiello G., A. D'Atri, M. Moscarini, Chordality Properties on Graphs and Minimal Conceptual Connections in Semantic Data Models. *Journal of Computer and System Sciences* **33:3**, pp. 179–202, October 1986.

[12] Bancilhon F., P. Richard, M. Scholl, On Line Processing of Compacted Relations. *Proceedings* 8th *VLDB*, pp. 263–269, Mexico City, 1982.

[13] Bancilhon F., N. Spyratos, Update Semantics of Relational Views. *Transactions on Database Systems* **6:4**, pp. 557–575, December 1981.

[14] Batini C., A. D'Atri, M. Moscarini, Formal Tools for Top-Down and Bottom-Up Generation of Acyclic Relational Schemata. *Proceedings* 7th *Int. Conference on Graph-Theoretic Concepts in Computer Science*, pp. 219–229, Hanser Verlag, Linz, 1981.

[15] Beeri C., On the Membership Problem for Functional and Multivalued Dependencies. *Transactions on Database Systems* **5:3**, pp. 241–259, September 1980.

[16] Beeri C., P.A. Bernstein, Computational Problems Related to the Design of Normal Form Relation Schemes. *Transactions on Database Systems* **4:1**, pp. 30–59, March 1979.

[17] Beeri C., R. Fagin, D. Maier, A.O. Mendelzon, J.D. Ullman, M. Yannakakis, Properties of Acyclic Database Schemes. *Proceedings* 13th *Symposium on the Theory of Computing*, pp. 355–362, New York, 1981.

[18] Beeri C., R. Fagin, D. Maier, M. Yannakakis, On the Desirability of Acyclic Database Schemes. *Journal of the ACM* **30:3**, pp. 479–513, July 1983.

[19] Beeri C., M.Y. Vardi, The Implication Problem for Data Dependencies. *Proceedings* 8th *ICALP*, Acre, in *Lecture Notes in Computer Science* **115**, pp. 73–85, Springer-Verlag, 1981.

[20] Beeri C., M.Y. Vardi, Formal Systems for Tuple and Equality-Generating Dependencies. *SIAM Journal of Computing* **13:1**, pp. 76–98, February 1984.

[21] Beeri C., M. Vardi, On Acyclic Database Decompositions. *Information and Control* **61:2**, pp. 75–84, May 1984.

[22] Beeri C., M.Y. Vardi, A Proof Procedure for Data Dependencies. *Journal of the ACM* **31:4**, pp. 718–741, October 1984.

[23] Beeri C., M.Y. Vardi, Formal Systems for Join Dependencies. *Theoretical Computer Science* **38:1**, pp. 99–116, North-Holland, May 1985.

[24] Bidoit N., The Verso Algebra or how to Answer Queries with Fewer Joins. *Journal of Computer and System Sciences* **35:3**, pp. 321–364, December 1987.

[25] Biskup J., H.H. Brüggeman, Designing Acyclic Database Schemes. *Advances in Database Theory II*, H. Gallaire, J. Minker, J.-M. Nicolas, eds., pp. 3–26, Plenum Press, New York, 1983.

[26] Casanova M.A., R. Fagin, C.H. Papadimitriou, Inclusion Dependencies and Their Interaction with Functional Dependencies. *Journal of Computer and System Sciences* **28:1**, pp. 29–59, February 1984.

[27] Chamberlain D.D., et al., SEQUEL 2: A Unified Approach to Data Definition, Manipulation and Control. *IBM Journal of Research of Development* **20:6**, pp. 560–575, November 1976.

[28] Chandra A.K., M.Y. Vardi, The Implication Problem for Functional and Inclusion Dependencies is Undecidable. *SIAM Journal of Computing* **14:3**, pp. 671–677, August 1985.

[29] Codd E.F., A Relational Model of Data for Large Shared Data Banks. *Communications of the ACM* **13:6**, pp. 377–387, June 1970.

[30] Codd E.F., Further Normalizations of the Database Relational Model. *Data Base Systems*, R. Rustin, ed., pp. 33–64, Prentice Hall, Englewood Cliffs, 1972.

[31] Codd E.F., Relational Completeness of Data Base Sublanguages. *Data Base Systems*, R. Rustin, ed., pp. 65–98, Prentice Hall, Englewood Cliffs, 1972.

[32] Codd E.F., Extending the Database Relational Model to Capture More Meaning. *Transactions on Database Systems* **4:4**, pp. 397–434, December 1979.

[33] Cosmadakis S.S., P.C. Kanellakis, Functional and Inclusion Dependencies: A Graph Theoretic Approach. *The Theory of Databases, Advances in Computing Research III*, P.C. Kanellakis, ed., pp. 163–184, JAI Press, Greenwich, CT, 1986.

[34] Date C.J., An Introduction to Database Systems. Volume I. 4th edition, Addison-Wesley Publishing Company, 1986.

[35] D'Atri A., M. Moscarini, Recognition Algorithms and Design Methodologies for Acyclic Database Schemes. *The Theory of Databases, Advances in Computing Research III*, P.C. Kanellakis, ed., pp. 43–68, JAI Press, Greenwich, CT, 1986.

[36] De Bra P., J. Paredaens, An Algorithm for Horizontal Decompositions. *Information Processing Letters* **17:2**, pp. 91–95, North-Holland, 24 August 1983.

[37] De Bra P., J. Paredaens, Horizontal Decompositions for Handling Exceptions to Functional Dependencies. *Advances in Database Theory II*, H. Gallaire, J. Minker, J.-M. Nicolas, eds., pp. 123–144, Plenum Press, New York, 1984.

[38] De Bra P., Horizontal Decomposition Based on Functional-Dependency-Set-Implications. *Proceedings* 1st *ICDT*, Rome, in *Lecture Notes in Computer Science* **243**, pp. 157–170, Springer-Verlag, 1986.

[39] Fagin R., Multivalued Dependencies and a New Normal Form for Relational Databases. *Transactions on Database Systems* **2:3**, pp. 262–278, September 1977.

[40] Fagin R., Normal Forms and Relation Database Systems. *Proceedings SIGMOD Int. Conference on Management of Data*, pp. 153–160, Boston, 1979.

[41] Fagin R., A Normal Form for Relational Databases that is Based on Domains and Keys. *Transactions on Database Systems* **6:3**, pp. 387–415, September 1981.

[42] Fagin R., Armstrong Databases. *Proceedings* 7th *IBM Symposium on Mathematical Foundations of Computer Science*, Kanagawa, 1982. also: *IBM RJ* 3440 *research report*, San Jose, April 1982.

[43] Fagin R., Horn Clauses and Data Dependencies, *Journal of ACM* **29:4**, pp. 952–985, October 1982.

[44] Fagin R., Degrees of Acyclicity for Hypergraphs and Relational Database Schemes. *Journal of ACM* **30:3**, pp. 514–550, July 1983.

[45] Fagin R., Acyclic Database Schemes (of Various Degrees): A Painless Introduction. *Proceedings of CAAP*, L'Aquila, in *Lecture Notes in Computer Science* **159**, pp. 65–89, Springer-Verlag, 1983.

[46] Fagin R., A.O. Mendelzon, J.D. Ullman, A Simplified Universal Relation Assumption and its Properties. *Transactions on Database Systems* **7:3**, pp. 343–360, September 1982.

[47] Fagin R., J.D. Ullman, M. Vardi, On the Semantics of Updates in Databases. *Proceedings* 12th *Symposium on Principles of Database Systems*, pp. 352–365, Atlanta, 1983.

[48] Fagin R., M.Y. Vardi, The Theory of Data Dependencies - An Overview. *Proceedings of the* 11th *ICALP*, Antwerp, in *Lecture Notes in Computer Science* **194**, pp. 1–22, Springer-Verlag, 1984.

[49] Fischer P.C., L.V. Saxton, S.J. Thomas, D. Van Gucht, Interactions Between Dependencies and Nested Relational Structures. *Journal of Computer and System Sciences* **31:3**, pp. 343–354, December 1985.

[50] P.C. Fischer, D. Van Gucht, Weak Multivalued Dependencies. *Proceedings* 3rd *Symposium on Principles of Database Systems*, pp. 266–274, Waterloo, Ont., 1984.

[51] Fischer P.C., D. Van Gucht, Structure of Relations Satisfying Certain Families of Dependencies. *Proceedings* 2nd *Symposium on Theoretical Aspects of Computer Science*, in *Lecture Notes in Computer Science* **182**, pp. 132–142, Springer-Verlag, 1985.

[52] Fischer P.C., D. Van Gucht, Determining When a Structure is a Nested Relation, *Proceedings* 11th *VLDB*, pp. 171–180, Stockholm, 1985.

[53] Galil Z., An Almost Linear Algorithm for Computing a Dependency Basis in a Relational Database. *Journal of the ACM* **29:1**, pp. 96–102, January 1982.

[54] Ginsburg S., S.M. Zaiddan, Properties of Functional-Dependency Families. *Journal of the ACM* **29:3**, pp. 678–698, July 1982.

[55] Graham M.H., On the Universal Relation. *Computer Systems Research Group Report*, University of Toronto, December 1979.

[56] Grahne G., K.-J. Räihä, Dependency Characterizations for Acyclic Database Schemes. *The Theory of Databases, Advances in Computing Research III*, P.C. Kanellakis, ed., pp. 19–42, JAI Press, Greenwich, CT, 1986.

[57] Grant J., B.E. Jacobs, On the Family of Generalized Dependency Constraints. *Journal of the ACM* **29:4**, October 1982.

[58] Gurevich Y., H.R. Lewis, The Inference Problem for Template Dependencies. *Proceedings* 1st *Symposium on Principles of Database Systems*, pp. 199–204, Los Angeles, 1982.

[59] Gyssens M., J. Paredaens, Another View of Functional and Multivalued Dependencies in the Relational Database Model. *Int. Journal of Computer and Information Sciences* **12:4**, pp. 247–267, August 1983.

[60] Gyssens M., J. Paredaens, On the Decomposition of Join Dependencies. *The Theory of Databases, Advances in Computing Research III*, P.C. Kanellakis, ed., pp. 69–106, JAI Press, Greenwich, CT, 1986.

[61] Gyssens M., On the Complexity of Join Dependencies. *Transactions on Database Systems* **11:1**, pp. 81–108, March 1986.

[62] Gyssens M., D. Van Gucht, The Powerset Operator as an Algebraic Tool for Understanding Least Fixpoint Semantics in the Context of Nested Relations. *Technical Report* 233, Indiana University, 1987.

[63] Gyssens M., J. Paredaens, D. Van Gucht, A Uniform Approach Towards Handling Atomic and Structured Information in the Nested Relational Database Model. *Technical Report 88-17*, University of Antwerp, 1988.

[64] Gyssens M., D. Van Gucht, The Powerset Algebra as a Result of Adding Programming Constructs to the Nested Relation Algebra. *Proceedings SIGMOD Int. Conference on Management of Data*, pp. 225–232, Chicago, 1988.

[65] Honeyman P., Testing Satisfaction of Functional Dependencies. *Journal of the ACM* **26**, pp. 668–677, 1982.

[66] Imieliński T., W. Lipski, Incomplete Information in Relational Databases. *Journal of the ACM*, **31:4**, pp. 761–791, October 1984.

[67] Jaeschke G., H.-J. Schek, "Remarks on the Algebra on Non First Normal Form Relations", *Proceedings* 1st *Symposium on Principles of Database Systems*, pp. 124–138, Los Angeles, 1982.

[68] Kambayashi Y., K. Tanaka, K. Takeda, Synthesis of Unnormalized Relations Incorporating More Meaning. *Information Sciences* **29:2**, pp. 201–247, May 1983.

[69] Kanellakis P.C., S.S. Cosmadakis, M.Y. Vardi, Unary Inclusion Dependencies Have Polynomial Inference Problems. *Proceedings* 15th *Symposium on the Theory of Computing*, pp. 246–277, Boston, 1983.

[70] Karabeg A., D. Karabeg, K. Papakonstantinou, V. Vianu, Axiomatization and Simplification for Relational Transactions. *Proceedings 6th Symposium on Priciples of Database Systems*, pp. 254–259, San Diego, 1987.

[71] Kuper G., J. D. Ullman, M. Vardi, On the Equivalence of Logical Databases. *Proceedings* 3rd *Symposium on Principles of Database Systems*, Waterloo, Ont., 1984.

[72] Lien Y. E. On the Equivalence of Database Models. *Journal of the ACM* **29:2**, pp. 333–362, April 1982.

[73] Lucchesi C.L., S.L. Osborn, Candidate Keys for Relations, *Journal of Computer and System Sciences* **17:2**, pp. 270–279, October 1978.

[74] Maier D., The Theory of Relational Databases. Computer Science Press, Rockville, MD, 1983.

[75] Maier D., A.O. Mendelzon, Y. Sagiv, Testing Implications of Data Dependencies. *Transactions on Database Systems* **4:4**, pp. 455–469, December 1979.

[76] Maier D., Y. Sagiv, M. Yannakakis, On the Complexity of Testing Implications of Functional and Join Dependencies. *Journal of the ACM* **28:4**, pp. 680–695, October 1981.

[77] Maier D., J.D. Ullman, Connections in Acyclic Hypergraphs. *Journal of Computer and System Sciences* **32:1,2**, pp. 185–199, July 1984.

[78] Maier D., J.D. Ullman, M. Vardi, On the Foundations of the Universal Relation Model. *Transactions on Database Systems* **9:2**, pp. 283–308, June 1984.

[79] Makinouchi A., A Consideration of Normal Form of Not-Necessarily-Normalized Relations in the Relational Data Model. *Proceedings* 3rd *VLDB*, pp. 447–453, Tokyo, 1977.

[80] Mitchell J.C., Inference Rules for Functional and Inclusion Dependencies. *Information and Control* **56:3**, pp. 154–173, March 1983.

[81] Nicolas J.-M., Mutual Dependencies and Some Results on Undecomposable Relations. *Proceedings* 4th *VLDB*, pp. 360–367, West-Berlin, 1978.

[82] Özsoyoğlu G., Z.M. Özsoyoğlu, V. Matos, Extending Relational Algebra and Relational Calculus for Set-Valued Attributes and Aggregate Functions. *Transactions on Database Systems* **12:4**, pp. 566–592, December 1987.

[83] Özsoyoğlu Z.M., L.Y. Yuan, A Normal Form for Nested Relations. *Proceedings* 4th *Symposium on Principles of Database Systems*, pp. 251–260, Portland, OR, 1985.

[84] Paredaens J., About Functional Dependencies in a Database Structure and Their Coverings. *Philips MBLE Lab. Report* 342, Brussels, 1977.

[85] Paredaens J., The Interaction of Integrity Constraints in an Information System. *Journal of Computer and System Sciences* **20:3**, pp. 310–328, June 1980.

[86] Paredaens J., D. Janssens, Decompositions of Relations: A Comprehensive Approach. *Advances in Database Theory I*, H. Gallaire, J. Minker, J.-M. Nicolas, eds., pp. 73–100, Plenum Press, New York, 1981.

[87] Paredaens J., D. Van Gucht, An Application of the Theory of Graphs and Hypergraphs to the Decompositions of Relational Database Schemes. *Proceedings of CAAP*, L'Aquila, in *Lecture Notes in Computer Science* **159**, pp. 350–366, Springer-Verlag, 1983.

[88] Paredaens J., D. Van Gucht, Possibilities and Limitations of Using Flat Operators in Nested Algebra Expressions. *Proceedings* 7th *Symposium on Principles of Database Systems*, pp. 29–38, Austin, TX, 1988.

[89] Parker D.S.Jr., K. Parsaye-Ghomi, Inference Involving Embedded Multivalued Dependencies and Transitive Dependencies. *Proceedings SIGMOD Int. Conference on Management of Data*, pp. 52–57, Santa Monica, CA, 1980.

[90] Pistor P., R. Traunmueller, "A Database Language for Sets, Lists and Tables", *Information Systems* **11:4**, pp. 323–336, 1986.

[91] Rissanen J., Independent Components of Relations. *Transactions on Database Systems* **2:4**, pp. 317–325, December 1977.

[92] Roth M.A., H.F. Korth, D.S. Batory, SQL/NF: A Query Language for ¬1NF Relational Databases. *Information Systems* **12:1**, pp. 99–114, 1987

[93] Roth M.A., H.F. Korth, A. Silberschatz, Theory of Non-First-Normal-Form Relational Databases. *Technical Report* TR-84-36, University of Texas, Austin, 1984, revised 1986.

[94] Sacca D., On the Recognition of Coverings of Acyclic Database Hypergraphs. *Proceedings* 2nd *Symposium on Principles of Database Systems*, pp. 297–304, Atlanta, 1983.

[95] Sacca D., Closures of Database Hypergraphs, *Journal of the ACM*, **32:4**, pp. 774–803, October 1985.

[96] Sagiv Y., An Algorithm for Inferring Multivalued Dependencies with an Application to Propositional Logic. *Journal of the ACM* **27:4**, pp. 250–262, April 1980.

[97] Sagiv Y. and S. Walecka, Subset Dependencies and a Completeness Result for a Subclass of Embedded Multivalued Dependencies. *Journal of the ACM* **29:1**, pp. 103–117, January 1982.

[98] Schek H.-J., M.H. Scholl, The Relational Model with Relation-Valued Attributes, *Information Systems* **11:2**, pp. 137–147, 1986.

[99] Scholl M.H., Theoretical Foundation of Algebraic Optimization Utilizing Unnormalized Relations, *Proceedings* 1st *ICDT*, Rome, in *Lecture Notes in Computer Science* **243**, pp. 380–396, Springer-Verlag, 1986.

[100] Sciore E., A Complete Axiomatization of Full Join Dependencies. *Journal of the ACM* **29:2**, pp. 373–393, April 1982.

[101] Tarjan R.E., M. Yannakakis, Simple Linear Time Algorithms to Test Chordality of Graphs, Test Acyclicity of Hypergraphs, and Selectively Reduce Acyclic Hypergraphs. *SIAM Journal on Computing* **13:3**, pp. 566–579, August 1984.

[102] Thomas S.J., A Non-First-Normal Form Relational Database Model. *Ph.D. Dissertation*, Vanderbilt University, Nashville, TN, 1983.

[103] Thomas S.J., P.C. Fischer, Nested Relational Structures. *The Theory of Databases, Advances in Computing Research III*, P.C. Kanellakis, ed., pp. 269–307, JAI Press, Greenwich, CT, 1986.

[104] Ullman J.D., Principles of Database and Knowledge-Base Systems, Volume I. Computer Science Press, Rockville, MD, 1988.

[105] Van Gucht D., Theory of Unnormalized Relational Structures. *Ph.D. Dissertation*, Vanderbilt University, 1985.

[106] Van Gucht D., On the Expressive Power of the Extended Relational Algebra for the Unnormalized Relational Model. *Proceedings* 6th *Symposium on Principles of Database Systems*, San Diego, pp. 302–312, 1987.

[107] Van Gucht D., P.C. Fischer, MVDs, Weak MVDs and Nested Relational Structures. *Technical Report*, Vanderbilt University, Nashville, TN, 1984.

[108] Van Gucht D., P.C. Fischer, Multilevel Nested Relational Structures. *Journal of Computer and System Sciences* **36:1**, pp. 77–105, February 1988.

[109] Van Gucht D., P.C. Fischer, High Level Data Manipulation Languages for Unnormalized Relational Database Models. *Proceedings XP7.52 Workshop on Relational Database Theory*, Austin, TX, 1986.

[110] Vardi M.Y., The Implication and Finite Implication problems for Typed Template Dependencies. *Journal of Computer and System Sciences* **28:1**, pp. 3–28, February 1984.

[111] Yannakakis M., Algorithms for Acyclic Database Schemes. *Proceedings* 7th *VLDB*, pp. 82–94, New York, 1981.

[112] Yannakakis M., C. Papadimitriou, Algebraic Dependencies. *Journal of Computer and System Sciences* **25:2**, pp.3–41, October 1982.

[113] Yu C.T., Z.M. Özsoyoğlu, An Algorithm for Tree-Query Membership of a Distributed Query. *Proceedings IEEE Computer Software and Applications Conference*, pp. 306–312, Chicago, 1979.

[114] Yu C.T., Z.M. Özsoyoğlu, On Determinimg Tree-Query Membership of a Distributed Query. *Computer Science Report* 80-1, University of Alberta, Edmonton, 1980.

[115] Yuan L.Y., Z.M. Özsoyoğlu, Logical Design of Relational Database Schemes. *Proceedings 6th Symposium on Principles of Database Systems*, pp. 38–47, San Diego, 1987.

[116] Zaniolo C., Analysis and Design of Relational Schemata for Database Systems. *Technical Report* UCLA-ENG-7669, University of California, Los Angeles, 1976.

[117] Zaniolo C., Database Relations with Null Values. *Journal of Computer and System Sciences*, **28:1**, pp. 142–166, February 1984.

Index

EATCS Monographs on Theoretical Computer Science

Vol. 1: K. Mehlhorn: Data Structures and Algorithms 1: Sorting and Searching. XIV, 336 pages, 87 figs. 1984.

Vol. 2: K. Mehlhorn: Data Structures and Algorithms 2: Graph Algorithms and NP-Completeness. XII, 260 pages, 54 figs. 1984.

Vol. 3: K. Mehlhorn: Data Structures and Algorithms 3: Multidimensional Searching and Computational Geometry. XII, 284 pages, 134 figs. 1984.

Vol. 4: W. Reisig: Petri Nets. An Introduction. X, 161 pages, 111 figs. 1985.

Vol. 5: W. Kuich, A. Salomaa: Semirings, Automata, Languages. IX, 374 pages, 23 figs. 1986.

Vol. 6: H. Ehrig, B. Mahr: Fundamentals of Algebraic Specification 1. Equations and Initial Semantics. XI, 321 pages. 1985.

Vol. 7: F. Gécseg: Products of Automata. VIII, 107 pages, 18 figs. 1986.

Vol. 8: F. Kröger: Temporal Logic of Programs. VIII, 148 pages. 1987.

Vol. 9: K. Weihrauch: Computability. X, 517 pages. 1987.

Vol. 10: H. Edelsbrunner: Algorithms in Combinatorial Geometry. XV, 423 pages, 93 figs. 1987.

Vol. 11: J.L. Balcázar, J. Díaz, J. Gabarró: Structural Complexity I. IX, 191 pages, 57 figs. 1988.

Vol. 12: J. Berstel, C. Reutenauer: Rational Series and Their Languages. VIII, 151 pages. 1988.

Vol. 13: E. Best, C. Fernández C.: Nonsequential Processes. IX, 112 pages, 44 figs. 1988.

Vol. 14: M. Jantzen: Confluent String Rewriting. IX, 126 pages, 1988.

Vol. 15: S. Sippu, E. Soisalon-Soininen: Parsing Theory. Volume I: Languages and Parsing. VIII, 228 pages. 1988.

Vol. 16: P. Padawitz: Computing in Horn Clause Theories. XI, 322 pages, 7 figs. 1988.

Vol. 17: J. Paredaens, P. De Bra, M. Gyssens, D. Van Gucht: The Structure of the Relational Database Model. X, 231 pages, 53 figs. 1989.